THE STATE IN WESTERN EUROPE

The State in
Western Europe

Edited by
RICHARD SCASE

ST. MARTIN'S PRESS   NEW YORK

Library of Congress Cataloging in Publication Data

Main entry under title:

The State in Western Europe.

Based on papers from a symposium held in Paris, Dec. 1978, under the auspices of the Franco–British programme of the Maison des sciences de l'homme and the British Social Science Research Council.
Includes index.
1. Europe – – Politics and government – – 1945– – – Congress. I. Scase, Richard. II. Maison des sciences de l'homme, Paris. Franco–British programme. III. British Social Science Research Council.
JN94.A3 1980.S72   321'.0094   80-10364
ISBN 0-312-75610-0

Contents

Notes on Contributors

Pierre Birnbaum is Professor of Political Science at the University of Paris I. His many publications include, *La Fin du Politique* (The End of Politics), 1975; *Les Sommets de l'Etat* (The Summits of the State), 1977: *La Classe Dirigeante Française* (The French Ruling Class), 1978; and (with B. Badie), *Sociologie de l'Etat* (Sociology of the State), 1979.

Carlo Donolo is Professor of Political Sociology at the University of Salerno, Italy. He has completed several studies of the Italian state including articles which have appeared in *Quaderni Piacentini* and *Quaderni di Sociologia*, and a major work entitled *Mutamento o Transizione? Politica e società nella crisi Italiana* (Change or Transition? Politics and Society in the Italian Crisis), 1977. He is a member of the editorial board of *Quaderni Piacentini*.

Serras Gago is an assistant professor of Sociology in the Institute of Social Sciences at the Technical University of Lisbon.

Salvador Giner is Reader in Sociology at Brunel University, London. He is President of the Catalan Sociological Association and has completed many studies on contemporary Spain including analyses of social structure, labour migration, land tenure and culture. His publications include *Mass Society*, 1976, and *Sociology*, 1972. He is also joint editor, with Margaret Archer, of *Contemporary Europe: Class, Status and Power*, 1971, and *Contemporary Europe: Social Structures and Cultural Patterns*, 1978.

Joachim Hirsch is Professor of Political Science at Frankfurt University. His several publications include: *Wissenschaftlich-technischer Fortschritt und politisches System* (Technical Progress and the Political System), 1973, and *Staatsapparat und Reproduktion des Kapitals* (The State Apparatus and the Reproduction of Capital), 1974.

Bob Jessop is a lecturer in Government at the University of Essex. He is the author of *Social Order, Reform and Revolution*, 1972, and *Traditionalism, Conservatism and British Political Culture*, 1974. He has written several articles on corporatism and theories of the state and is currently working on the nature of liberal democracy and contemporary British politics.

Nicos Mouzelis is a senior lecturer in Sociology at the London School of Economics. He is the author of *Organisation and Bureaucracy: An Analysis of Modern Theories*, 1967, and *Modern Greece: Facets of Underdevelopment*, 1978. He has also written various articles on sociological theory, the state, and economic and political developments in Greece.

Casten von Otter is Professor of Public Administration at the Swedish Work Research Centre (Arbetlivscentrum), Stockholm. He is the author of several publications including *Lönebildningen på Arbetsplatsen* (The Determination of Wages in the Workplace), 1973; and *Försok med Förvaltningsdemokrati* (Experiments in Employee Participation in the Public Sector), 1975. He is currently investigating aspects of industrial democracy in the Swedish public sector.

Nuno Portas is currently teaching at the Technical University of Lisbon. Between 1974 and 1975 he was Secretary of State for Housing and Town Planning in Portugal.

Richard Scase is a senior lecturer in Sociology at the University of Kent. He is the author of *Social Democracy in Capitalist Society*, 1977, and has edited *Readings in the Swedish Class Structure*, 1976, and *Industrial Society: Class, Cleavage and Control*, 1977. He is currently working with Robert Goffee on processes of small-scale capital accumulation.

Eduardo Sevilla is Professor of Agricultural Economics and Rural Sociology in the School of Agricultural Engineering at the University of Cordoba, Spain. He is Vice-President of the European Association for Rural Sociology and his many studies include *La Evolución del Campesinado en España* (The Evolution of the Peasantry in Spain), 1979.

Preface

This collection of essays is the product of a symposium on 'The State in Western Europe' held in Paris, December 1978. The symposium was jointly organised by Manuel Castells and Richard Scase under the auspices of the Franco–British programme of the Maison des Sciences de l'Homme and the Social Science Research Council. The organisers are grateful to Clemens Heller and Garry Runciman for their encouragement and support and to Hélène Lydenberg and Caryle Dean for their administrative and secretarial efforts. I am also thankful to Howard Davis, Mark Grimshaw, Michael Fuller and Janet Miller for their respective translations of the chapters by Birnbaum, Donolo, Portas and Gago, and Hirsch.

R.S.

Introduction

RICHARD SCASE

In recent years the state has been the subject of considerable discussion such that theoretical analyses are now more sophisticated although sometimes no less confusing. Indeed, there is often the predominance of a complex 'formalism' which fails to be 'empirically' grounded.[1] However, there have been substantial conceptual clarifications so that somewhat more 'empirical' work can now be usefully undertaken. Considerations of the state now go beyond the rather 'vague' perspectives which tended to polarise the debate during the late 1960s and the early 1970s. Then, it was possible to identify two essential approaches: the 'liberal–democratic' and the 'Marxist'.

Briefly, the 'liberal–democratic' tradition conceived of the state as an autonomous complex of institutions, politically neutral and external to structurally-determined social forces.[2] It is, then, 'up for grabs', to be 'captured' by elected régimes and used as an instrument for their own specific political purposes. Within this perspective, the state is regarded as necessary for the purposes of creating, defining and enforcing 'the rules' within which various socio-economic and political forces operate. It is, furthermore, seen as the institutional basis for the 'political' as distinct from the 'economic' sector of society. Thus, there are two essential assumptions within this perspective. First, that Western capitalist societies are 'pluralistic' if only because economic and political power are institutionally separated. Secondly, that the political – as an institutional system of power – is structurally and internally differentiated not only in terms of the functions exercised by the executive, the legislative and the judiciary, but also because of the existence of various pressure groups and political parties. The 'political', then, is regarded as irreducible to the 'economic'; indeed, this is seen to be one of the major differences between Western capitalist and East European societies. Within the former, there are 'economic' (industrial) and 'political' rights, roles and obligations

11

which are quite separable both institutionally and legally. Any social forces that would be likely to lead to an erosion of this distinction are seen as 'dangerous' since they would undermine the essential characteristics of the liberal–democratic state.[3]

This liberal–democratic perspective, however, may be further sub-divided. On the one hand, there is the 'conservative–liberal' which claims that the sole function of the state should be 'facilitative'; that is, to provide the general framework within which economic enterprises can operate and, under exceptional circumstances, ameliorate the 'problems' created by the market economy. In essence, therefore, the state is seen to be a 'passive' instrument, inappropriate as a force for social change; at best, it can only *respond* to changes initiated within the economic system.[4] On the other hand, there is the 'social–democratic' tradition which tends to regard the state as an institution which can be 'captured' and then used for the purposes of not only 'reforms' within a market economy but also for the long-term transformation of capitalism as a mode of production.[5] Thus, within the Social Democratic Parties of Western Europe a rhetoric has developed which emphasises the unique features of 'welfare capitalism', 'parliamentary socialism', 'democratic socialism', and so on. In a sense these ideologies owe much less to Marxism, out of which some of these parties developed, than to the liberal–democratic tradition.[6]

The 'Marxist' approach – the second major perspective of the late 1960s – tended to regard the state as simply a 'tool' of the ruling class; it unambiguously and deliberately furthers the economic and ideological interests of capital. It is a *capitalist* state which, contrary to Social Democratic claims, cannot be 'occupied' and used as a force for the transformation of society.[7] According to many Marxist theorists the state must, by its very nature, inevitably serve the needs of capital and, hence, those of the ruling class. This view has been most explicitly stated in recent years by proponents of 'state derivation'.[8] To put their case crudely, they argue that the structure and function of the state can only be adequately explained by reference to the global requirements of capital. Consequently they claim that the changing role of the state, particularly in terms of its greater *direct* intervention within the productive process, can mainly be explained as a 'counter-tendency' to the tendency for the rate of profit to fall; brought about in late capitalism by, for example, an increase in the organic composition of capital, the over-extended capacity of productive forces, and the heightened intensity of class struggle.[9] Therefore the state is increasingly forced to 'underwrite' the costs of capitalist production by *direct* involvement in renewing and maintaining the forces of production, both in terms of various technological processes and in the reproduction of labour power. It is with this assumption that Marxist writers account for the increase in functions of the state in all Western capitalist societies, ranging from the provision of health and social welfare facilities and the direct sponsorship and supervision of technological research, to the expansion of state subsidies to capitalist corporations and the growth of state capitalist enterprises.

Of course in the last instance, the state in any capitalist country must try to meet the needs of capital; it has to provide conditions under which the accumulation process can take place.[10] But this is not to assume that there will always be a 'fit' between the functions of capital and those of the state; indeed, one of the shortcomings of the theory of 'derivation' is its under-estimation of the tensions and contradictions that exist in the relationship between capital and the state. This is inevitable since neither are homogeneous entities; both are characterised by fractional forces that are often in conflict and in contradiction with each other. For example, capital is often internally fragmented in terms of the interests of small and large capitals, national and multinational capitals, and financial and industrial capitals.[11] Consequently, the state, in attempting to meet the needs of capital *in general*, often finds itself at any particular point of time in conflict with any of one or more of these specific fractions.

As a consequence of the growing recognition of these tensions and divisions, the state is now increasingly seen to be *relatively* autonomous, partially removed from the direct control of capital and of ruling-class interests.[12] It is only when the state is removed from a direct relationship with *particular* fractions that it can provide the necessary conditions for *general* capitalist production. Furthermore, it is in the provision of these that the state is able to function in variable ways such that important structural variations between different national social formations persist which, despite the internationalisation of capital, continue to be the essential sites for the capitalist mode of production. It follows from this, then, that the state cannot be conceived to be simply a servant of capital; although it has to cope with the *general* needs of the capitalist mode of production, the manner and directions in which it does this will be highly variable, depending upon the conjuncture of a wide range of not only economic but also social and political forces as they operate within the context of specific national social formations.[13]

This point may be clarified by reference to the availability of labour power. One of the necessary pre-conditions for capitalist production is the existence of propertyless labourers who can sell their labour power. This is a *universal* feature of the capitalist mode of production.[14] However, the conditions under which this labour power is sold and the character of the labourers that are available to specific units of capital are determined not only by capital but also by the state as it stipulates the conditions of an economy within which units of capital operate. It is important to stress that in providing these conditions the state is only *relatively* autonomous since, as stated above, it is subject to various political, social and economic forces. Nevertheless, there is sufficient autonomy to enable the state to implement policies which cannot always be seen as reducible to the needs of capital except at the general level. Thus, in the provision of wage labour, for example, the state can cope with any shortages confronting capital in a number of different ways; allowing for the permanent immigration of labourers and their families, issuing short-term work permits for migrants (without their families), or increasing the work participation rates of those who in a national population have been traditionally defined as 'marginal'.[15] Thus, although capital needs labour power for the accumulation process, this can be resolved by the state in a number of different ways. Similarly, the material conditions of groups of workers such as, for example, migrants and women as they differ between national economies cannot *solely* be explained by reference to the logic of capital.[16] Although the capitalist mode of production predominates within the national economies of such countries as the United States, Sweden and West Germany, the state has not met similar 'needs' of capital in a uniform manner. Witness, for example, the differences that exist between countries in the extent to which the state has directly intervened in determining contracts of employment, systems of industrial relations and wage bargaining structures, as well as in the provision of facilities necessary for the reproduction of labour power, such as housing and education.

It is within this context that it is necessary to consider the nature of political régimes since, as the expression of specific interests and forces within particular national social formations, they can exercise 'political will' which can have important consequences for the operation of an economy and, hence, the dynamics of the accumulation process. For example, it is through the election of Social Democratic régimes that many of the short-term 'reformist' interests of the dominated classes can be represented within the state. This can lead to the implementation of legislation in such areas as employment protection, health and safety at work, industrial retraining, and so on, such that although the essential nature of the relationship between wage labour and capital is unchanged, the material circumstances of workers are improved.[17] Indeed, 'reformist' political régimes may be instrumental in reinforcing crises within the accumulation process. Although the state may act as a 'counter-tendency' to the tendency for the rate of profit to fall, 'reformist' legislation may create contradictions in this. It may, for example, increase the 'costs' of labour power and hence, those of capitalist production such that the long-term reproduction of capital within a specific national social formation becomes problematic. Under these circumstances the state is further compelled to intervene directly in the production process as a 'counter-tendency' and, indeed, as a consequence of its own 'reformist' policies. The outcome will tend to be the creation of various corporatist and state capitalist structures.

These brief comments, then, are intended to suggest no more than the need to move from general, formal theories of the state to more specific, empirically-related theories. In other words, to develop theories in relation to specific national social formations. Within this context, it is important to relate the structure and function of the state to the development of the forces and the social relations of production. Clearly, the role of the state will differ considerably in a 'dependent' or 'peripheral' economy compared with one in which the development of large-scale monopoly capitalism has reached an advanced stage. In the case of the former, the state has to cope with the contradictions created by the persistence of small-scale commodity producers, the development of national capitals, and the growing dependence of an economy upon multinational monopoly capital.[18] Furthermore, any theory must recognise that the state is shaped by civil society; that is, by the conjuncture of a wide range of social, cultural and political as well as economic forces.[19] Only by an historical analysis of these is it possible to understand the formation of the state in terms of its structure, function and legitimacy. In order to investigate the origins and characteristics of present-day states in Western Europe, for example, it is necessary to consider the *political* history of Europe as well as the dynamics of the capitalist mode of production. In addition, conjunctures of various social and political forces have created national 'cultures' which legitimate the role of the state and stipulate the spheres of social and economic activity within which it is considered appropriate for the state to intervene. In this sense there are considerable differences between Britain, Italy and Scandinavia. But if civil society conditions the nature of the state, it is also the case that the state conditions civil society; not merely as an instrument of capital, but as a relatively autonomous entity. It is within these terms that the state and its role in class struggle must be considered. Clearly the state is a bourgeois state since it must guarantee the conditions of existence for capital. But, as stated earlier, it is not simply a tool of ruling-class interest; it is also an institutional outcome of class struggle. In other words, it is an 'uneasy compromise' of class interests in which some of the aspirations of the dominated classes become, at least partially, incorporated.[20] This is, of course, often the case when wage labour is well organised in trade unions and represented by 'reformist' political régimes.

From these points, it follows that there need to be more theorised historical analyses of specific national states. Within this context, detailed comparative studies are necessary in order to describe and explain similarities and differences in terms of such factors as, for example, the structure and function of national states, the development of their various institutions, their varying autonomy in relation to specific social, economic and political forces – particularly those of capital, wage labour and other class forces – and their internal contradictions, tensions and dynamics of social change.[21] It is only in these terms that it will be possible to determine the specificity of national states and their role within the context of cleavages, struggles and conflicts as they exist within national social formations. However, an emphasis upon specific national states should not detract from the consideration of more broadly-based socio-economic forces. Indeed, an understanding of these forces must provide the framework within which any particular analysis must be undertaken. This is particularly the case during the present stage of capitalist development when the increasing internationalisation of capital has brought about the creation of dependent national economies as well as a wide range of supranational economic and political institutions. Consequently, it is possible to identify a number of common trends in the development of national states, all of which would need to be considered in any specific analysis. Briefly, these may be summarised as follows.

First, in all Western capitalist countries the state has increasingly taken over functions necessary for the maintenance and reproduction of labour power in terms of such matters as the provision of education, housing, health and welfare. This has created some discussion about the 'legitimate' areas of state involvement and the extent to which facilities that may be perceived as 'benevolent' are, in fact, a further extension of state 'repression'. In a number of countries this has led to widespread popular reaction and the election of rightist political régimes committed to the virtues of self-help and 'cut-backs' in the extent of government intervention in everyday life.[22] In any case, the increasing provision of state-financed welfare services has rendered as problematic the liberal—democratic distinction between 'private' and 'public' spheres and highlighted the essential contradictions inherent within the provision of these resources.

Secondly, the state has become explicitly more repressive, reinforcing its functions of control and surveillance. This has generally been a consequence of 'rationalisation' within the accumulation process with all that this has entailed for the mobility of labour and the destruction of 'traditional' community and family structures.[23] Thus, 'informal' sources of control, structured upon these institutions, have been replaced by formally-prescribed agencies of the state; not only the police but also social workers and other functionaries in the health services. Again, such developments have created widespread concern about the deterioration of 'human rights' and 'political freedoms' and revealed an essential contradiction of the state; as *both* 'protector' and 'despot'.

Thirdly, the functions of the state have become more centralised. In every Western capitalist country there has been the 'rationalisation' of local and regional state activities and their integration within centralised, national bureaucracies. This is evident within all branches of the state, ranging from education and police services through, paradoxically, to the execution of regional economic and social policies. Furthermore, as part of this trend, both national and 'local' political parties have become less relevant as effective power has increasingly passed to the executive. This, in turn, has led to a crisis in the legitimacy of political institutions, particularly in terms of parliamentarianism and traditional notions of representative democracy. Thus, there has been the growth of forms of 'direct action' which seek to obtain results from the state by bypassing the legitimate political procedures. Strategies of protest have emerged ranging from the formation of grass-roots pressure groups (both within communities and institutions) to the development of urban terrorism. In addition, the trend towards centralised decision-making has intensified demands for 'local' and 'regional' autonomy and for experiments in self-management. If, then, the accumulation process requires further centralisation within state apparatuses, this has rendered more acute the legitimacy of these institutions, highlighting yet again the contradictions created by the capitalist mode of production.

A fourth trend that can be readily identified is the growing direct intervention of the state within the productive process.[24] There has been a shift from general Keynesian macro-economic management to direct state intervention through loans, subsidies and the formation of state capitalist enterprises. This, of course, would have been unnecessary if capitalism was 'doing well'; the trend can only be explained by the state acting as a 'counter-tendency'. In this, it has become involved in the 'modernisation' and 'rationalisation' of the forces of production both in terms of labour power (for example, industrial and occupational retraining) and in various technological processes (for example, grants, loans and subsidies for investment projects). This trend has led some observers to suggest that contemporary capitalist economies have developed corporatist structures. Although corporatism is an ill-defined concept it is clear that it implies a direct intervention by the state in the relationship between wage labour and capital; it attempts to reduce the intensity of class struggle by the institutionalisation of industrial relations and the incorporation of subordinated classes. If, then, increasing direct state intervention and corporatism are responses to the crisis of profitability this, in turn, has created a fiscal crisis for the state. Its activities have become 'over-extended' when the sources available for the funding of its operations have become more restricted; deficit budgeting causes inflation while a reduction in the living standards of wage labour limits the scope for further revenue through taxation.[25]

Finally, it can be seen that there is a growing contradiction between the internationalisation of capital and the maintenance of national states. Although national social formations remain the essential sites for the capitalist mode of production, the growth of large-scale financial and industrial capitals have reduced their autonomy. Within the international division of labour, there is the increasing economic and political dependence of 'peripheral' states upon the 'central' capitalist countries particularly, of course, the United States. Even among the most developed capitalist economies, the dynamics of the accumulation process have questioned the relevance of the national state. Consequently, there has been the growth of 'supra-national' institutions created for the purposes of regulating financial, industrial and political relationships.[26] Nevertheless, fundamental tensions remain; increasingly, states must 'compete' with each other in order to attract capital. In this they must guarantee conditions which international capital will find acceptable. Indeed, the most 'moderate' 'reformist' policies of Social Democratic régimes (for example, protection of employment legislation) may lead capital to perceive of a particular national economy as an inappropriate site for investment.

These, then, are some of the common trends affecting the structure and function of the state in Western capitalist countries. The purpose of the present book is to bring together a number of accounts of national states so that emerging similarities and differences can be more readily identified. Although these reflect a number of different theoretical perspectives, they nevertheless delineate important specificities as they continue to exist between the national states of Western Europe.

As the chapters by Birnbaum, Donolo and Jessop suggest, there are variations in the centralisation of state functions; compare for example, the national states of France, Italy and Britain. In Italy, according to Donolo, the state is rather like an 'archipelago' since it is decentralised and enmeshed within the political system at all levels through 'clientelism' and patterns of mediation. In France, on the other hand, Birnbaum shows how the centralisation of functions reinforces the persistence of a 'strong' and 'autonomous' state. In Britain, by contrast, the state has been unable to formulate national economic plans and implement planning agreements with large-scale capitals in the same manner as in France.

This leads to a further difference; national states in Western Europe vary in the degree to which they are autonomous from the interests of capital. Although in every case the state has to guarantee the necessary conditions for the reproduction of capital, the chapters by Birnbaum and von Otter suggest that the 'separation' of the state from capital appears to be more pronounced in France and Sweden while, according to Mouzelis, and Giner and Sevilla, the national states of Greece and Spain are increasingly dependent upon the requirements of large-scale multinational capital. Donolo argues that the Italian state has only limited autonomy because it is structured within a variety of economic and political interests, organised around the Christian Democratic Party. If, however, as a general process, the autonomy of the state is in decline because of its increasing direct intervention within the accumulation process, the *forms* which this has taken differ between national economies.[27] In some, such as in Britain and France, there has been the creation of state capitalist enterprises while in others – for instance, Sweden and West Germany – more corporatist strategies have been adopted; financial assistance has been extended to capitals in return for compliance to state economic policies. Furthermore, the state as a 'counter-tendency' has intervened in variable ways in the relationship between wage labour and capital. Thus, as the chapters by Jessop, Hirsch and von Otter confirm, there are important contrasts in the labour market policies and industrial relations systems of Britain, West Germany and Sweden, for which any explanation must take into account the various conjunctures of class forces and the formation and development of different political régimes.

It is in terms of these class forces that there are variations in the extent to which dominated class interests are represented within state apparatuses; compare, for example, the chapters by Jessop, Donolo and Mouzelis. The expression of these is probably greater in Sweden than elsewhere in Western Europe if only because of the tradition of 'reformist' Social Democratic régimes and a well-organised working-class movement. Thus, there has been the development of a range of industrial, social and welfare facilities which have been beneficial to the material condition of the industrial working-class. This, however, has created contradictions within the Swedish state since it also has to maintain conditions suitable for the reproduction of capital. Since health and welfare provisions are partly financed by charges imposed by the state upon capital, unless these can be compensated by lower production costs, capitals may prefer to invest elsewhere. This, as many of the chapters suggest, illustrates a contradiction confronting national states in Western Europe; in the attempt to 'resolve' class antagonisms as a necessary pre-condition for capitalist production, dominated class interests are met, if only partially, through various 'reformist' welfare and industrial measures. Since, however, these can increase capital's costs of production, capitals may move to 'peripheral' economies where such conditions do not prevail because of the relative weakness of working-class movements. As Mouzelis argues, this reinforces the dependence of these national states upon large-scale multinational capitals.

If, then, despite a number of common trends, national states differ in degrees of centralisation, autonomy and incorporation of dominated class interests, these can only be explained – as stated earlier – by undertaking historico-comparative analyses of specific social formations. Thus, in Western Europe there are considerable differences in the stage of capitalist development; while in Britain, West Germany, France and Scandinavia there is the growing dominance of monopoly capital, in Southern Europe there are severe contradictions brought about by the uneven development of the capitalist mode of production. But if the structure and function of the state are partially shaped by such forces it is important to stress that these, in turn, are conditioned by the state. Consequently, any *specific* theory of the state must take into account these inter-dependencies.[28]

Notes

1. See, for example, the work of N. Poulantzas, particularly his *Political Power and Social Classes* (New Left Books, London, 1972); and *Social Classes in Contemporary Capitalism* (New Left Books, London, 1975).

2. For a brief summary of 'liberal–democratic' assumptions see R. Dahl, *A Preface to Democratic Theory* (Phoenix Books, London, 1965); and S. Lipset, *Political Man* (Heinemann, London, 1960).

3. Hence the perceived 'dangers' of corporatism. See J. Winkler, 'The Corporatist Economy: Theory and Administration' in R. Scase (ed.), *Industrial Society; Class, Cleavage and Control* (Allen and Unwin, London, 1977).

4. This tends to be the authentic philosophy of many of the Conservative and Christian Democratic political parties in Western Europe. The material circumstances confronting these parties when they have formed political régimes have often prevented the articulation of this philosophy in policies. However, the present British Conservative government is attempting to implement policies which are consistent with this philosophy.

5. For example, the Swedish Social Democratic Party; see R. Scase, *Social Democracy in Capitalist Society* (Croom Helm, London, 1977). For a collection of essays on the various European Social Democratic parties see W. Paterson and A. Thomas (eds.), *Social Democratic Parties in Western Europe* (Croom Helm, London, 1977).

6. The German and Swedish Social Democratic Parties, for example, have stronger Marxist origins than the British Labour Party.

7. See, for example, R. Miliband, *The State in Capitalist Society* (Weidenfeld and Nicolson, London, 1969); and J. Westergaard and H. Resler, *Class in a Capitalist Society* (Heinemann, London, 1975).

8. For a collection of essays which reflect the 'core' features of this perspective among a number of German writers, see J. Holloway and S. Picciotto (eds.), *State and Capital* (Edward Arnold, London, 1978).

9. The chapter by Hirsch in the present collection closely adheres to this perspective.

10. Hence the state is inevitably a *capitalist* state.

11. For a discussion of these, see N. Poulantzas, *Political Power and Social Classes*. For an empirical discussion of the often conflicting interests of financial and industrial capitals in Britain see A. Glyn and B. Sutcliffe, *British Capitalism, Workers and the Profits Squeeze* (Penguin, Harmondsworth, 1972).

12. The debate over the state's relative autonomy has been primarily motivated by the work of Poulantzas. However, 'relative autonomy' remains a problematic concept not least because of the considerable *empirical* difficulties that it entails. For a severe criticism of its usefulness see, for example, A. Cutler, B. Hindess, P. Hirst and A. Hussain, *Marx's 'Capital' and Capitalism Today* (Routledge and Kegan Paul, London, 1977/8), vols. I and II.

13. See, for example, N. Poulantzas, *Social Classes in Contemporary Capitalism*.

14. K. Marx, *Capital*, vol. I.

15. Compare, for instance, the policies of the British and West German states during the labour market shortages of the 1950s and 60s.

16. Wage differentials between men and women, for example, are much narrower in Sweden than in Britain; partly as a result of more 'effective' legislation.

17. For a discussion of these in Sweden see W. Korpi, *The Working Class in Welfare Capitalism* (Routledge and Kegan Paul, London, 1978); and R. Scase, *Social Democracy in Capitalist Society*.

18. See, for example, the chapters on Greece, Portugal and Spain in the present collection.

19. This point is emphasised by, among others, N. Poulantzas, *Political Power and Social Classes*.

20. It is the incorporation of these interests within various apparatuses of the state which has led to the contemporary interest in corporatism as a strategy of control. For a discussion of corporatism in Britain, see J. Winkler, 'The Corporatist Economy: Theory and Administration'; and the chapter by Jessop in the present volume. The usefulness of the notion has been criticised by J. Westergaard, 'Class, Inequality and Corporatism', in A. Hunt (ed.), *Class and Class Structure* (Lawrence and Wishart, London, 1977). The present Conservative régime is attempting to dismantle corporatist structures.

21. As stated in note 12 above, there are considerable empirical problems in determining the 'varying autonomy' of the state. As yet, theoretical discussions have not been 'backed up' by empirical analyses.

22. It remains an open question whether such policies can be pursued in anything but the very short-term in view of the present stage of the development of the capitalist mode of production and the nature of the present crisis. For an elaboration of this point by reference to Britain, see the chapter by Jessop.

23. Hirsch refers to this trend in his chapter on West Germany.

24. The Conservative régime in Britain is trying to reverse this trend. But see note 22 above.

25. Hence the contemporary appeal of 'monetarist' economics to rightist political parties.

26. Ranging, for example, from the development of 'informal' trading agreements between national states to the creation of the EEC.

27. As implied in note 22 above, it is probably more appropriate to regard the reversal of this trend in Britain as short-term and temporary.

28. I am grateful to Robert Goffee, University of Kent, for his comments on an earlier draft of this introduction.

1 The Transformation of the State in Post-war Britain

BOB JESSOP

This chapter investigates the reorganisation of the state in post-war Britain. It focuses on four interrelated sets of political relations: (a) the structure of political representation, (b) the social bases of state power, (c) the structure of the state apparatus, and (d) the nature and scope of state intervention. In addition to her involvement in various international economic and political organisations and her integration since 1973 in the European Economic Community, Britain has also experienced major changes in her domestic state system.[1] The main *tendencies* here are: the increasing importance of functional as opposed to parliamentary representation, the fundamental social democratisation and incipient corporatisation of the social bases of state power, the growing concentration and centralisation of the state system (including the growth of para-state bodies, the strengthening of the coercive apparatus, and involvement in an emergent European state), the development of economic and social programming, and the increasing 'politicisation' and 'étatisation' of social relations in the economy and civil society.[2]

These tendencies are indirectly attributable to the chronic structural and cyclical crises in Britain's economy, to its declining weight in an international economy which was itself entering a period of instability and prolonged crisis, to an emergent crisis of representation (centred on the political parties, trade unions, and capitalists' associations), and to a growing crisis of hegemony in the political sphere. More directly they are the outcome of struggles over the most suitable economic and political strategies to resolve these crises and create conditions more favourable to economic growth and political stability. Thus attention is also focused on the complex interplay between these crises and the principal political forces involved in this reorganisation. The chapter concludes with some comments on the future of the British State.

The International Context

The reorganisation of the imperialist system under the hegemony of American capital and the development of a socialist bloc following the Second World War had major repercussions on the international position and domestic situation of Britain. For not only was Britain externally vulnerable to these changes due to its worldwide colonial possessions, overseas investments, and defence commitments, its major rôle in the international monetary system and world trade, and its longstanding dependence on trade for half its food supplies and almost all essential raw materials; it was also affected internally throughout this period by the continuing internationalisation of both financial and industrial capital. The transformation of the British State since 1945 cannot be fully comprehended unless account is taken of these fundamental changes in the international system and their effects on British society.

The principal growth areas for international capital accumulation since the Second World War have increasingly proved to be mutual trade and cross-investment among metropolitan nation-states, whereas economic exploitation of colonies and other dependent societies through unequal exchange, protected markets, political tribute, or investments, became less significant. Moreover, whilst capital investment in metropolitan areas was typically channelled to capital-intensive, high technology, and high productivity industries with a high growth potential, that in peripheral areas was generally limited to extractive industries and/or light manufacturing employing cheap labour and inferior technologies. It was monopoly capital which took the lead in restructuring the world economy and this is reflected in the tremendous growth of multinational companies. In turn this both presupposes and reinforces the tendential internationalisation of capital markets and industrial production.

This reorganisation of the imperialist system followed mainly from the growing international mobility of financial and industrial capital. This mobility rested in turn on the creation of a stable international monetary system, the increasing liberalisation of trade and investment, a commitment to peaceful co-existence between the capitalist and socialist blocs, and military and political co-operation among the major capitalist powers. For capital accumulation on a world scale presupposes not only favourable conditions within national markets but also an adequate institutional framework and a suitable balance of forces on an international level. How these conditions are secured is influenced by the twin considerations that the international circuit of 'capital in general' is realised only through competition among individual capitals and that the political structure of the world market involves a plurality of national states. Since no single capital and no one nation-state can secure the international conditions required for capital accumulation, some supranational organs are required to articulate and promote the common interests of different capitals and states. Moreover, since different states and capitals will still disagree about the most appropriate '*Ordnungspolitik*' and accumulation strategies, these supranational bodies will be most effective when organised under the hegemony of one dominant state.

In this context it was American capital that secured an initially predominant position owing to its industrial strength (its production was twice that of the rest of the world in 1945), the great demand for investment capital, means of production, and finished products in Europe and Japan during post-war reconstruction, and the paramount position of the dollar in the international monetary system. The last factor was increasingly important in sustaining American investment abroad in the face of growing European and Japanese competition after reconstruction. But the Bretton Woods system eventually collapsed in the late sixties under the combined weight of an international recession, a long-term reversal in America's post-war surplus on trade and invisible earnings coupled with escalating foreign investment and government expenditure, the decline of sterling as a significant international reserve and trading medium, and the growing strength of the German, Japanese, and other economies.[3] The instability and contradictions of the reorganised, Smithsonian international monetary system constitute a fundamental obstacle for the resolution of the international crisis still facing capitalism today.

It is not only in maintaining a stable international monetary and legal order favourable to capital accumulation that individual nation-states are constrained in their conduct of economic management but also in securing the infrastructural, political, and social preconditions of capitalist production within the context of a developing international division of labour. The complex relation between the nation-state and multinational capital is particularly significant in this respect. For the central contradiction between 'capital in general' and 'particular capitals' finds a major focus here and is also overdetermined by class and popular-democratic struggles. While the nation-state has to secure conditions for multinational capital to expand, it is subject to constraints imposed by the international mobility of the latter. Thus the use of monetary and fiscal policy to manage demand

and to influence the balance of payments is limited through multinational firms' access to international capital markets (including the virtually uncontrolled Eurocurrency and Eurobond markets), their routine and/or speculative transactions on international money markets (especially since the crisis of the Bretton Woods system became apparent), and their ability to manipulate accounts to minimise tax liabilities. Similar considerations obtain in the case of exchange rate policy. Likewise the development of an international division of labour within multinational firms reduces the opportunities to influence the ratio of imports to exports as specific quantities of goods must flow between interdependent enterprises in different nations without regard to short-term policy changes in any one society.

Since multinationals also tend to be the most advanced capitals, however, there is also pressure to encourage their activities. This is apparent in various forms of subsidy, concession, infrastructural support, etc., to assist multinationals in making capital investments and reorganising production. This is a complex process with contradictory effects. For the short-term gains from the domestic investment and foreign sales of alien multinationals may be reversed through the long-term expatriation of profits. Conversely foreign investment by a domestic multinational can lead to short-term losses from the export of capital (together with jobs) and to long-term benefits from the repatriation of foreign income (in so far as this is not re-invested abroad). Similar problems arise in relation to technological dependency and potential positive 'spillover' effects. The overall impact of this complex process will obviously depend on the relative weight of domestic and foreign capital in each society and the weight of international trade and capital flows in relation to its gross national product. But its effects become more significant in all cases as internationalisation continues to expand.[4]

In addition to these changes in the international economic order, there have also been major developments in the international political system. The most fundamental of these are: the creation and subsequent economic and military development of a socialist world system in Europe and the Far East, the development of national liberation struggles and the dissolution of British and other European empires, the emergence of a bipolar nuclear system focused on the Soviet Union and United States, the growth of supranational economic and political associations on both a regional level (e.g., the EEC) and that of the capitalist bloc (e.g., the IMF, OECD, and GATT), the development of a multilateral balance of power following the Sino–Soviet split, the continued expansion of the European and Japanese economies, and, most recently, the emergence of a series of medium powers among the industrialising societies of the Third World (e.g., Brazil, Mexico, Iran). These changes have had major repercussions on international politics and have also fundamentally affected politics in many of the countries involved.

The combined impact of these economic and political changes has been particularly marked in the case of Britain. Crucial factors here were the traditional rôle of sterling as a major international reserve and trading currency, the loss of empire combined with massive defence commitments overseas, and, even after the former problems were largely solved through the City's diversification into Euro-currency operations and the drastic reduction of Britain's military rôle East of Suez, the continued dependence on foreign trade for economic survival. But the irreversible long-term decline in Britain's relative position in world economic and political affairs was masked by various short-term forces which delayed the onset of crises and measures to resolve them. Thus, although Britain was already in a weak economic and political position at the end of the Second World War, it still had the Empire to sustain it with food, raw materials, markets, political tribute, and military support, it continued to receive some support from the United States, the Soviet Union was pre-occupied with post-war reconstruction and still lacked a nuclear capability, and continental Europe, Japan, and China were also weakened by war and occupation.[5] Moreover, although these forces proved short-lived, they were replaced by economic recovery, a favourable shift in the terms of trade, and the initial political and economic success of the overseas sterling area in sustaining the unity of the Commonwealth and the international rôle of sterling.[6] But the beneficial effect of these factors was in turn much reduced towards the end of the fifties and Britain's long-term international decline had meanwhile become more deep-seated and pervasive. It is in this broad context that one must locate the attempts to secure British entry into the EEC and the radical reorganisation of the British state during the sixties. But the internal situation must also be examined in greater detail and it is to this task that we now turn.

The Post-war Settlement

At the close of the Second World War the Labour Party won a major victory in the 1945 general election and proceeded to implement a social democratic programme based on macro-level management of a mixed economy and the extension and consolidation of a welfare state. This produced a major transformation in the British state and also implied a fundamental social democratisation of the political system. These basic shifts were closely interrelated. Both developed out of the economic and political conditions of the interwar period and the Second World War. Chief among these conditions were the realignment of the party system following the introduction of near-universal suffrage in 1918, the major repercussions of the General Strike in 1926, the manifest failure of orthodox economic policies based on 'sound finance' to secure conditions favouring growth and full employment, the ignominious disintegration of the second Labour government in 1931, and the total mobilisation of the population in the Second World War. These conditions encouraged far-reaching reappraisals of economic and political strategies within the major political parties, the trade union movement, the City and industry, the civil service, and intellectual circles. There was a general movement in favour of class collaboration and state intervention in the interests of economic growth and improved social conditions for the whole people. This was apparent in the post-1926 consultations among trade union leaders and industrial statesmen, the elaboration within the post 1931 Labour Party of a social democratic programme based on nationalisation and the welfare state, the integration of trade unions and employers' associations into the wartime state apparatus, and the commitment of the wartime coalition government to a post-war programme of full employment, the reform of social security in line with the Beveridge Report, educational reform, and other welfare measures.[7] The electoral victory of the Labour Party in 1945 confirmed this fundamental political and ideological realignment and the incoming Labour government proceeded to give it material expression in the reorganisation of the form and scope of state intervention in the economy and civil society.

The creation of the mixed economy and the welfare state during the post-war Labour administration laid the foundations for the economic and political settlement between capital and labour in the next two decades. For these changes signified a reorganisation of the bases of capitalist hegemony through the integration of the economic and political wings of the social democratic movement. This is clear not only in the successful political containment of the Labour Party (although one must stress here that it was never a revolutionary organisation) but also in the acceptance of free collective bargaining and official consultation over the unions' economic-corporate demands in a context of state-induced full employment and in the implementation of programmes and policies concerned to reduce insecurity and improve social conditions. This realignment of economic and political forces also required a reorganisation of the state itself to secure means of maintaining full employment and economic growth. Thus, although the Conservatives and many industrialists opposed several of Labour's nationalisation schemes, these did give additional leverage in demand management as well as enabling major reconstruction of key infrastructural and industrial sectors. The rise of the welfare state also involved a major increase in public spending and taxation (as well as in public employment) and this provided still more leverage. Hence, through varying its current and capital spending in the public sector and welfare state and/or altering the incidence and level of taxation and/or manipulating the money supply through orthodox open-market operations in government securities, the Bank rate, reserve requirements, etc., the state is supposed to affect the aggregate level of demand and thus engage in contra-cyclical activities to eliminate or reduce the effects of the business cycle on employment, production, and prices. Further, since demand management acts at the macro-level and does not involve direct controls on either capital or labour, there was little opposition to the principle of such interventions from financial and industrial capital or their political representatives in parliament and the administration. Thus, when the Labour government was defeated in the 1951 general election, the incoming Conservative government was careful to retain the institutional basis of the post-war settlement and to maintain the commitment to full employment and welfare state.

In retrospect the continuity between the two administrations seems more obvious than it did to contemporary observers. For the Labour government was not only identified with nationalisation but also with the physical planning and controls retained from the wartime economy. However, far from using these extensive powers to introduce a planned, socialist economy, it was the Labour administration that began the 'bonfire of controls'. In this it was prompted as much by the unions' desire to return to free collective bargaining and popular dissatisfaction with rationing as it was by growing hostility from industry, the City, and the Opposition.[8] The Conservatives merely accelerated the process of physical decontrol and de-nationalised the iron and steel industry and road haulage, whilst maintaining indirect controls based on manipulation of market forces.

The success of the post-war settlement depended on continuing class collaboration within the economic and political domains and on economic growth to secure rising real wages and welfare benefits without threats to continuing capital accumulation. But these conditions were unstable and were gradually attenuated during the years of Conservative office. The causes for this gradual collapse are complex and a major factor was the drastic relative decline of Britain within the international order. However, if the international decline was largely due to irresistible external forces, it was aggravated by internal forces that delayed and distorted British adaptation to the changed conditions. Of particular importance in this respect have been the organisation and activities of the trade union movement and the hegemony of financial over industrial capital. The interaction of these forces within the framework of the capitalist system and a 'Keynesian-welfare state'[9] is at the heart of the long-term structural decline of the British economy and the current economic and political crisis. Since financial capital was the central mediating link between the international system and domestic affairs in this period, we examine the rôle of the City before considering that of the labour movement.

The Role of Financial Capital

The British economy is characterised by a distinctive dislocation between financial and industrial capital. For, owing to the favourable nineteenth-century combination of British domination in world trade and industrial production, an international monetary system based on gold and sterling, and international political stability associated with *pax Britannica*, the City was able to establish itself as the most important international financial centre. This domination was firmly established by 1870 and reached its zenith in the decade before the First World War. Early leadership in world trade and finance plus high yields encouraged the City to specialise in servicing international commerce and foreign capital markets. So long as Britain was the principal 'workshop of the world' for both capital and consumer goods, this specialisation did not constitute a serious obstacle to industrial accumulation in Britain but actually stimulated it through the creation of overseas demand. It was this initial community of interest that consolidated the political and ideological hegemony of financial capital in the British Establishment (or power bloc) and, although the economic basis for this situation was undermined before 1900 by the superior strength of German and American industrial capital and was further weakened by the instability of the international monetary system after 1918 and the subsequent rise of the dollar, the City was still able to maintain its hegemony more or less unchecked until the sixties.[10] This was evident in the protracted and ultimately unsuccessful interwar attempt to return sterling to the gold standard at its pre-1914 parity – since this involved long-term deflation which worsened unemployment and produced relative stagnation in the industrial sector. It has also been evident in the economic policies pursued by successive governments since the Second World War.

For, despite the major decline in Britain's economic and political position in the international system, there was a concerted attempt to maintain sterling's rôle as a top international reserve and financial medium and to operate as a superpower with worldwide commitments. This attempt was also made in the context of a marked disequilibrium between short-term liabilities (loans and deposits from abroad) and short-term assets (gold and foreign currency reserves), a chronic deficit in trade in food, raw materials and (semi-)manufactured goods, and the gradual disintegration of the British Empire. Three further policy constraints were the commitment to maintain a fixed and stable exchange rate within the Bretton Woods system, the structurally-determined greater marginal propensity to import than to export with economic expansion, and a firm rejection of direct state intervention to restructure British industry to facilitate capital accumulation.[11] And, since this attempt required a free flow of capital for portfolio and industrial investment overseas and entailed heavy expenditure on foreign aid to maintain the overseas sterling area, production of arms and military material, and defence of foreign investments, markets, and vital sources of supply, governments were forced to concentrate their efforts on increasing the reserves and eliminating the deficit on visible trade. However, since the state was also operating in the context of the post-war settlement between capital and labour, it could not pursue these policies to the point where full employment and welfare expenditure were threatened. The overall effect of these complex structural and political constraints on the conduct of the government's policy was continual oscillation between deflation and reflation triggered in turn by sterling crises and rising unemployment. In short, the result was Britain's famous and unique 'stop–go' cycle.[12]

In pursuing this 'stop–go' policy the state not only failed to halt the long-term decline in the rôles of sterling and Britain in the international system, it also reinforced the conditions making for continued industrial decline across successive cycles and even tended to produce pro-cyclical effects. For the policies intended to maintain the position of sterling discouraged and distorted industrial investment through high interest rates to attract foreign funds and prevent the flight of 'hot money', restrictions on investment outside the sterling area (while continental Europe and North America were the key growth areas open to foreign investment[13]), and recurrent bouts of deflation to restrain home demand and 'free' resources for export production. The defence of the overseas sterling area and the empire also inhibited and distorted industrial growth due to the resulting high 'unproductive'[14] state expenditure on the military sector – especially in comparison with Japan and Britain's competitors in Europe.[15] At the same time the reflationary measures intended to *restore full employment* after each 'stop' phase tended to prevent the onset of economic crisis which could have precipitated the restructuring of industrial capital in the interests of more streamlined and profitable production. Nor did the state pursue active industrial policies ('*Strukturpolitik*') to compensate for this lack of crisis-induced industrial modernisation. Indeed, although the relative stagnation from the 'stop–go' cycle did lead to some measure of industrial concentration in the fifties,[16] the basic international competitiveness of British capital as a whole continued to decline. In addition, while the state avoided an active industrial policy in favour of reliance on market forces, the state sector continued to grow under the impact of the post-war settlement and the escalating state expenditure required to maintain full employment in the context of this structural decline. This constituted an additional burden on declining industrial profits and also contributed to the slowly increasing inflation of this period.[17] In short, within the framework of the 'stop–go' cycle, there was a steady deterioration in the performance of the British economy.[18]

However, during the late fifties and early sixties, the balance of forces mobilised behind this economic and political strategy started to disintegrate. The débâcle of the Anglo–French intervention at Suez made it apparent that Britain was no longer able to act as a superpower and called the extensive defence commitments overseas increasingly into question. Spokesmen for industrial capital began to debate the wisdom of the restrictions on domestic growth and investment outside the overseas sterling area and to press for changes in the strategy for capital accumulation. This shift was particularly clear in the growing support for indicative planning to stimulate economic expansion at home and in increasing interest in British membership of the EEC to achieve greater access to the fast-expanding European market. Important changes were also taking place in the City. There had been increasing association between financial and industrial capital as City institutions acquired an increasing equity stake in industrial and commercial enterprises,[19] entered the medium- and long-term industrial capital market as well as increasing their consumer credit operations, and provided an expanding range of financial and managerial services. At the same time sterling became less important in its overseas operations as the European and American financial markets became increasingly integrated after 1958[20] and the City diversified into the fast-expanding Eurocurrency and Eurobond markets. Thus an increasing weight of financial opinion also began to question the costs of the commitment to sterling and to consider other economic strategies.[21] Within the trade union movement there was also growing pressure to break out of the 'stop–go' cycle. Nor were the major political parties immune from this general reorientation in strategy. Thus, spurred by the Suez fiasco in 1956, a balance of payments crisis in 1960, and a sterling crisis in 1961, the Conservative Party started to reconsider its attitude towards state intervention in the framework of the changing international order and the post-war settlement between capital and labour. It began to implement new programmes in the early sixties to encourage rationalisation and modernisation, introduced an incomes policy, and made the first British application to the European Common Market. Likewise, prompted by its third successive electoral defeat in 1959 and seeking to capitalise on the relatively poor growth record of the economy under the Conservatives, the Labour Party joined the movement to planning and industrial reorganisation.[22] This shift of strategy was consolidated during the sixties despite important, if residual, opposition from various economic and political tendencies in the Establishment, the petite bourgeoisie, and the labour movement.

Industrial Capital and the Working-class

Britain is characterised not only by the historical separation of financial and industrial capital but also by the relative backwardness of its industrial base and the *defensive* economic power of its working-class. And, just as the separation and hegemony of financial capital can be explained in terms of the development of British capitalism, so one can relate the industrial backwardness and working-class defensive strength to the nature and timing of Britain's industrialisation and its nineteenth-century dominance in the international system. Since these characteristics generate continuing problems and provide a major focus for state intervention since the Second World War, it is perhaps worthwhile to sketch in their background.

Early leadership in manufacturing meant that British capital was locked into areas and techniques of production that became obsolescent as more advanced products and technologies were discovered. Moreover, because of the low levels of concentration and centralisation characteristic of industrial capital in nineteenth-century Britain, it tended to be so fragmented that enterprises lacked adequate individual market power and/or cartel organisation and/or City co-ordination to permit a fundamental restructuring of declining industries or diversification into expanding industries. Instead, faced with increasing competition from foreign capital, British industry extended and intensified trade and investment links with the growing but protected imperial markets. This reinforced the strategic position of the City in Britain since it retained its international hegemony into the interwar period and was a crucial source of revenue to compensate for the overall trade deficit. Thus British capital tended to neglect its domestic industrial base in favour of industrial and portfolio investment overseas and acting as a middleman in international transactions. Its domestic investments were often lower than those overseas and they were all too often confined to refurbishing and complementing existing facilities instead of scrapping obsolescent plant and re-equipping with the most advanced and efficient means of production. Indeed, despite massive overseas disinvestment to finance two World Wars and a switch to domestic investment in new technologies and products in the great depression (accompanied by defensive mergers and cartellisation in traditional staple industries), this pattern has continued well into the post-war period. Thus British capital became increasingly vulnerable to foreign competition and faced serious problems once the empire and overseas sterling area began to dissolve and its home and foreign markets were penetrated with the liberalisation of post-war trade and the development of its imperialist rivals.[23]

The early industrialisation in Britain is also reflected in trade union and employer organisation, the industrial relations system, and the organisation of the labour process. Its early lead in manufacturing meant that Britain developed an industrial base with a large range of products, a complex mixture of technologies, a correspondingly elaborate system of occupational groups, skill levels, and work tasks, and an initially low level of concentration and centralisation of industrial capital. These characteristics are reproduced in the traditional weakness of employers' organisations in Britain and in the existence of a complex trade union movement with major unions organised on a variety of craft, general, and industrial lines.[24] In turn this has inhibited the development of a centralised collective bargaining system and also encouraged strong union organisation at plant and company level. Moreover, given the high level of union membership in industry, the lack of religious and political divisions that might undermine union solidarity during disputes, and the strength of union organisation at shop-floor level, the better organised workers were able to establish significant areas and forms of control over the labour process.[25] This is evident in restrictive practices concerning demarcation, apprenticeships, manning levels, work rates, overtime, etc., and in shop-floor resistance to reorganisation of the labour process. These essentially defensive attempts to achieve some control at the point of production were reinforced by the interwar experience of mass unemployment and facilitated by the continuity of organisation through a World War which saw unions in many other countries destroyed by fascism. Thus, if the availability of protected markets for traditional staple products was one major factor in delaying industrial reorganisation in Britain, another cause was the veto power of organised labour. Hence industrial capital was reluctant to re-equip and restructure and/or failed to secure expected increases in the rate of exploitation.[26] Moreover, excluding periods when overseas investment was impossible (such as the great depression and the Second World War), this also stimulated the export of capital to areas where labour was more compliant, wages were lower, and the rate of exploitation higher. This was compensated in part through an increasing flow of American and other foreign investment since the war (especially in technologically-advanced, capital-intensive production on 'greenfield' sites with a new labour force).[27] Yet this did not stem the long-term decline of British *national* capital due to working-class strength at the point of production but merely highlighted it.

This situation was aggravated after the Second World War owing to the high level of employment maintained through resort to macro-level demand management. For this encouraged the development of plant- and company-level bargaining over wages in manufacturing industries and reinforced attempts to influence the terms on which plant- and company-level (and, more recently, even industry-wide) reorganisation would occur, if at all.[28] Moreover, to the extent that production none the less becomes more capital-intensive, the labour process becomes more dependent on uninterrupted production, and continuing socialisation leads to greater interdependence among units of production, there is a parallel increase in the effective short-term economic 'strike-power' of labour. In conjunction with the strength of shop-floor organisation and state-induced full employment, this presented a growing threat to industrial capital. Thus, once the rising real wages produced by the Korean boom, a shift in the terms of trade, and a reduction in arms expenditure were attenuated through the 'stagflationary' effects of 'stop–go' policy and the increasing burden of taxation on wages due to the expansion of the public sector, the increase of state expenditure on transfer payments, and a redistribution of taxation on to earned income and consumption to compensate industrial capital for a decline in gross profits as its international competitiveness diminished, there was a marked increase in trade union militancy and industrial disputes in both the private and public sectors of the economy. The nature of these disputes varied much over time but there was growing concern in the Establishment about the 'strike problem', 'bad industrial practices', and 'wage-push inflation'.[29] Thus the sixties and seventies also revealed a 'crisis in industrial relations'.

Another factor in Britain's industrial decline in this period was the steady expansion of the public sector and public expenditure. The existence of a large public sector and/or large public expenditure is a precondition of effective Keynesian demand management. Moreover, if nationalisation was necessary to permit the restructuring of declining industries essential to the reproduction of capital in general and the state is also obliged to socialise the provision of infrastructure and 'public goods' to facilitate accumulation, equally necessary is the implementation of basic social and economic policies and programmes to ensure the reproduction of labour power and capitalist relations of production. Indeed, without a significant peasantry or traditional urban petite bourgeoisie to mobilise as allied or supporting classes and faced with an homogeneous and well-organised working-class, it is also politically essential for a national bourgeoisie operating in a liberal democratic system to consolidate support in the working-class through social imperialism and/or social democratic policies.[30] But within this framework there is considerable room for variation in the form and scope of state intervention in the economy and civil society and the causes and effects of such variation must also be considered.

In Britain the expansion of the state sector and public spending was stimulated by several forces. Chief among these were the decline of British industry, the requirements and effects of the unique 'stop–go' policy, and the impact of electoral competition. For, granted the commitment to full employment and social welfare embodied in the post-war settlement and the comparatively slow growth of British industry, there was growing pressure for expansion of the state sector from the late fifties to provide employment as well as maintain demand.[31] The approximate balance in electoral support for the two main parties also encouraged 'pensioneering'[32] and other forms of competitive bidding to secure marginal votes. Moreover, since public spending was planned on the assumption that the economy would expand faster than actually occurred, there was a regular upward bias in the share of public spending beyond that intended.[33] In turn this reinforced pressure on taxation and/or the government borrowing require-ment – reducing take-home wages and/or net profits and/or con-tributing to inflation to the extent that the borrowing was met through treasury bills and/or attracting capital that might otherwise be lent to the industrial sector.[34] Finally, as the industrial crisis deepened, it was more and more necessary for the state to provide financial support to stimulate demand and further investment. This generated a growing fiscal crisis in the British state towards the end of the sixties.

In conclusion, in attempting to sketch the economic background to the reorganisation of the British state since the Second World War, we have emphasised four main factors. First, Britain was characterised by the separation of financial and industrial capital and the economic and political hegemony of the former to the long-term detriment of the latter. Secondly, owing to the possibilities of a retreat into imperial trade and investment and to the defensive strength of key sections of the labour force, industrial capital in Britain became increasingly less competitive in international markets. Thirdly, despite the major decline in Britain's economic and political position in the international order by 1945, a concerted attempt was made to restore sterling and empire to a central position in the new world system. And, finally, within the framework of the post-war settlement between capital and labour, the state was obliged to maintain full employment and increase social welfare. The combined impact of these factors was crystallised in the 'stop–go' cycle, the 'crisis of industrial relations', the worsening 'profitability crisis', a growing 'fiscal crisis', and a growing tendency towards 'stagflation'. Moreover, within the apparently stable framework of 'stop–go', the underlying position deteriorated steadily. With each new cycle of 'stop–go', the peak balance of payments deficit tended to grow larger, the peak rate of unemployment increased, the inflation rate reached new heights, and the overall increase in national production tended to decline.[35] The need for action was increasingly apparent to all sections of the Establishment and there was increasing discussion about the best strategies for promoting capital accumulation.

This analysis implies that the British crisis cannot be explained simply through the tendency of the rate of profit to fall (or 'TRPF'). The internationalisation of capital means that the latter (and, indeed, its equally important counter-tendencies) now works on a world scale as well as a national level and that the international TRPF overdetermines national tendencies. An international crisis due to the TRPF has certainly aggravated British problems, heightened inter-imperialist rivalries, and precluded a purely domestic solution to the British crisis. But the latter *pre-dates* the global collapse of the post-war boom and is based on a long-term failure to restructure British capital and provide the most appropriate framework for accumulation. British capital has encountered abnormal problems in *valorisation* (or adding value) and in *realisation* (meeting an effective demand to permit the appropriation of this value). Thus it tends to receive below-average profits and/or to depend on below-average wages. This situation is reinforced by other factors reviewed above: the hegemony of financial capital, the nature of state intervention, the defensive strength of organised labour. In short the current crisis is much more the expression of the overall weakness of British capital than the effect of some abstract, tendential fall in the rate of profit.

State Intervention and the Crisis of Keynesianism

State intervention was fundamentally restructured after the Second World War through the introduction of macro-level demand management in a mixed economy and the massive expansion of social welfare programmes. But there are definite limits to both forms of intervention in securing the reorganisation of production and moderating the growth of crises in social relations. Thus the welfare state involves the bureaucratic or rational-legal distribution of financial resources and social services on the basis of entitlements embodied in the institution of citizenship and is concerned with alleviating the effects on individual citizens or family units of adverse economic, social, or personal contingencies. It does not eliminate the continued reproduction of these contingencies in the course of capital accumulation (to the extent that it is responsible) nor does it alleviate contingencies, such as urban crises, whose effects manifest themselves principally at a supra-individual or supra-family level. Likewise, although Keynesian techniques are supposed to eliminate or alleviate economic crises, their effects on production are necessarily indirect and mediated through the monetary system and the level of aggregate demand. For this reason they are inappropriate for resolving structural crises (of the kind that underlay the economic and political decline of Britain) and must be complemented through direct intervention in the reorganisation of industrial production. Moreover, although Keynesian techniques presuppose that an expansion of effective demand in a closed economy will stimulate additional production, money is integrated into the international circuit of capital and it can function there either as revenue or as capital. Given the openness and structural crisis of Britain's economy, increases in effective demand were just as likely to finance capital exports and the import of consumer goods and/or to enable capital to engage in speculative activities or to raise prices and/or to permit labour to raise its money wage as they were to stimulate further production and the reorganisation of industry. Without such increased production and industrial reorganisation, Keynesian increases in the money supply to maintain full employment merely served to intensify the structural crisis and to fuel stagflation. In this sense the problems discussed in the preceding two sections also manifested themselves as a crisis of Keynesianism as a mode of state intervention and led to increasing interest in alternative modes of regulating the British economy and securing its reorganisation.

The most significant initiative in this respect was the movement to *economic planning* in the early sixties in association with measures to promote rationalisation and competition. Moreover, just as the radical reorganisation of state intervention in the immediate aftermath of the last war was congruent with a broad shift in economic and political strategy within the Establishment, so was the movement towards economic planning. Indeed, whilst it was the principal national federation of industrial capital (the FBI) that articulated the need for planning at its annual conference in 1960, it was the Conservative Party that initiated the National Economic Development Council in 1962 as a tripartite forum for national planning. The Conservative government also pursued a series of policies (ending retail price maintenance, major government spending programmes to modernise education and the social services, incentives for regional investment, etc.[36]) intended to promote modernisation and rationalisation. But it was the Labour Party, after a narrow electoral victory in 1964, that gave planning a high priority. In its policies during the Wilson government of 1964–70, the Labour government not only continued or implemented many policies that originated in the preceding Conservative administration but also began a more active, interventionist structural policy. It is with the nature and limits of this concerted attempt at economic planning in response to the serious crisis of Keynesianism that this section is concerned.

Economic planning in Britain has been handicapped by the institutional weakness of the state planning apparatus in relation to the central axis of the overall system of state economic apparatuses, i.e., the Treasury and Bank of England. Thus, whilst the National Economic Development Council (NEDC or 'Neddy') has been formally located outside the institutional complex of central government since its creation in 1962 and the institutions created under the recent Labour administrations to restructure industrial capital (the Industrial Reorganisation Corporation, 1966–71, and the National Enterprise Board, 1975–) have likewise been para-state apparatuses, even the state planning apparatus (Department of Economic Affairs) and the main intervention apparatus (Ministry of Technology) established by the incoming Labour government in 1964 were set apart from the central axis. This is important because the Treasury and the Bank have retained control over the instruments of short-term economic policy and over central government expenditure because of the vulnerability of sterling.[37] This dissociation between state economic apparatuses has thus meant that the Treasury–Bank axis was able to reassert the priority of the balance of payments and the reserves against the priority of growth (and full employment) entailed in the commitment to planning. The dominance of the short-term could have been broken by a devaluation of sterling to provide the breathing space necessary for industrial reorganisation and long-term planning. But the balance of political forces (especially at the international level) tended to oppose this.[38] This was particularly clear during the 1964–70 Labour administration. For, in both 1964 and 1966, when faced with the choice between devaluation as a precondition of planned growth and deflation to safeguard the reserves and protect sterling, the Labour government decided in favour of another 'stop'.[39] Moreover, even after the inevitable but long-delayed devaluation of sterling in 1967, priority was still given to continued deflation in order to repay international debt and accumulate a payments surplus rather than resort to economic planning and industrial reorganisation.

If the subordination of the planning apparatus due to the overall disarticulation of the state economic apparatus was a principal cause for the failure of planning, another was the very nature of the planning system itself. For the national plans drawn up by the NEDC in 1962 and the Department of Economic Affairs (DEA) in 1965 were essentially indicative (if not purely subjunctive) in character and there were no policy instruments for directly or indirectly securing compliance with the growth targets. Planning by the nation-state is a notoriously difficult exercise owing to the growing internationalisation of capital, the contradictions between 'capital in general' and individual competing capitals, and the effects of class struggle.[40] It is not made easier through reluctance to employ measures to secure compliance and trusting instead in voluntary co-operation.

But the indicative, voluntary nature of economic planning in this period expresses a fundamental problem at the heart of state intervention in Britain. For, whereas organised labour has considerable 'veto' power at the point of production and monopoly capital has considerable scope for international mobility, the 'social partners' of government in the management of the economy are weak, decentralised, and fragmented. The Trades Union Congress (TUC) is a loose confederation of craft, general and industrial unions – many of which are themselves somewhat decentralised bodies. And, owing to the complex industrial base, the historically low levels of concentration and centralisation of industrial capital, the economic and political hegemony of financial capital, the weakness of the TUC, and the absence of a strongly interventionist state, the political representation of industrial capital is also comparatively weak and ineffective. Indeed, until the formation of the Confederation of British Industry (CBI) was sponsored by the Labour administration in 1965, there was no single peak organisation to represent industrial capital in Britain. Even this organisation does not represent all fractions of capital (excluding both financial and commercial capital) and it lacks effective control over its members.[41] The nature of these 'social partners' means that, if their participation in economic planning is to be secured, it must be indicative and voluntary in character and/or must imply little sacrifice on the part of individual capitals and individual unions or groups of workers. In turn this means that, however fruitful participation may be in generating an economic plan and consensus over economic strategy between the government and peak organisations, the state and the social partners alike are unable to enforce compliance with the requirements of such a plan at the micro-level.

This problem is also evident in the successive *attempts of the state to regulate incomes* (especially wages) to promote capital accumulation. These attempts have tended to acquire legal and/or *ad hoc* administrative force and to be associated with institutional supports in the state or para-state system.[42] Thus, whereas the first post-war Labour and Conservative governments pursued voluntary policies which were, at most, subject to review only by para-state bodies with no substantive powers, the second post-war Labour administration established the National Board for Prices and Incomes (NBPI) to advise on specific cases and to police the official powers of delay.[43] A new Conservative administration abolished the NBPI in 1970 and pursued a voluntary policy for two years; it then imposed a pay freeze and later created a Price Commission and a Pay Board to advise on, implement, and enforce its price and pay codes. The last Labour government followed a similar path. It abolished the Pay Board in 1974 and adopted a 'voluntary' incomes policy as part of the Social Contract (see below). But there were significant elements of compulsion in this policy – including pressure on arbitrators and Wages Councils, exemplary resistance and/or 'cash limits' in the public sector, the operation of a 'black-list' for government aid and contracts in cases where private employers went beyond official guidelines, and the refusal of price increases in line with cost increases where firms broke these guidelines. The whole policy came under increasing pressure in the winter of 1978/9 and the new Conservative administration has promised a return to 'responsible' (sic) free collective bargaining in a context of monetary restraint, 'cash limits', and, in the background, a possible pay freeze (likely to begin the cycle once more?)

All these policies, apart from that of 1948–50 (associated with a manpower policy and the diversion of increased peacetime production into exports), have occurred in reaction to the crisis of Keynesianism. For industrial capital needed encouragement to invest in the face of a long-term structural decline, working class resistance, 'stop–go', and a growing public sector share in national income. And, given the reluctance to devalue sterling and/or pursue an active structural policy as well as the ability of organised labour to disarticulate demand management strategies, the state was obliged to act on wage-costs through incomes, price, and fiscal policies. It was hoped to improve profits and stimulate investment by ensuring that wage increases did not keep pace with productivity, price-inflation, and fiscal drag. But, although every incomes policy has helped in reducing the rate of increase in take home pay (discounting price and tax effects) or even reducing net real income, the resulting shift of resources to the private sector and/or the state has not been fully utilised for industrial investment at home. In part this failure is attributable to the imposition of a 'stop' phase at some point during each period of incomes policy (thus discouraging investment) but it is also a result of the continued operation of other disincentives to investment. At the same time the effect of incomes policies on real wages (especially in the public sector and in those industries where wages did not keep pace with inflation) and on the level of unemployment stimulated growing discontent and militancy among rank-and-file trade unionists. This precipitated increased strike action in opposition to wage restraint (often without the support of the national union leadership when the restraint was operated by a Labour administration) and also produced a wage explosion at the end of the incomes policy. Indeed, since another effect of wage restraint has been to make union leaders less moderate in order to reflect and/or contain the growing militancy of their members with each new period of incomes policy, it has become increasingly difficult to secure even TUC support for wage restraint and the government has therefore been obliged to offer more concessions and/or to impose more powerful sanctions with each successive period of restraint.[44] In turn this has aggravated the crisis of industrial relations and union organisation in Britain.

Thus neither economic planning nor incomes policies have succeeded in resolving the emerging crisis of Keynesianism in the British context and enabling industrial capital to escape from the economic straitjacket of 'stop–go' policies. Indeed both the planning apparatus and the operation of incomes policies have been subordinated to short-term considerations and thereby rendered ineffective in promoting a long-term regeneration of British industry. In contrast a certain degree of *industrial reorganisation* has been achieved through the activities of certain other state and para-state institutions. Thus, in addition to the reports of the tripartite little Neddies concerned with promoting technical efficiency in various industrial sectors,[45] we may note the important rôle of the Industrial Reorganisation Corporation (IRC), the National Enterprise Board (NEB), the Ministry of Technology (Mintech), and Mintech's various successors in the central government system. In different ways each of these bodies has been concerned with industrial reorganisation.

Whereas the Conservative administration of 1951–64 had restricted its economic intervention largely to monetary and fiscal policies, wage restraint, and changes in *Ordnungspolitik* (e.g., legislation on monopolies, retail price maintenance, company law, etc.), the Labour government of 1964–70 established important new forms of *direct intervention* in industry. The IRC was formed in 1966 as a quasi-non-governmental organisation ('quango') empowered to use its own money capital (initially £150m) to promote or assist the reorganisation or development of any industry and/or to promote or assist the establishment and development of any industrial enterprise. It was a major force behind the reorganisation of the nuclear industry, the electrical industry, and the indigenous motor industry; and it also intervened in other areas to encourage centralisation and concentration of industrial capital.[46] The Labour administration also established Mintech in 1964 and introduced the Industrial Expansion Act in 1968 to encourage scientific and technical innovations and their application in industry (e.g., in modernising the machine tool industry and promoting the British computer industry).[47] The activities of the various 'sponsoring departments' (initiated during the last World War as the appropriate Whitehall departments promoted the interests and/or demands of different branches of industry) were also stepped up and co-ordinated with those of the IRC and Mintech.[48] Moreover, although the incoming Conservative government in 1970 abolished the IRC and dismantled Mintech under pressure from small and medium capital opposed to state intervention,[49] it created two super-ministries for more effective co-ordination of infrastructural provision (the Department of the Environment) and of commercial and industrial policies (the Department of Trade and Industry). Within two years the Conservatives also undertook a major U-turn with the Industry Act (1972) which gave the state even more extensive powers of intervention than before as well as establishing an Industrial Development Unit to implement these policies and an Advisory Board for independent advice.[50] This resulted in state support for the modernisation of several industries (wool textiles, ferrous foundries, machine tools, printing machinery, and non-ferrous foundries) and for a number of investment plans in other industries. Such interventionist policies were continued and extended under the last Labour administration with the passage of a further Industry Act (1975) and the concomitant introduction of the National Enterprise Board (NEB) as an independent state holding company. These measures have provided the state with a broad-based institutional complex able to offer extensive financial and infrastructural incentives to the private sector and to permit extensive state intervention in this sector.[51]

These developments originated in the search for a viable alternative to past government policies and have become increasingly significant in the overall economic strategy of the state. It remains to be seen how far the present Conservative régime will disengage from an active

Strukturpolitik as opposed to more politically inspired programmes such as state-sponsored co-operatives or job preservation. In contrast to Keynesianism, indicative planning, and wage restraint, this approach involves direct intervention in the organisation of production and is thus akin to the restructuring that accompanies nationalisation. Thus, whereas Keynesian techniques can influence the 'supply side' at best indirectly and haphazardly, the new industrial policies attempt to integrate government money directly into the circuit of productive capital and to ensure that it promotes further accumulation of capital. This is apparent not only in the increasing utilisation of general and/or selective incentives for industrial investment (e.g., accelerated depreciation, free depreciation, investment relief under the Price Code, investment grants of various kinds, regional employment subsidies, etc.) but also in the growth of state participation in the private sector in the form of equity and/or loan capital subscribed by state-financed bodies such as the Industrial Reorganisation Corporation, the National Research Development Corporation, and the National Enterprise Board.

State interventions to rescue 'lame ducks' and preserve jobs are also increasingly associated with attempts to restructure industry and/or redeploy labour. This is evident in the last Conservative government's restructuring of Upper Clyde Shipbuilders as well as in the Labour government's planning agreement with Chrysler.[52] And there has also been increasing emphasis on rationalisation and restructuring in the public sector with the nationalised industries obliged to increase productivity, reduce their labour force, accept cash limits on government support, and achieve a target rate of return on capital. The British Steel Corporation provides the most important example here but these pressures are also significant in the case of British Leyland, British Shipbuilders, the British Transport Docks Board, British Rail, and the Post Office. In short, whether in the form of intervention in the private sector or reorganisation of the public sector, the state has become increasingly integrated into the circuit of productive capital since the mid-sixties.

However, although *industrial policy* has become an important element in the accumulation strategy of British capital, it is *not yet dominant*. In part this is due to the continued significance of short-term problems associated with the balance of payments and the reserves, the management of the national debt and the financing of the public sector borrowing requirement, and the control of 'wage-push' inflation. But, although an apparent collapse of the pound in June,

1975, coupled with an escalating budget deficit and accelerating inflation, forced the Labour government to impose a 'voluntary' incomes
policy and begin moving to a much firmer control over the money
supply and public expenditure, these measures were more closely
articulated than hitherto with industrial policy. For the Labour
government was particularly concerned not only to reduce public
spending and control the money supply but also to restructure the
state sector and ensure that tax revenues and domestic credit expansion functioned as far as possible as productive capital or (in)directly
productive social expenditure.[53] With certain modifications this
approach will be continued by the current Conservative administration. But the relative weakness of industrial policy within the overall
strategy of British capital also stems from division and conflicts in the
Establishment and from the continued resistance of organised labour
to any economic strategy which involves an immediate threat to its
economic-corporate interests and/or not subject to workers' control
or consent. Thus Labour legislation to provide certain institutional
and financial conditions for an active industrial policy was opposed by
important sectors of industry (including the CBI), influential City
institutions, the Conservative Party, and most of the press. Even
under the past Labour government the NEB was a pale shadow of the
projected state holding company, only an indigent Chrysler signed a
planning agreement, plans to set up company-level industrial
democracy were shelved, the operations of the British National Oil
Corporation were attenuated, and plans to nationalise major firms in
banking, insurance, and industry to provide the basis for an active
meso-level industrial policy were jettisoned. The new Conservative
régime is most unlikely to be more interventionist in the immediate
future than its Labour predecessor. Business opposition is partly
rooted in commitment to monetarism and market forces and partly in
disquiet over the likely influence of organised labour on industrial
policy. Organised labour has been opposed in turn because of worries
that industrial policy would involve a decline in living standards,
increased unemployment and inflation, an attack on the welfare state,
continuing wage restraint, and increased economic exploitation. But
there is also support for industrial policy provided that it is operated
under workers' control or, at least, is formulated after consultation
with the TUC and union officials. In this sense the state has been
restricted and partially paralysed in this field by opposition from both
sides of industry.

Indeed, far from industrial policy being a consensual panacea for solving the British crisis, it is a major focus of economic, political, and ideological struggle. For, whereas Keynesianism is compatible with considerable freedom of market forces and does not fundamentally undermine managerial prerogatives or collective bargaining, an active structural policy involves discriminating among economic agents, intervening in individual firms and industries, restricting and channelling market forces, and the deliberate devalorisation of capitals and unemployment of workers. Its effective operation requires certain conditions in the field of economic and political representation that do not exist in contemporary Britain. It is to problems in this area that we now turn.

Corporatism and the Crisis of Industrial Relations

The structural crisis of the British economy has also manifested itself as a 'crisis of industrial relations'. This in turn has various facets: it is apparent in working-class resistance to the reorganisation of the labour process, in increasing trade union militancy in wage negotiations, in the development of rank-and-file movements opposed to official union policies at local and national level, and in the elaboration of more effective forms of strike action. Individual capitals have attempted to overcome some of these problems through productivity bargaining, the introduction of new payment schemes (e.g., measured day work), the introduction of new production techniques, and the development of schemes for employee participation and consultation.[54] But the extent of these initiatives has varied considerably, as has their level of success in securing greater managerial control over the labour force and reducing labour costs. Moreover, since it is the overall structure of the trade union movement and the system of decentralised bargaining within the framework of full employment that is largely responsible for this crisis, there has also been growing pressure on the state to reorganise the whole industrial relations system in the absence of union or managerial initiatives. For, given the specific conditions of capital–labour relations in Britain both at the point of production and at the level of national organisation for political and economic representation and co-ordination, neither capital nor labour, whether acting alone or together, could accomplish the necessary restructuring of industrial relations to facilitate accumulation. In turn, given the real strength of shop-floor organisation and the weakness of national industrial and union organisation, the state has increasingly been forced to intervene in an effort to neutralise shop-floor power and to reinforce the 'peak' organisations.

This is evident not only in the continued resort to incomes policies throughout the post-war period and in the two (soon to be three?) unsuccessful attempts to reorganise industrial relations and the trade union movement through legislation, but also in the integration of industrial and trade union representatives into the state apparatus and the 'corporatisation' of the economic and political representation of the so-called 'two sides of industry' in Britain.

Official encouragement and sponsorship of trade union organisation and integration of union leaders into the state started on a large scale in the First World War but were reversed or at least allowed to atrophy in the interwar period. These policies were revived in the Second World War and, as part of the post-war settlement, continued under both Labour and Conservative administrations. This is evident not only in official support for collective bargaining in the private as well as public sector and in the activities of the Ministry of Labour (and its successors) in the fields of conciliation, arbitration, and industrial inquiries – support and activities which have been greatly reinforced by the late Labour administration through its industrial relations legislation and the creation of the tripartite Arbitration, Conciliation, and Advisory Service; but also in the growing number of state and para-state bodies on which trade unions are formally or informally represented and in the increasing contacts between trade union officials and ministers or civil servants.[55] Such involvement extends beyond advisory and investigative organs to include state and para-state apparatuses responsible for the formulation and implementation of programmes and policies at national, regional, and local level. Major stimuli here have been the introduction of economic planning (especially in relation to Neddy, the various little Neddies, Regional Economic Development Councils, and, recently, the Manpower Services Commission) and the attempt to strengthen and effectuate wage restraint policies (especially under the Social Contract). Moreover in both these areas trade union involvement has been promoted less to obtain technical information and detailed advice than to secure active support or at least passive acquiescence in measures intended to facilitate accumulation. Thus union participation in Neddy was sought by the Conservative administration not only to secure information and advice but also to encourage union acquiescence in wage restraint along with union co-operation in efforts to increase productivity.[56] This emphasis is also apparent in the fact that both Labour and Conservative administrations have frequently undertaken major policy initiatives directly affecting the unions (and not just concerned with overall economic management) without prior consultation or after rejecting any TUC or union advice.[57] This is very clear in the case of industrial relations legislation (e.g., Labour's 1969 Industrial Relations Bill and the Conservatives' Industrial Relations Act in 1971) and in the resort to wage freezes in early stages of incomes policies. It is thus crucial to consider the precise rôle of union integration and participation and the general function of the tendency towards corporatism or tripartism.

In part union involvement simply reflects the significance of the labour movement in the post-war settlement and this aspect is evident in the largely *symbolic* representation of trade unionism on royal commissions, advisory bodies, the benches of the House of Lords, the Court of the Bank of England, etc. But this is increasingly coupled with trade union participation in bodies charged with policy formulation and execution. This reflects the changing imperatives of economic intervention in the context of the British crisis. Three aspects are important here – the crisis of Keynesianism, the structural crisis, and the industrial relations crisis. The manipulation of monetary and fiscal instruments to maintain full employment (or, alternatively, to deflate the national economy in the interests of sterling) does not require the co-operation of organised labour since it relies on the reaction of market forces to changes in aggregate demand. But Keynesianism cannot solve structural crises and, in the context of a strong and militant labour movement, is also liable to generate inflation.[58] Moreover, since these conditions also entail that a monetarist policy coupled with non-intervention and disengagement will produce economic and political consequences that are unacceptable (bankruptcies, high unemployment, electoral defeat, etc.), it has become necessary to adopt active structural policies and impose wage restraint. Both sorts of intervention directly affect the unions. For the co-operation of organised labour is required to improve productivity through the elimination of restrictive practices, the repudiation of strike action, the introduction of new machinery and techniques, and the large-scale redeployment and retraining of labour-power. Such co-operation is also required in the reorganisation and restructuring of the welfare state in order to reduce the burden of social expenditure on capital and to ensure that the state sector contributes more effectively to accumulation. And it is also required to implement and police wage restraint on a voluntary basis or, failing that, to acquiesce in a compulsory incomes policy. In short, whereas the Keynesian pursuit of full employment and/or defence of sterling did not require integration of the union movement into the state apparatus, the regeneration of industrial capital and the battle against inflation do necessitate active involvement of organised labour.

Similar considerations apply to the participation and integration of capital. The relations between the state and particular capitals in the fifties were characterised by the system of 'sponsorship' in which different departments promoted the interests of relevant sectors of industry. This system is rooted in the *dirigisme* of the Second World War when 'sponsoring departments' enforced or supervised wartime controls and promoted or channelled the demands of industries and individual enterprises. It continued after the dissolution of wartime planning and the departments tended simply to transmit information and requests from trade associations and individual companies and to mediate on their behalf in relation to other departments and the Treasury.[59] This pattern of economic and political representation was necessarily fragmented and also tended to be *ad hoc*, informal, and intermittent in character. But the increasing resort to economic planning and state intervention meant there was a growing need for a forum to represent the interests of capital in general and for permanent formal bodies in which to elaborate industrial strategies. Moreover, since industrial reorganisation and regeneration presupposes union co-operation, these bodies are often tripartite in contrast to the bilateral form of the sponsorship system. And, in order to facilitate the operation of both government-business and tripartite bodies, the state has also sponsored a major reorganisation of industrial and commercial representation since the early sixties and encouraged the formation of various trade associations, the Retail Consortium, the Confederation of British Industry, and the City Liaison Committee.[60] Such reorganisation has not only occurred at the national level but also at the regional level.

The development of functional representation and tripartism is not peculiar to Britain but is also found to a greater or lesser degree in other European societies. Thus, although it is correct to focus on the distinctive rôle of the British crisis and especially on the importance of the crises of Keynesianism, industrial relations, and structural decline, it is also essential to consider whether there are more general developmental tendencies which are mediated and/or reinforced through these distinctive British characteristics. Chief among these general tendencies are the consolidation and internationalisation of capitalist relations of production, the increasing socialisation of the forces of production, and the increasing rôle of the state in securing the social conditions of capital accumulation and mobilising counter-tendencies to the rate of profit to fall. Together these changes result in a simplification of class relations through the tendential elimination of pre-capitalist classes and the expansion of the wage-earning classes (thus requiring a reorientation of strategies of political domination), in an increased complexity and interdependence of the circuit of capital and increasing vulnerability to breaks in the circuit (thus requiring ever-increasing centralisation and control over different moments and forces in the accumulation process), and in increasing integration of the state into the circuit of capital (thus transforming the institutional separation between the economic and political instances characteristic of capitalism). In turn this implies a need to reorganise the social bases of political domination and to restructure the system of political representation and state intervention.

One solution to these problems is the social democratisation of state power and the institutionalisation of a corporatist form of state. For, while social democracy transforms wage-earners into a 'supporting class' of the bourgeoisie through the integration of their economic and political organisations into the public sphere and political order and through concessions to their economic-corporate demands, corporatism transcends the separation between the economic and political instances of capitalist formations through the development of functional representation and functional intervention. In this sense the partial evolution of social democratic corporatism in Britain corresponds to more general developmental tendencies.

But it is also obvious that corporatism is far from being dominant or stable and that it is subject to major contradictions internally and in its articulation with the parliamentary-bureaucratic form of state. For the consolidation of corporatism requires effective representation of the 'two sides of industry' through organisations with a strong base in their respective functional constituencies and it also demands forms of intervention adequate to class collaboration in industrial restructuring and wage restraint. It also requires an institutional framework within which to articulate functional representation with parliamentary representation and to co-ordinate intervention through corporatist channels with that through rational-legal administration. Little progress has been achieved in meeting any of these requirements despite frequent attempts and pious appeals to develop and extend corporatism.

In particular, although the consolidation of corporatism requires a mass base as well as the effective co-operation of the business community, the structure of the labour movement in Britain and the continued weakness of business representation preclude this. For, while the Labour Party has never had a mass individual membership and no longer has deep roots in the organisational life of working-class communities, the trade union movement is decentralised and fragmented and the TUC lacks the power to commit individual unions (let alone particular groups of trade union members) to implement its decisions. Moreover, despite the creation of a TUC–Labour Party Liaison Committee in 1972 and the strong organisational links between the trade union movement and the Labour Party, there is a strong continuing commitment to the separation of economic and political action and their confinement within the limits of the market relation and liberal parliamentarism respectively. But, whilst this separation was appropriate in the 'Keynesian-welfare state' system, it is inappropriate when the state is integrated into the circuit of productive capital and social policy is programme-based rather than redistributional in nature. The resulting disarticulation of economic and political strategies is reinforced through the fragmentation of the union movement and the strength of shop-floor organisation. The obvious crisis in the Social Contract between the two wings of the labour movement is compelling evidence of this contradiction and reflects the weakness of social democracy as well as the major structural crisis affecting the British economy. In short, despite the continuing effort to co-ordinate economic and political action through the Social Contract and the TUC–Labour Party Liaison Committee, the British labour movement is unable to organise the mass base required for a full-fledged corporatist system. This means that corporatism is restricted to tripartite discussions between top union officials, industrial statesmen, politicians, and government bureaucrats. In turn this means that corporatism cannot provide a stable basis of political mobilisation or economic intervention and that other forms of representation and intervention must be employed.

It is in this context that we can locate the continuing government attempts since the mid-sixties to restructure the trade union movement. For, whilst the principal objective of these attempts has been to eliminate or alleviate working-class resistance at the point of production and to secure greater control over wage costs, the means employed have been based on the bureaucratisation of shop-floor organisation and its integration into the national trade union movement and/or the displacement of shop-floor organisation through a combination of centralisation and subjection to legal and judicial regulation. Successful reorganisation along these lines would have created conditions more favourable to the operation of a corporatist system but attempts to reform industrial relations through legislative means have met with concerted union opposition.[61] None the less there has been some movement in this direction due to the gradual and uneven bureaucratisation of the shop steward movement and its partial incorporation into managerial and/or official union hierarchies. The initial successes of the voluntary government–union wage restraint from 1975 owed much to the ability of national officials to win the support of major convenors who were in turn able to secure the acquiescence of other shop stewards and ordinary workers.[62] This informal mediation subsequently collapsed because of a sharp decline in real disposable wages (amounting to 10 per cent in 1975–7) and the intensificiation of attempts to restructure the labour process and reorganise the welfare state in the interests of restoring capital accumulation.[63] For, since the Social Contract had been 'sold' to the labour movement as the most effective means to produce a massive shift in the distribution of wealth, power, and income in favour of the working-class while restoring economic growth and full employment, its apparent perversion into a means of attack on the living standards and organisation of the working-class was bound to produce a crisis in the labour movement. In this respect it should also be noted that, since corporatism tends to fuse organs of representation and intervention on functional lines, the representational crisis within the labour movement also tends to undermine the effectiveness of corporatist forms of intervention.

Indeed the history of the Social Contract underlines the general contradictions at the heart of corporatism. For, not only does it involve an attempt to transcend the separation between the economic and political instances through the introduction of functional representation, it also attempts to transcend the separation between representation and administration through the voluntary self-regulation of corporations. In contrast to the pluralisation of political forces and the independent rational–legal administration charac-teristic of the parliamentary-bureaucratic system, therefore, cor-poratism requires the constitution of a system of corporations enjoy-ing a representational monopoly and a high degree of centralisation to ensure effective self-administration. But, whilst the recent Labour industrial relations legislation moved some way in this direction for the trade union movement and the major professions have long approximated this position, neither the union movement nor the business community are sufficiently 'incorporated' (organised into corporations) to ensure the effective operation of a corporatist system. In the absence of these conditions other means of representation and intervention are necessary to secure favourable conditions for capital accumulation and bourgeois political domination.

However, if corporatist forms have traditionally been marginalised through restriction to professional self-government and are still fundamentally limited to a relatively ineffective system of tripartite discussions among incompletely incorporated and fragmented peak organisations and representatives of the parliamentary-bureaucratic state system, the latter is itself subject to increasing contradictions and strains in the reproduction of capital accumulation and political domination. This is evident in the decline of parliament as an organ of political representation (with a concomitant shift in the rôle of political parties) and in the decline of rational-legal administration and Keynesianism as modes of political intervention. Since neither the incipient corporatist system nor the traditional parliamentary-bureaucratic system appear to be functioning effectively, we are witnessing a general crisis of the British state. This is reflected in current discussions of 'ungovernability' and 'political overload'.[64] It is in this context that tendencies towards the 'strong state' in Britain can best be understood.

The Decline of Parliament and the Rise of the Strong State

Parliament displaced the 'Court' as the principal national forum of political representation following the English Civil War.[65] It was initially confined to the representatives of propertied interests but, as the franchise was progressively extended, Parliament acquired a key rôle in an emergent liberal–democratic state. Although the latter was always hybrid in form, it was increasingly dominated by parliamentary representation and rational-legal intervention. Thus, whereas political representation was mediated through the suffrage and other political rights enjoyed by the people as 'citizens' in relation to government, state intervention occurred through the parliamentary enactment and subsequent impartial, rational-legal bureaucratic implementation of general legislative codes concerning private and public activities and/or through the provision of general external conditions facilitating or supporting such activities without directly controlling them.[66] This system was gradually extended and consolidated during the nineteenth and early twentieth centuries but, beginning with the First World War and accelerating with the Second World War, it has also been circumscribed and modified through the development of other forms of representation and intervention. Thus, whilst the rise of pressure groups and corporatist organs as well as mass parties has altered the nature and significance of parliamentary representation, state intervention has tended towards more discriminatory, *ad hoc*, delegated, directive forms and, even where it retains a rational–legal, bureaucratic form, has tended to escape from effective parliamentary control. However, although parliamentarism in Britain appears to be in decline and there seems to be a movement towards corporatism and/or an independent and authoritarian executive, the institution of parliamentary sovereignty still means that control of Parliament is critical in the *formal* exercise of state power. In this context it is the Cabinet that remains the most important institution within the con- temporary British state.[67]

The Cabinet is the principal forum in which ministers consider new programmes and policies, determine executive and legislative priorities, try to resolve internal disputes, and discuss issues or events likely to have major economic or political repercussions. Its central position at the apex of the different departments and branches of the state apparatus gives the Cabinet a unique mediating and co- ordinating rôle in the state system – especially as there is only a limited separation of legislative, executive, and judicial powers in Britain. This has been reinforced with the growth of delegated legisla- tion and administrative tribunals but is also characteristic of the traditional state system.[68] Thus, as far as parliamentary legislation is concerned, the Cabinet is usually more restricted by the changing balance of party forces than the relatively unchanging rules and con- ventions of Parliament itself. This follows from the partial fusion of executive and legislative power rooted in the recruitment of the government from the dominant party (or parties) in the Commons. Thus, although it must adhere to certain minimal legal requirements in the conduct of its parliamentary business, the ability of the govern- ment to manipulate and circumvent other procedural rules and con- ventions depends on the movement of factions, tendencies, and alliances and the relative strength of different parties. The rôle of its own backbenchers is generally more important here than movements in opposition parties. Likewise, whilst the traditional judiciary has a large measure of formal independence and is broadly insulated from direct political pressures, it has no power to review the constitutional status of executive or legislative actions provided that due process is observed. Its function is therefore confined to the interpretation of statutes and the elaboration of common law and equity and, whilst its judgements have often significantly modified the law relating to trade disputes, public order, and similar strategic issues, it is within the competence of the Crown-in-Parliament to change judicial precedents in subsequent legislation. Through its ministers the Cabinet is also responsible in law and/or to Parliament for the actions of the executive branch (but see below on quangos and quagos) and collectively it must command the confidence of a majority of MPs in order to retain office. This highlights once again the importance of control over a Parliament subject to the interplay of party politics but it does not alter the position of the Cabinet as the dominant executive apparatus and the linchpin of the state system as a whole. Indeed, although the development of corporatism and para-state organs involves a decline in parliamentarism, it has reinforced the need for an apparatus to mediate among different forms of representation and to co-ordinate the manifold interventions of the state. It is the Cabinet that attempts to fulfil these essential and interrelated political tasks.

The growth of state intervention and its changing forms are associated with significant changes in Cabinet organisation as well as other aspects of the state apparatus. This reorganisation was initiated with the War Cabinet in 1916–18 and experienced a further boost during the sixties and seventies.[69] Among the most significant changes recorded since the last war are the extension and consolidation of the committee system, the further growth of the Cabinet Office as a co-ordinating and advisory body, the foundation of the Central Policy Review Staff in 1970 to assess the long-term strategy of the government and examine specific programmes, and the increasing resort to special advisers in individual departments or attached to the Policy Unit (1974–) as a source of alternative, non-official advice to the Cabinet and individual ministers.[70] These changes are linked with others elsewhere in the executive branch. There has been a marked tendency towards the formation of giant, unitary departments, each with its own Cabinet minister, to develop a coherent, general strategy in its field of interest and sponsor it in relation to the Cabinet, Treasury, and Cabinet Office. This is evident in the formation and reorganisation of such departments as Trade, Industry, Health and Social Security, Energy, Defence, Environment, and Employment.[71] The concentration and centralisation of state power is also apparent in the introduction of the Public Expenditure Survey Committee (PESC) and Programme Analysis and Review (PAR) to co-ordinate strategy across the whole range of government policies involving significant use of resources, to assess departmental objectives and priorities, and to control public expenditure more effectively.[72] The PESC–PAR system was also intended to establish a closer articulation between central government and the local authorities in the development of expenditure programmes (especially as many of the fastest expanding programmes, such as roads, law and order, education, and social services, are predominantly undertaken at a local level).[73] In conjunction with these changes there has also been growing resort to central forecasting techniques, statistical services, etc., in order to improve government planning and co-ordination. The main effect of this reorganisation is to strengthen the central rôle of the Cabinet, Treasury, and Cabinet Office in the overall co-ordination of departmental strategies, programmes, and policies and to emphasise the financial cost and practical effect of state intervention.

However, although there have been increasing attempts to establish greater coherence in central and local government policies through such forms of concentration and centralisation of state power, it is evident that they have been far from successful. Indeed, since government cannot be reduced to technique, this is hardly surprising. The state is a complex institutional ensemble in whose institutions and interstices is reproduced the contradictory, conflicting interplay of political forces and its policies necessarily reflect the constantly shifting equilibria of compromise that emerge from political struggles within and among departments and branches of the state apparatus. Moreover, given the inherent contradictions of the capitalist economy and its complex articulation with the state system, state interventions will necessarily produce contradictory effects. Thus, whether one focuses on the financial costs and/or on the policy content of government actions, their overall coherence and effectiveness will be continually disturbed through their economic and political repercussions.

In this context it should be emphasised that the policies of central government are not solely determined by prime ministerial or ministerial initiative but also derive from sources such as declared party policy, departmental recommendations, demands from pressure groups and 'corporations', opposition parties, the mass media, local and regional government bodies, the European community, clients of the sponsoring departments, para-state organs, international institutions, and foreign allies. Indeed, even when policies represent an immediate response to economic crises or other urgent problems, they must reflect the current balance of forces within government. In this sense the Cabinet is the principal locus of political struggles and mediates the complex play of political forces within the social formation. In turn this means it is essential to consider the relationship between the Cabinet and other institutions and forces and the ways in which this has changed since 1945.

There are three principal functions traditionally ascribed to Parliament. These are the enactment of laws, the control of taxation and public expenditure, and scrutiny of government coupled with redress of grievances. But the collective power of Parliament in all three domains has declined substantially in the last century and especially since the outbreak of the Second World War. The decline was initially associated with the extension of the franchise and growth of mass parties and the concomitant transformation of Parliament from a forum in which propertied interests could establish common needs, negotiate compromises, and formulate shared strategies into an institution in which the broad mass of the population could be represented and whose function was accordingly restricted to legitimation and surveillance. But it was subsequently reinforced through the transformation of state intervention from liberal facilitation of private enterprise and guaranteeing public order to more supportive and directive functions in relation to economy and civil society alike. The latter set of changes was accelerated during the First World War (cf. the transformation in the Cabinet) and again with the onset of the Second World War; and, as we have seen above, the development of state intervention has further intensified since the early sixties. In this sense British entry into the EEC (on which see below) was simply a further step in the decline of Parliament as an institution and, whatever its significance in other respects, cannot be said to mark a decisive turning point in its secular decay.

Thus we find that the deliberative stage of legislation has been fundamentally absorbed into the executive branch with the extensive consultation between government and affected interests. The massive growth in subordinate legislation through the exercise of the royal prerogative and delegated powers has also removed the details of economic management and intervention and of social administration from parliamentary control and vested them in the executive and/or advisory bodies. Indeed, not only is such legislation subject only to the most perfunctory parliamentary scrutiny and even more limited judicial review, even the Cabinet necessarily permits a relatively free hand to the various departments, boards, commissions, public corporations, and other public bodies involved. There has also been a growing tendency for legislation to take the form of 'enabling' acts giving wide, unspecified powers to the executive and/or for significant powers to be vested in para-state institutions with little or no accountability to Parliament. The expanding institutional complex concerned with industrial reorganisation, prices, profits, and incomes, regional planning, social administration, etc., is the area *par excellence* here. Lack of parliamentary control is also increasingly evident in the field of taxation and expenditure. For the Cabinet still wields the royal prerogative of initiating financial legislation and can generally manage to enact it fundamentally unchanged. This also applies to the government's budget strategy and its estimates on government expenditure. Moreover, although there have been innovations in the work and organisation of parliamentary committees concerned with financial and economic matters (e.g., the Public Accounts Committee, the Estimates Committee, and the Select Committee on the Nationalised Industries), back-benchers are still restricted in their scrutiny of government by lack of information, the inevitable complexities of economic management, and the ability of the government effectively to ignore committee reports. Finally, whilst formal opportunities for general scrutiny and the redress of grievances are many and varied, the committee system has been widened in recent years, and Ombudsmen have been appointed to investigate maladministration, it is still difficult for Parliament to translate these formal powers into effective control.

This said, it should be emphasised that, *pace* those who fetishise rules and conventions, the ability of the Cabinet to utilise procedure to dominate Parliament depends on the balance of party forces. It must explain, defend, and justify its policies in Parliament and must mobilise the votes necessary to sustain its programme. Furthermore, whilst government whips can wield a certain amount of influence in this field, parliamentary time is not infinitely extensible and there are limits to the use of the guillotine and other methods of closure. Likewise, even though the House of Lords is essentially a paper tiger, opposition and obstruction from peers can also damage or delay government business.[74] This means it is prudent for the government to adapt its policies and programmes to facilitate their acceptance. Indeed, during periods of national crisis and/or minority government, it is essential to consider the movement of opinion and shift of political forces in the opposition and minor parties as well as among the government's own supporters in Parliament. This is particularly clear in the period culminating in the short-lived pact between the Labour government and parliamentary Liberal Party and the subsequent mobilisation of support from nationalist parties to sustain that government in office. In short, although Parliament operates along party lines under the dominance of the Cabinet, its procedures do no more than favour such dominance and certainly do not unconditionally guarantee it. This means that crises in the relations between parties and their supporters in the country, between factions and tendencies in parliamentary parties, or between different parties in Parliament could well have major repercussions on the conduct of government business. And, to the extent that it proved impossible to compensate for such crises through resort to alternative forms of representation and intervention (such as corporatism or prerogative powers), the government would be paralysed.

The decline of Parliament is not only evident in the gradual consolidation of Cabinet dominance but also in the powers accruing to the administrative staff of state and para-state bodies. For the increase in state intervention has necessarily enhanced the political weight of permanent officials at the expense of Cabinet and Parliament. For top officials are not only entrusted with the co-determination (in association with recognised and responsible affected interests) of the growing mass of subordinate legislation but also play a more significant rôle in the initiation, deliberation, and formulation of new policies as well as the continuing review of current programmes. In all three respects it should be noted how official influence has been reinforced through their strategic rôle in consultations with pressure groups and through the establishment of links with outside experts through advisory committees, study groups, research institutes, dining clubs, etc. In turn this is reflected in intensified competition to secure direct representation in Whitehall and the local state and in increasing conflicts about policies and programmes within and between departments.

The foundation of independent bodies to perform public functions has also contributed to the loss of control by Parliament and Cabinet. Thus, not only have certain routine tasks traditionally executed under the immediate formal control of a minister been 'hived off' to independent agencies, there has also been a remarkable growth in the number (now more than 600) and importance of such bodies in new fields of administration. While 'quasi-government organisations' (or quagos) have been established either as a means of hiving off central government responsibilities (such as regulatory and quasi-judicial powers or the financing of universities) or because they can finance themselves more or less independently of the Treasury (such as nationalised industries, organisations which rely on levies or fees, and state-backed secondary banks with revolving funds), 'quasi-non-governmental organisations' (or quangos) have been established primarily to export certain awkward or controversial problems from parliamentary control to *ad hoc* public bodies (such as those concerned with science or arts patronage) and to facilitate the partial control or self-regulation of dominant institutions and élites (such as the press, broadcasting, advertising, and the professions).[75] Certain of these bodies are subject to more or less substantial ministerial or Cabinet interference – especially the regulatory commissions concerned with prices, profits, pay, etc., and the nationalised industries. Many also have either 'dignified' or 'efficient' representation of functional groups and/or other sections of the community – such as the Manpower Services Commission, Health and Safety Executive, Race Relations Commission, and Equal Opportunities Commission.

This proliferation of quagos and quangos involves a massive extension of bureaucratic domination over economy and civil society and, indeed, within this context, a significant increase in *ad hoc*, discriminatory intervention oriented to specific goals at the expense of general rational–legal administration. Thus, although some of these bodies are responsible for implementing certain economic–corporate and/or popular-democratic reform programmes that benefit subordinate classes and/or oppressed social categories, this proliferation nonetheless reinforces the separation of the people from control over the state in the area of political and ideological domination as well as capital accumulation and/or imposes a framework of bourgeois social relations upon popular participation.[76] In turn this encourages the private appropriation of public functions either directly (as with the Press Council) or indirectly (as with the various regulatory commissions) and/or leads to the dissemination of a still concentrated state power among different institutions so that parliamentary (let alone popular) control is made more difficult. However, unless the executive is able to mediate among these various public bodies and co-ordinate their activities, the growth of quagos and quangos can also result in incoherence and contradictions in state intervention. This is evident not only in the co-existence of quagos with contrary or inconsistent goals (such as the promotion of industrial reorganisation, regulation of monopolies, control of mergers and takeovers, and job preservation), but also in the long-standing failure to develop integrated strategies in areas such as transport and energy. In such cases the dissemination of state power among various independent bodies tends to limit control from the centre and to reproduce the contradictions of economy and civil society within the state.

The growth of state intervention and the proliferation of para-state institutions has also reinforced official domination over economy and civil society. The most general basis for such domination is the specialisation of officials in routine administration so that it is exceptional for ministers or the Cabinet to intervene in this area. For, just as the operation of the law is largely silent so that litigation and prosecution rarely occur compared with the number of lawful and law-governed actions, so there is also a vast substratum of administrative practices which proceed in the shadow of the more dramatic changes in government policies and programmes but which nonetheless have enormous cumulative effects on social relations. Moreover, as the rule of law is replaced in the interventionist state by administrative discretion, the impact of such 'routine' administration tends to become more far-reaching and significant. This effect is reinforced through the increasing involvement of officials in the formulation of policies and programmes. For senior officials constantly provide information and recommendations based on departmental views, interdepartmental consultations, and external representations; and they frequently 'pre-select' policies for ministers through the presentation of limited alternatives. This is particularly significant where the Cabinet or individual ministers are inadequately prepared and/or lack outside support to overcome bureaucratic inertia, official secrecy, ministerial isolation, and departmental or interdepartmental opposition. It is also true, of course, that departmental (as opposed to ministerial) proposals must secure Cabinet and parliamentary approval in most cases and this places a premium on adequate preparation not only in relation to departmental views and affected interests but also in relation to ministerial preferences, known party policies, and the degree of government support within Parliament. Thus one should not isolate the political actions of officials from the milieu within which they operate and one must also examine the sources of departmental policies in organisational habits, the movement of political forces within and outside the administration, and changing economic and social conditions on a national and international level.

So far this discussion has focused on the articulation between the parliamentary arena and the administrative apparatuses as this is mediated through the Cabinet. But the development of the 'strong state' in Britain is also evident in the reorganisation of the machinery for maintaining law and order. Indeed, if the explosion of para-state administrative apparatuses is one striking characteristic of the post-war state in Britain, another is the concentration and centralisation of the repressive apparatuses.

Recent changes have strengthened the repressive potential of this system. In part these changes reflect the general tendency towards increasing concentration and centralisation of state power related to the growing socialisation of production and the increasing interdependence of all social relations. This is the case, for example, with the formation of regional crime squads in 1964. But other changes reflect the escalation of industrial and political conflict in Britain and/or the development of the civil rights movement and urban guerilla warfare in Northern Ireland. Thus, in addition to the police acquisition of the most comprehensive system of computerised information in the world and the development of pre-emptive sur-veillance and policing of industrial and political dissent and social deviance, the police have gained new powers under the Prevention of Terrorism (Temporary Provisions) Act of 1974 and the Prevention of Terrorism Act, 1976, as well as recent legislation to control illegal immigration and illegal drug use.[77] Specialised police forces have also been established to control short-term and isolated outbreaks of dissent (Special Patrol Group), to safeguard foreign diplomats and VIPs (Diplomatic Protection Group), to combat terrorist activity (Anti-Terrorist Squad), to protect Britain's nuclear installations (Atomic Energy Authority Constabulary), and so forth.[78] There has also been increasing co-operation between the police force and the military and an increasing number of joint police–military actions. The armed forces themselves have acquired an extensive range of weapons and armour for use in civilian disturbances, a highly sophisticated and technologically complex range of surveillance and control devices, and new techniques of interrogation based on sleep or sensory deprivation. Finally, in addition to these changes in the organisation and equipment of the repressive apparatuses, there has been an intensification of official contingency planning for military and civilian emergencies. The much increased use of emergency powers during industrial disputes (permitting *inter alia* the use of troops for strike-breaking) is one aspect of these changes. Other examples could be cited.[79] In general, then, we may observe a substantial reorganisation of the repressive apparatus in Britain since the mid-sixties and increasing preparation for the use of repression in future crises.

The high-point in the repressive conduct of the 'strong state' occurred in 1970–72 under the 'Selsdon' régime of Mr Heath (before his remarkable conversion to corporatism) and was fundamentally checked in a series of confrontations with organised labour over pay restraint and the legal regulation of union activities.[80] However, whilst there has been a partial retreat from open judicial and police confrontation with the trade union movement (evident in the repeal of the 1971 Industrial Relations Act and the extension of trade union prerogatives and immunities under the Social Contract as well as the subsequent collapse of the Labour government's policies of wage restraint in a massive upsurge of strike action in the winter of 1978/9), the apparatus of repression has been further refined in terms of both organisation and the content of the law and there has been continuing use of both judicial and police repression against more marginal social and political groups (such as immigrants, coloured youths, students, 'extremist' political groups, squatters, and drug-takers).[81] This consolidation of a 'strong state' has been associated with a general shift toward 'authoritarian populism' in the ideological field. This shift has been promoted by various political and ideological groups, orchestrated by the mass media and Conservative Party, and facilitated by the left's neglect of the fight for intellectual and moral leadership of the nation. It is apparent in the popular swing against 'progressive education', 'welfare scroungers', 'alien immigrant groups', 'faceless bureaucrats', 'union robber barons', 'oppressive taxation', 'the rising tide of crime', and so forth; and, at the same time, in the mobilisation of popular support behind more authoritarian forms of social control legitimated by demands for 'law and order'.[82] Thus, even though the field of economic relations has recently been dominated by a voluntary avoidance of repression coupled with macro-economic measures to activate the discipline of market forces and an increasingly vain reliance on central control by national trade union leaders over their own rank-and-file, the field of political and ideological relations has witnessed a distinct shift towards police and judicial repression coupled with state-sponsored incorporation through participation conditional on responsible behaviour.[83] Together with a decline of parliamentarism in favour of independent executive action and/or an emergent corporatism marked by a growing crisis of voluntary self-regulation, this suggests a basic shift in the balance between coercion and consent in reproducing bourgeois domination. This is not to argue that the state is now 'fascist' nor that the moment of 'force' dominates that of 'consent'.

But it is to argue that the growth of the interventionist state in Britain is increasingly overdetermined by a deep-seated crisis of hegemony in the whole field of social relations.

Nonetheless, despite such changes in the British state system, the Cabinet is still the dominant political apparatus. Indeed, while it retains its leading rôle in the traditional parliamentary-bureaucratic system (albeit one modified by the explosion of quagos and quangos), it has gained a central rôle in the new corporatist system (subject to the rule of concurrent majorities typical of corporatist decision-making). However, as it occupies so crucial a mediating and co-ordinating rôle in relation to both systems, the Cabinet also tends to reproduce in itself their various conflicts and contradictions. This is evident in the increasing strain placed on the principle of collective responsibility in recent years. But a disunited Cabinet that is unable to mobilise support behind realistic policies cannot impose a coherent strategy on the interventionist state. Thus even a so-called 'strong state' can prove weak and ineffective if subject to weak and ineffective direction along with opposition from organised labour and/or major fractions of capital.

The Reorganisation of the Welfare State

The post-war settlement involved the extension of the welfare state as well as the utilisation of Keynesian techniques in a mixed economy to maintain full employment. The welfare state involves the rational–legal administration of welfare benefits to which individual citizens and/or their dependants are entitled. It is principally concerned with assuring them a minimum income regardless of the market value of their labour-power or capital, enabling them to meet particular contingencies (e.g., unemployment, homelessness, sickness, and old age) which might otherwise lead to domestic crisis, and, thirdly, providing them, irrespective of ability to pay, with approved standards of care across an agreed range of social and medical services.[84] Thus, not only does it entail state intervention in the operation of market forces to effect a redistribution of income and/or to socialise the provision and costs of certain forms of consumption, it is also premised on the institution of citizenship (and welfare rights) and organised to support the family as a primary unit of civil society. In this sense the welfare state both presupposes and reinforces the institutional separation of the state and civil society from capitalist relations of production and reflects the juridico–political forms of the parliamentary–bureaucratic system. But this separation of the welfare state and its mode of operation also involves specific limitations and contradictions. Thus, not only is the welfare state restricted to operating on the symptoms of capital accumulation and so able to influence its functioning only indirectly, it is dependent on continued accumulation for the revenues from which welfare measures are financed. In turn this leads to pressures for more direct intervention to eliminate or moderate the causes of social need and/or to adapt the level and/or nature of welfare provision to the demands of capital accumulation. In both cases this can involve conflicts between citizenship and market rationality and create political and ideological as well as economic problems. Let us now consider how such limitations and contradictions have manifested themselves in Britain since 1945.

The welfare state as a specific form of social intervention by the British state grew out of the great depression and the Second World War and was established under the first post-war Labour government. For, although certain measures of insurance and assistance were initiated in the Liberal government of 1906–14 and extended between the wars, they were partial, limited, short-term, and supplemented rather than replaced the old Poor Law. Indeed, not only did mass unemployment overwhelm all the existing schemes of insurance and poor relief during the depression, the provision and rates of unemployment benefit and assistance were the focus of bitter struggles.[85] These events were reinforced by the concern for national efficiency and social justice engendered by total war. This is reflected in the fact that the principal welfare state measures enacted by the post-war Labour government were based on commitments entered into by the wartime coalition government. The three major institutions associated with the welfare state at this time were all introduced in 1948 – National Assistance, the new National Insurance Act, and the National Health Service; and, in contrast to previous welfare measures, the emphasis was on a universal 'national minimum' to which every citizen was entitled. The framework established by this legislation was maintained by the succeeding Conservative governments and extended in a number of respects. However, although welfare expenditure continued to rise under the Conservatives (especially under Macmillan after 1957[86]), there was also a progressive attenuation of the basic principles of the welfare state. Indeed, if we consider its development from the initial proposals through enactment to subsequent administration, it is evident that the retreat from these principles began at the very outset.

Thus, whilst flat-rate benefits in the universal insurance scheme were initially set at a minimum subsistence level (and their real value soon diminished by inflation), the purportedly transitional scheme of means-tested, tax-financed benefits for those without sufficient insurance cover became a permanent, integral feature of social security.[87] There has also been increasing differentiation of benefits through the introduction of earnings-related contributions in exchange for earnings-related benefits. Moreover, caught in the contradiction between market rationality and welfare rights, policy toward the low paid and/or large families oscillated between an emphasis on the need to maintain the work ethic and labour market and a stress on the needs of the citizen and his/her family.[88] In turn this was associated with an increase in the discretion exercised by the administration and in the conditions associated with entitlement to benefits. Later, although replacement of national assistance with 'supplementary benefits' involved widening the range of benefits (e.g., rent and rate rebates, fuel allowances, clothing grants), it was also linked with increasing discretion, conditions, disqualifications, and special investigations. In addition much more supervision and control, as well as discretion, was introduced for the poorest claimants. This is evident in the increasing use of social workers with statutory powers of intervention in the lives of claimants and their families and able to make benefits conditional on alterations in behaviour and/or acceptance of close supervision.[89] Conversely, if we consider the realm of 'fiscal welfare', there has been a major rise in tax concessions and subsidies for private welfare provision in areas such as pensions, housing, life insurance, child care, and so forth. In short, instead of the Beveridge system of universal rights to agreed standards of income and services, there has been a steady shift towards a highly differentiated, fragmented system of welfare rights and privileges with a tendential polarisation between a growing number of means-tested and state-supervised claimants and a growing number of those reliant on tax-aided and state-encouraged private provision.[90] Moreover, although this polarisation is still tendential and most full-time workers belong to neither the new pauper stratum nor the fiscal élite, such changes have combined with the escalation of public expenditure and tax revenues to generate struggles over welfare rights among various claimant groups as well as an incipient 'welfare backlash'.

Not only have there been a complex series of molecular changes in the organisation and administration of the post-Beveridge welfare state, it has also been subject to two major crises that have pre-cipitated more radical forms of reorganisation. Thus, whilst the financial and resource costs of implementing the welfare state imposed a growing burden on central and local state budgets and contributed to the industrial decline of the British economy because of its disarticulation with the requirements of capital accumulation, it also proved increasingly inadequate and ineffective in resolving the social problems threatening the reproduction of capital and bourgeois hegemony. Although recurrent attempts were made to reduce and/or control welfare expenditure under the post-war Labour government (especially in connection with rearmament) as well as the succeeding Conservative governments (note the implementation of the Plowden Report on the control of public expenditure in 1962), it was the second crisis that produced the first major reorganisation in the social policy of the state. Beginning in the mid-sixties there was a massive extension of social services and socio-economic programmes concerned to attack the causes of the contingencies affecting individual citizens rather than treating their symptoms through an essentially redistributive system of financial support. Thus, alongside the welfare measures introduced in the aftermath of the Second World War, there has arisen a complex of local, regional, and national programmes to alleviate such problems as urban poverty, educational deprivation, inner city decline, urban disorder, imbalance in the spatial organisation of economic and social life, regional underdevelopment, and so on. In particular we may note the implementation of educational programmes aimed at inner city areas and educational priority areas; the rapid expansion of a wide range of urban programmes (e.g., Urban Aid, National Community Development Projects, planners' comprehensive development areas, neighbourhood councils, general improvement areas, partnerships between local authorities, central government, and industry, etc.); the adoption of a poverty programme to overcome the 'cycle of transmitted deprivation'; the implementation of programmes to attract industry back to older urban areas; and various other local policies and programmes.[91] This was also associated with an enormous expansion of regional level apparatuses, programmes, and policies. Thus, in addition to the growth of regional development policies through increasing resort to capital grants, tax allowances, employment subsidies, infrastructural support, government training programmes, land-use planning, and so forth, there has also been a growing movement towards the regionalisation of government with the formation of Regional Economic Planning Boards, Regional Health Authorities, Regional Water Authorities, etc., at the expense of local authority control.[92] In short, whilst the welfare state is concerned with the redistribution of income and the provision of services to enable individuals and families to cope with specific contingencies, social policy has increasingly been reoriented toward intervention concerned with the structural roots of poverty and social need and/or with the social control and integration of those affected rather than their treatment as autonomous citizens with an entitlement to social welfare.

However, despite this qualitative change in social policy as well as its increasing cost, it has proved about as ineffective as the economic intervention of the state. Thus, not only is the so-called inter-generational 'cycle of deprivation' still operative and the pauperisation process (reflected in growing numbers in receipt of supplementary benefits and the extension of the 'poverty trap') still occurring, also still much in evidence are the underlying urban and regional crises and the crises in social relations with which they are associated. In turn this reflects the inability of essentially redistributive welfare measures at individual and/or local levels to reverse the long-term structural decline of the British economy and, indeed, the fact that much intervention is concerned simply to cushion the political effects of this decline and/or to shore up backward capitals. Moreover, even where the policies pursued have proved effective on some criteria (such as state-induced job creation in underdeveloping regions), they have often worsened problems elsewhere (such as fuelling the fiscal crisis and inflation). At the same time the expansion and transformation of the welfare state has produced a general politicisation of urban relations (witness the growth of urban protest movements as well as welfare rights groups) and, indeed, of state employees in the public welfare agencies (particularly among social workers and the now closed community action and development programmes) as well as in areas such as education and health. In addition the unproductive nature of state intervention and the fiscal crisis of the state have been aggravated through these changes.

The latter crisis has assumed more political and economic significance in the seventies and has produced a major restructuring of state expenditure in the context of a hoped-for gradual reduction in the proportion of GNP taken by the state sector. Two aspects here merit special mention. First, there has been much stress on increasing directly or indirectly productive expenditure and reducing unproductive spending. This is reflected in spending cuts on education, health, and housing and spending increases on industrial assistance, industrial reorganisation, economic infrastructure, and, mainly for political reasons, social security.[93] Secondly, this restructuring of expenditure has been accompanied by attempts to re-impose bourgeois political and ideological domination through a reorganisation of social relations within the state sector. This is evident in efforts to restructure the social relations of education, to incorporate tenants' and squatters' movements, to restore control over public expenditure through 'cash limits', to subordinate welfare provision to corporate management criteria rather than to the welfare needs of citizens, to integrate health service workers into hospital management, to displace the loci of decision-making from local authorities, vulnerable to popular-democratic pressures to regional and central government bodies more insulated from such pressures and accessible to business influence.[94] In this sense we find an obvious parallel between attempts to ensure that government money is translated immediately into productive capital through the new industrial policies in response to the crisis of Keynesianism and attempts to re-impose bourgeois relations of political and ideological domination in response to the fiscal crisis and welfare crisis of the British state.

European Integration and British Capital

The original arguments for British entry into Europe were largely political in character but changes in Britain's position in the international economy were the principal factor behind the realignment of forces that eventually led to British membership of the Common Market. In the sixties there was a substantial switch in the relative importance of Western Europe and the Commonwealth in the pattern of Britain's economic relations. With growing Commonwealth industrialisation and the increasing penetration of Commonwealth markets by Japan, the USA, and the EEC, there was a marked drop in the proportion of British trade with this market. Moreover the Commonwealth market was also growing at a relatively slow rate in comparison with the metropolitan markets. In contrast, within a European market expanding twice as fast as the home market in Britain, British trade was increasing so rapidly that by 1968 two-fifths of overseas trade was with Europe. Overseas investment was also directed more and more to Europe and away from the Commonwealth. Indeed, given the structural decline of British industry and its worsening profitability, expansion into the European market through exports of financial, industrial, and commercial capital as well as of finished goods seemed essential to industrial regeneration. Moreover, once the formation of a North Atlantic Free Trade Area was effectively ruled out by the dollar crisis and growing American protectionism, Common Market membership was the only realistic alternative to a continued and ultimately self-destructive retreat into a disintegrating Commonwealth.

The City also subscribed to the European strategy. For financial capital began to recognise it could no longer rely on the international rôle of sterling to ensure continued accumulation and, indeed, was actually hindered by the 'stop–go' measures intended to maintain that rôle. For the policies involved in internal demand management had inhibited short-term money flows, limited *entrepôt* trade, reduced the rate of industrial accumulation and thus the surplus available for new investment, hindered the free flow of capital, and otherwise restricted the business activities of the City. The growth of the Eurocurrency market and the continued predominance of the City in insurance, banking, commodity and gold markets, stock exchange services, etc., were expected to provide a solid base for rapid accumulation. Moreover, as the Bretton Woods system became increasingly unstable, the City began to seek ways to reduce its identification with the dollar. These constraints and arguments were reinforced during the third, ultimately successful round of negotiations for membership by the worsening American trade and overall deficits and the resulting instabilities in international markets and world industrial production.

Moreover, while the industrial and financial arguments for joining grew stronger in the late sixties, the original political case for European integration was also strengthened. The deterioration in its economic position meant that Britain could no longer afford an independent nuclear deterrent and world-wide military commitments nor finance them indirectly through the supply of sterling to other countries' gold and foreign currency reserves. Yet, despite the continuing decline in domestic economic strength and international influence, there was still a steady expansion in overseas trade and investment that indicated a growing need for political institutions able to protect and promote the interests of British capital. Indeed, even if Britain focused its main efforts on the European front (where an increasing proportion of new investment was directed), it would still be necessary to share the cost of defence with its allies in Europe. These arguments were reinforced by other political considerations. Post-war British foreign policy was based on exploiting a unique position at the heart of three intersecting spheres of influence – the Anglo–American relationship, the Commonwealth, and Europe. However, not only was the Commonwealth dissolving (with the old dominions increasingly integrated directly into the American empire and the new Commonwealth states tending towards neutrality or alignment with the Soviet Union or China), but the rather unilateral 'special relationship' with the United States was also subject to growing strain in the wake of Suez, the Cuban missile crisis, the Macnamara doctrine, and the development of bilateral negotiations with the Soviet Union. These changes strengthened the case for increased association with Europe and were themselves overdetermined by economic constraints.

Thus the European strategy of the Establishment represented a response to the increasingly apparent decline in the economic and political position of Britain in the international system. It was promoted through the activities of the CBI, the City, the European Movement, and the NFU, the propaganda of various mass media, and the three main political parties (albeit with varying degrees of conviction and consent). There were also important shifts in favour within the Foreign Office (hitherto committed to a global rather than regional rôle for Britain) and in the Treasury—Bank axis (hitherto committed to defending sterling rather than promoting the interests of British industrial capital). In addition, while the United States and most of Europe and of the Commonwealth favoured the general idea of British membership of the EEC, even the opinion of the French government changed as the French economy suffered from the aftermath of May 1968, the instability of the international monetary system, and the increasing domination of Germany within Europe. Thus, despite opposition from a majority of trade union leaders and small businessmen, many farmers, about half the electorate, and a third of MPs, the balance of forces shifted decisively in favour of integration into the European Economic Community. British membership began in 1973 under a Conservative administration and was subsequently ratified in a consultative referendum held in 1975 under a Labour administration.

However, although the European strategy was shaped by fundamental constraints associated with Britain's international position, integration into the EEC has not relieved the state of external or interiorised limits on state power. But there has been a major reorganisation of these limits in several important respects. Chief among these has been a partial loss of sovereignty to regional institutions – symbolised in the fact that British accession to the Common Market entailed adoption of ten volumes of treaties and 142 volumes of detailed rules and regulations as well as a commitment to implement future European legislation and judicial decisions. These laws and judgements seem most likely to tend in the direction of European harmonisation of company law, accounting practice, taxation, financial institutions, etc., the development of monetary union, and further movement towards economic union. There will also be increased co-operation between Community institutions and individual states in the field of regional, social, industrial, and environmental policies. The introduction of direct elections to the European Parliament will also have repercussions in the field of political representation alongside the above-mentioned changes in intervention.

But the European Community is a developing state power rather than a fully-constituted system of state apparatuses and it provides a field of struggle between many contradictory economic and political forces in the same was as any other state system. Indeed it is quite fallacious to regard the development of the EEC in terms of a simple contradiction between nation-states and supranational institutions. For individual nation-states are themselves necessarily involved in securing essential conditions for the internationalisation of the total circuit of capital as well as in promoting the interests of their own national or interior bourgeoisies within such a framework. In this context it should be emphasised that individual states may well improve their opportunities or capacities to promote these interests through a 'pooling' of individual sovereignties to centralise state power and/or adapt the structures of representation and intervention to the scale of capital accumulation. In any case European state and para-state institutions are just as much the focus of various intra- and inter-class struggles and/or popular-democratic struggles as political institutions at the national or local level. Indeed the structure of the European state permits the articulation of such conflicts and provides significant opportunities for member states to modify or veto European initiatives within the Council of Ministers, the European Commission, the various committees, and the European Parliament and/or to ameliorate, distort, or neutralise European decisions at the time of implementation. The extent to which this conduct is successful depends on the balance of forces rather than constitutional questions concerning the distribution of sovereignties.

In this context it must be recognised that the European state is increasingly dominated by German capital (in alliance with French capital) and that this developing German hegemony will decisively shape the future development of the European Community. The proposals for monetary union are just one indication of this. It is the balance of forces in this and other matters that will limit the British state in pursuit of 'national' interests and not the formal distribution of sovereignty.

The Emergent Crisis in the Party System

Although the British state is increasingly hybrid in form owing to the gradual development of functional representation and intervention, the parliamentary-bureaucratic form is still dominant. But, while some theorists argue that 'parliamentarism' is the ideological linchpin of bourgeois society and guarantees the reproduction of bourgeois political domination, it must be stressed that the latter depends on the successful articulation within the party system of the needs of capital accumulation with the economic–corporate and popular-democratic demands of the electorate. It is this ability to bridge the gap between the electoral market and the realities of state power that distinguishes the dominant party or parties in a liberal political system from minor parties and ensures the reproduction of bourgeois political domination through the parliamentary-bureaucratic system.[95] But, since the major parties are increasingly unable alone or together to operate the latter in accordance with the needs of economic growth and political stability, we find an emergent crisis in the party system in contemporary Britain.

Following the development of mass parties in the late nineteenth century, it was the Conservative Party that established itself as the natural governing party. In this respect it was thrice blessed. For it was able to mobilise and unify the principal fractions of the dominant class and to identify itself with the dominant institutional and moral order.[96] It has also gained from the disarray of opposing parties from the 1880s to 1940 – with splits in the Liberal Party over Irish Home Rule and Free Trade followed by the breakdown of the Lib–Lab electoral pact, the gradual emergence of Labour as the alternative governing party, and, lastly, the split in the Labour Party in 1931. This disarray, coupled with the simple plurality voting system, necessarily favoured the Conservative Party. But the opportunity to hold office is certainly not a sufficient condition to establish any party as the natural governing party. In the latter task the Conservative Party has benefited from its close ties with the whole 'Establishment' and from its own leaders' emphasis on the accommodation of popular support to the realities and limits of political office. Thus, whilst Conservative leaders have long been aware of the problems involved in representing bourgeois interests in a society with a large, enfranchised working-class (hence the importance of their 'One Nation' electoral approach), they have generally avoided crude appeals to economic–corporate and/or populist demands that would be incompatible with continued accumulation and bourgeois domination. Instead they have emphasised national and individual interests, the alleged Tory monopoly of economic and political acumen (implying a passive rôle for the rest of the British people), and the need to protect the dominant institutional and moral order against internal and external threats alike. This does not mean that the Conservative Party has not pursued policies to benefit subordinate classes and groups (far from it) but it does mean that such measures have been fashioned with close regard to the needs of state power.

Following the last war it was the 'right progressive' tendency that dominated the Conservative Party. This tendency is especially concerned with the politics of power as well as electoral support and has much in common with democratic socialism.[97] Under its hegemony the Conservative Party supported state intervention in the mixed economy to promote full employment as well as to secure the conditions for capital accumulation and it has backed the welfare state as a means of promoting social justice as well as accomplishing piecemeal social engineering. But, as the post-war boom turned into stagflation and economic crisis, it became increasingly difficult to pursue these policies and, at the same time, maintain the traditional social bases of Tory support. For, precisely because Conservative leaders have generally subordinated the politics of electoral support to those of state power, the burden of Conservative policies on accumulation and of Conservative concessions to organised labour has fallen unequally on Tory supporters. Thus, whilst the City and multinational firms gained from policies intended to promote the interests of financial capital and/or the internationalisation of capital, the brunt of these policies has been borne by small and medium industrial capital and the old petite bourgeoisie. Together with the non-unionised new petite bourgeoisie and the non-unionised working class, these groups have also borne the cost of full employment policies, public welfare programmes, rising state expenditure, and inflation. This has caused serious problems at constituency level, where these groups retain a strong presence. In turn this has prompted the growth of the 'new right' with its renewed emphasis on the need to safeguard the traditional institutional and moral order against threats from trade union power, socialism, corporatism, immigration, vandalism, crime, pornography, etc., and its revamped political economy of monetarism and market forces. This tendency is more concerned with problems of electoral support than state power and has therefore been forced to revert to a more interventionist stance when the Conservatives have regained office and tried to pursue 'neo-liberal' policies with only moderate (if any) success. This was clear during the 1970–4 government under a Heath Cabinet and is likely to occur again under Mrs Thatcher.

Whereas the Conservative Party has been largely concerned with the politics of power, the Labour Party has been mainly concerned with that of representation and electoral mobilisation. From its foundation it has been linked organically with the trade union movement and adopted a consistently parliamentary strategy. Its original organisational bases were in the local trades councils, the co-operative movement, and institutions such as socialist Sunday schools and, although these have withered since the 1920s, the Labour Party managed to retain the electoral support of a majority of organised labour. At the same time the unions are essentially economistic in orientation and see their chief field of action as sectional and/or localised industrial bargaining. This separation of the economic and political wings of the labour movement and the absence of any mass base for the Labour Party posed no serious problems whilst the latter was in office during 1945–51. For it was occupied implementing a social democratic programme supported by the trade union movement and, despite the austerity of this period, it was also able to secure full employment. However, with the deepening structural crisis of the British economy and the growing crisis of the 'Keynesian-welfare state', this separation poses increasing problems and is aggravated by the absence of a mass individual membership. For, as we noted in our discussion of direct state intervention and corporatism, industrial regeneration and the 'fight against inflation' require close co-operation between organised labour and the state. Yet, although leading Labour politicians have come to accept the logic of capital accumulation and bourgeois domination and have attempted to bridge the gap between the electoral market and the realities of state power with their 'Social Contract' electoral approach, the Labour Party has proved unable to secure the necessary electoral support and grass-roots union backing for the policies required to reorganise and regenerate British industry. Indeed, just as the Conservative Party's economic and political strategies have tended to undermine and alienate its traditional social base, the Labour Party has tended to undermine and alienate its own basis of support among organised labour (especially skilled labour) through the effects of inflation and taxation on net disposable income.

Along with the general ideological shift towards 'authoritarian populism', this erosion of real wages has provided a favourable climate for the Conservative Party to detach significant numbers of organised workers from their now largely *habitual* allegiance to the Labour Party.[98]

In short, whereas the Conservative Party has become more concerned with the politics of electoral support at the expense of realistic policies, the Labour Party has become a would-be natural governing party without the organisational base to enable it to implement its policies. This paradox reflects the combined impact of an increasing structural underdetermination of electoral behaviour (owing to the decline of the traditional institutional and moral order that sustained Tory support and the general disintegration of working-class communities and culture that sustained Labour support) and of significant changes in the political preconditions of economic and social reproduction (especially the increased importance of union co-operation and direct state intervention in the organisation of production). It should be emphasised that these changes in the party system have not been uncontested. However, whilst the 'Labour left' (a tendency comprising *marxisant* social democrats and Labourist populists) has tried to impose an alternative, socialist economic and social policy on recent Labour governments, its commitment to parliamentary politics and consequent isolation from class and popular-democratic movements outside parliament have contributed as much to its lack of influence as the unrelenting opposition of the whole Establishment to such a policy. The 'right progressive' tendency in the Conservative Party has also fought a rearguard action against the 'new right' and, in contrast to the weakness of the 'Labour left', has contrived to temper somewhat its policies on both trade union reform and industrial policy. Moreover, whilst the Labour Party will probably move leftward in opposition and adopt a more corporatist, interventionist, socialist programme, it is nearly certain that the currently dominant 'new right' will be tamed in office by the combined forces of the Treasury, interventionist ministries, the interventionist pressures of the CBI and ailing industries, the worsening international economic crisis and its domestic repercussions (especially in Scotland and Northern England), the opposition of organised labour to wage control (whether in the form of monetary restraint, cash limits, or, perhaps, a wage freeze), rising unemployment, renewed inflation, and cuts in state expenditure, and, lastly, the resurgence of the 'right progressive' tendency within the Conservative Party. But, whatever the medium-term outlook for the party system, it has not been operating adequately in the recent past. Thus, in addition to the alienation of the traditional social bases of the two major parties and the growing divorce between the politics of electoral support and the politics of state power, there has also been growing disenchantment with party politics more generally and increasing involvement in extra-parliamentary and non-party political action. This emergent crisis in the party system helps to explain the increasing 'ungovernability' of Britain – especially as the alternative of a corporatist system is also proving impossible to stabilise.

Conclusions

We have now discussed certain aspects of the reorganisation of the British state since 1945. This has been a continuous process but there have been several peaks of activity. The first substantial reorganisation was begun during the Second World War itself under the coalition government and continued under the incoming Labour administration. It involved the major extension of the mixed economy through the nationalisation of important infrastructural, energy, and industrial sectors which had previously been privately or municipally owned; the switch of the radically increased wartime state expenditure programme to predominantly civilian ends rather than the retrenchment of public spending; and the introduction of the major pillars of the post-war welfare state. It must also be noted that the Labour government presided over the dismantling of the wartime planning system and its extensive range of corporatist or tripartite planning agencies and began the shift towards a predominantly Keynesian mode of economic intervention. Moreover, whereas in the first two years of Labour government it could be argued that the working class was the dominant political force due to wartime circumstances, the ensuing years of Labour rule saw its effective demobilisation as a radical political force and the reassertion of bourgeois political hegemony under the leadership of financial capital. This is apparent in the premature attempt to return to sterling convertibility in 1947 (abandoned within five weeks) at an unrealistically high parity (leading to devaluation in 1949) as well as the austerity measures associated with the exports-and-investment strategy followed in this period. Nonetheless, although it lost the political initiative, organised labour was closely integrated into the political system and formed the principal social basis of state power. For there was a fundamental social democratis-ation of the state mediated through limited economic–corporate concessions and integration of the trade union movement into the operation of the state apparatuses.

The fifties represented a period of the gradual extension of this 'Keynesian-welfare state' under the hegemony of financial capital and in the context of the post-war settlement between capital and labour. It is this particular balance of forces together with the system of state intervention that explains the unique 'stop–go' cycle in the economy. The 'stop' phases correspond to the dominance of financial capital mediated through the Bank–Treasury axis and the 'go' phases correspond to the increased political weight of the labour movement mediated through electoral reactions to rising unemployment. Within this framework industrial capital was represented within the state apparatus through 'sponsoring departments', the complex system of trade associations and industrial representation, and the Conservative Party (which was none the less also dominated by financial capital); and, within the constraints of 'stop–go', various measures conducive to industrial capital were implemented. It should also be noted that organised labour had its own 'sponsoring department' in the Ministry of Labour and there was also indirect pressure for concessions mediated through the electoral system. But, despite the representation of both industrial capital and the labour movement in the state apparatus itself, the pursuit of their interests and demands was limited by the dominance of the Bank–Treasury axis over short-term economic management and the control exercised by the Treasury over state expenditure and over interdepartmental consultation. This period seemed to be one of growing economic prosperity and political stability but the underlying economic and political position continued to deteriorate. We find this reflected in growing public discussion about 'what is wrong with Britain' and questioning of all major institutions (civil service, parliament, unions, management, universities, welfare state, etc.). The consequences of this become increasingly apparent in the sixties.

The sixties represented a period of major institutional change in the British state. In the early sixties the various experiments in economic planning began that have continued intermittently and on a growing scale up to the present. There was also an intensification of attempts to regulate wages and to strengthen these attempts through legal and/or administrative measures enforced through new state or para-state organs. Towards the end of the sixties there also began the important reorientation of economic intervention towards ensuring that public money functions directly as capital (initially as private or public productive capital and more recently – albeit less successfully because more obviously and heavily influenced by political considerations – as variable capital in the form of manpower services and job-creation) and ensuring that state and para-state intervention is guided less by rational–legal norms ('rule of law') than by its effects on capital accumulation. These tendencies are associated with increasing concern with uneven spatial development and urban and regional disorganisation and thus with the creation of various programmes to alleviate or reverse these changes. Also linked with these new forms of state intervention have been the continued reorganisation of central government and the proliferation of 'quangos' and 'quagos' – tendencies motivated by the attempt to ensure greater co-ordination and control of the executive branch and/or to insulate state intervention from parliamentary supervision and interference. This has led to an increasing autonomisation and separation of the state from the 'people' as represented through Parliament and to a growing reliance on functional representation as a 'dignified' and/or 'efficient' element in the conduct of state affairs. In turn this has meant an atrophy of the electoral system as an 'efficient' means of representation (evident in the growing volatility of electoral support, the rise and fall of minor parties, and, in particular, the increasingly arbitrary relation between manifesto commitments and actual governmental policies) as well as a transformation in the rôle of the two major parties in the organisation of bourgeois hegemony (with the loss of its traditional 'natural governing party' status by the Conservative Party and the increasing centrality of the Labour Party as the mediating link between parliamentary and functional representation). In short, during the sixties, there began a second major transformation in the forms of intervention and representation.

This transformation continued in the seventies under both Conservative and Labour governments. Indeed, although the first two years of the Heath administration witnessed an attempt at 'disengagement' and a reassertion of monetarist and neo-liberal policies (associated with a speculative boom in land and property as well as a major shakeout of labour in manufacturing and increased productivity), the experiment foundered on the rocks of structural crisis and an inability (reflected in the increased importance of police and judicial activities) to mobilise a social base for the neo-liberal state. From 1972 onwards there were continuing efforts to construct the social base adequate to a corporatist state based on functional representation and direct state intervention in the circuit of productive capital. These efforts were begun by the Conservative government but the latter was handicapped by trade union hostility deriving from the earlier Industrial Relations Act and the subsequent imposition of wage restraint. There was also increasing dissent among members of the CBI (especially among smaller firms but also among several major multinational or national capitals) over growing state intervention. Moreover, alongside the growing trade union militancy of this period, since 1968 there had also been increasing popular dissent. This is evident in a wide range of extra-parliamentary movements concerned with economic and/or popular-democratic issues ranging from the civil rights movement and republican violence in Northern Ireland to the student movement, tenants' movements, squatting, the anti-apartheid movement, claimants' unions, opposition to motorway and urban redevelopment programmes, racial violence, women's libera-tion, etc. In short, if the continuing structural decline of the fifties and early sixties witnessed a prolonged social peace based on the post-war settlement, the late sixties and the seventies have been characterised by an apparent crisis of hegemony as well as the intensification of the crisis of British capitalism. In this sense one can talk of a shift in the relations of forces towards the working-class and popular forces at an 'economic–corporate' level; but without a fully corresponding shift at the level of 'intellectual, moral, and political leadership' or at the level of 'political–military' relations.[99]

The late Labour government is particularly important here because it presided over a counter-attack to restore conditions more favour-able to capital accumulation. Elected in the political crisis engendered by a miners' strike intended to break the Conservative incomes policy and accompanied by the 'three day week' for much of British industry, the Labour government at once set about 'buying' economic and social peace through its implementation of the Social Contract and the restoration of free collective bargaining. With the second general elec-tion of 1974 and the 1975 EEC referendum safely behind it and prompted by the growing profitability crisis of British industry, accelerating inflation, and a deteriorating balance of payments, the Labour Party then started to reverse its policies and to reorganise the balance of forces. In this it was assisted by the framework of TUC–Labour Party consultation (which displaced economic conflict to the national level where the short-term strike power of organised labour was ineffective and bourgeois political and ideological hegemony was still relatively secure) and by the mobilisation of inter-national forces (signified above all by the intervention of the IMF in alliance with the Treasury–Bank axis). Thus, in addition to the progressive withdrawal of concessions such as food subsidies and the imposition of public expenditure cuts and wage restraint, the government also stepped up the attempt to ensure that state intervention functions directly in favour of capital accumulation. Moreover, if there was some success in rolling back the economic–corporate advance of organised labour, there was also success in demobilising and containing the rising tide of popular-democratic struggle. This is most clear in the reorganisation of the welfare state and the channelling of popular discontent into state-controlled or state-sponsored organisational forms. At the same time there was further growth in the capacities and strength of the repressive state apparatus and a further development of contingency planning against future internal disorder and civil unrest.

This recomposition of the balance of forces initially occurred under the aegis of a 'Social Contract' in which the Labour Party and the TUC negotiated as equal partners. But the inability of the TUC to control rank-and-file union activities forced the Labour Cabinet to employ administrative measures and fiscal and monetary policies to support its overall economic strategy. For, in the absence of forms of political representation of the 'two sides of industry' that are adequate to the demands of effective corporatism and confronted with the need to intervene immediately and massively in the economy and civil society (so that the traditional parliamentary-bureaucratic system is no longer adequate), it was found necessary to accelerate the movement towards a '*strong state*' which relies on a complex range of administrative and repressive measures to secure compliance with its programmes and policies. The imposition of 'incomes policies' which lack parliamentary enactment or legal force through administrative measures and sanctions is the most striking illustration of this growing tendency. This should not be attributed to the shift from an erstwhile parliamentary-bureaucratic system to a corporatist form of state but to the *crisis of both parliamentarism and corporatism* as forms of securing active consent to state intervention needed to restore, maintain, and extend capital accumulation and bourgeois political domination. In short, the 'strong state' has developed in Britain because parliamentarism has already lost, and corporatism has not yet acquired, the faculty of securing bourgeois rule.[100] But this dual crisis also suggests that the 'strong state' could well prove ineffective in its exercise of power through monetary, administrative, and repressive measures. For it, too, lacks an adequate social base.

This crisis is also apparent in the party system. For, whilst the Conservative Party established itself as the natural governing party in the traditional parliamentary-bureaucratic system, it is the Labour Party that meets more of the conditions for this status in the emergent corporatism. In particular it has organic links with the TUC and trade union movement as well as a continuing (if increasingly fragile) electoral base in the working-class; and, because it is not too closely tied to specific fractions of capital (in contrast with the Tory Party[101]), it is better placed to consider the interests of capital in general. However, although the initial success of the 'Social Contract' in safeguarding capital accumulation indicates the advantages of Labour administration, the subsequent history of the Wilson–Callaghan régime points to the continuing obstacles to a stable corporatist system orchestrated through the Labour Party. The structure of the trade union movement does not satisfy the requirements of effective corporatism and the Labour Party itself is structurally prone to major conflicts between a Cabinet committed to the 'politics of power' and a Conference committed to the 'politics of representation' and also dominated by trade union bloc votes. Hence there is an ambivalent relationship between a Labour government and the trade union movement characterised by bilateral negotiations and a frequent resort to unilateral state and/or trade union action when the costs (especially in the short-term) of compromise seem excessive to either partner. Thus the rise of the 'strong state' also corresponds in a certain sense to a crisis of 'social democracy'.

It is in this context that we must locate the Conservative victory in the recent general election. Major factors here were the shift towards 'authoritarian populism', growing resentment among the working-class (especially skilled labour) over the inflation–taxation scissors, the collapse of the Callaghan administration's wage restraint policy in a long winter of trade union confrontation, and the continuing economic crisis. Although it is too early to predict the future of the new government, certain tendencies can be expected on the basis of our analysis. There will be a continued strengthening of the coercive apparatus and 'authoritarian populism' together with fresh attempts to place the burden of economic crisis on marginal social groups (such as ethnic minorities, youth, the elderly, the sick) and those currently occupied in backward sectors of the economy (including capitals as well as wage-earners). This will be combined with attempts to consolidate support among the new petite bourgeoisie and skilled workers in advanced sectors of the economy through a redistribution of the tax burden from income to expenditure, material concessions (e.g., in housing policy), and, to the extent that it proves possible, reductions in the total tax burden. At the same time there will be attempts at trade union reform to reinforce bureaucratic control over the rank-and-file, to reinforce moderation against militancy at all levels (e.g., through state-aided secret ballots along with campaigns orchestrated by the popular press), and to alter the balance of forces in collective bargaining and industrial action (e.g., through laws on secondary picketing and strike pay). The Conservative government will also step up the reorganisation of the welfare state and public sector to reduce its cost to the exchequer and increase its directly or indirectly productive character for capital at the expense of unproductive projects and marginal groups. Consultation will continue with organised labour as well as capital (e.g., on future industrial policy, synchronising wage claims, pay guidelines, reforming industrial relations) but there will also be greater readiness on all sides to engage in unilateral action. The economic and political strategy of the Conservative government (if 'strategy' is not too strong a word to describe a partial and contradictory programme) is long-term in nature; but, especially as it will be pursued in the context of growing international recession, it will entail short-term costs whose economic and political repercussions will tend to weaken rather than consolidate support. There will be growing opposition to wage restraint, public spending cuts, rising inflation, increasing unemployment, the burden of indirect taxation, and so forth; this will lead to growing trade union militancy (with union officials forced to follow suit) and growing business pressure to intervene to sustain output, employment, profits, and investment (at least until the international recession abates). This will be reflected within the state apparatus and intensify conflicts within the Cabinet between the 'new right' and 'right progressives' and it is likely to lead to the resurgence of the latter over the 'Two Nations' approach of the neo-liberal tendency symbolised by Mrs Thatcher.

Finally we should note that the decline of Parliament and the rise of para-state bodies do not obviate the need for a central co-ordinating apparatus able to formulate and implement the interests of capital in general. In the last resort the needs of capital must be combined with the main economic–corporate and reformist democratic demands of subordinate social forces in order to maintain bourgeois hegemony. But how is this to be accomplished with the decline of Parliament and the explosion of para-state bodies and delegated powers? The rôle of the Cabinet continues to be paramount here. For, despite the emergence of corporatist institutions such as Neddy, there are serious obstacles to their effective operation in economic policy-making and they are ill-adapted for the resolution of many kinds of popular-democratic issue. Thus, for all the emphasis on corporatism and the decline of Parliament, the Cabinet still occupies the central position in the British state. Moreover, while the Treasury–Bank axis is still dominant in the administrative sphere, the alliance between Prime Minister and Chancellor is still dominant in the Cabinet itself. Within this framework the complex cabinet committee system (with its parallel network of interdepartmental committees) provides the principal field of political struggle in the heart of the state apparatus. And it is here that the coming battle over the most appropriate degree and forms of state intervention will be fought out against the background of economic, political, and ideological struggles outside the central state system. In this limited sense the development of the British state since the Second World War illustrates (perhaps too well) the aphorism of 'plus ça change, plus c'est la même chose'. However, if this is partly due to the flexibility of the British constitution, it is also partly due to the frailty of alternative forms of political co-ordination. Nonetheless the continued dominance of the Cabinet also disguises the other tendencies noted above – the increasing importance of functional as opposed to parliamentary representation, the fundamental social democratisation and incipient corporatisation of the social bases of state power, the growing concentration and centralisation of the state system, the development of economic and social programming, and the growing 'politicisation' and 'étatisation' of social relations in economy and civil society.

Notes

1. It is, of course, hard to isolate changes in the international and national state system and we must refer to this problem further on.
2. In this Chapter 'politicisation' refers to the transformation of social relations into foci of political struggles and 'étatisation' to their incorporation into the field of state intervention: there is no necessary relation between the two forms of political action and both are relevant.
3. On the collapse of the Bretton Woods system, see H. L. Robinson, 'The Downfall of the Dollar', in *The Socialist Register 1973*, pp. 397–450; S. Strange, 'International Monetary Relations', in A. Shonfield (ed.), *International Economic Relations of the Western World 1959–1971* (Oxford University Press, London, 1976), vol. 2, pp. 263–99; and H. G. Grubel, *The International Monetary System*, 3rd edn (Penguin, Harmondsworth, 1977), pp. 127–98.
4. On the contradictions involved in the relations between the nation-state and international capital, see H. Radice (ed.), *International Firms and Modern*

Imperialism (Penguin, Harmondsworth, 1975); N. Poulantzas, *Classes in Contemporary Capitalism* (New Left Books, London, 1975), pp. 33–88; E. Mandel, *Late Capitalism* (New Left Books, London, 1975), pp. 310–76.

5. Cf. J. Frankel, *British Foreign Policy 1945–73* (Oxford University Press, London, 1975), pp. 10–13 and *passim*.

6. Cf. J. C. R. Dow, *The Management of the British Economy* (Cambridge University Press, London, 1964), pp. 29–53 on recovery, pp. 39 and 55–8 on terms of trade; and S. Strange, *Sterling and British Policy* (Oxford University Press, London, 1971), pp. 55–70 on the contribution and problems of sterling.

7. On these developments, see N. Harris, *Competition and the Corporate Society* (Methuen, London, 1972), pp. 32–47; L. P. Carpenter, 'Corporatism in Britain, 1930–45', *Journal of Contemporary History*, 11 (1976), pp. 3–25; J. Leruez, *Economic Planning and Politics in Britain* (Martin Robertson, London, 1975), pp. 1–16; D. F. MacDonald, *The State and the Trade Unions*, 2nd edn (Macmillan, London, 1976), pp. 97–136; D. Howell, *British Social Democracy* (Croom Helm, London, 1976), pp. 52–95; M. Bruce, *The Coming of the Welfare State* (Batsford, London, 1971), *passim*.

8. Cf. S. H. Beer, *Modern British Politics* (Faber and Faber, London, 1965), pp. 188–216; J. Leruez, *Economic Planning and Politics*, pp. 37–81; L. Panitch, *Social Democracy and Industrial Militancy* (Cambridge University Press, London, 1976), pp. 30–40; D. Howell, *British Social Democracy*, pp. 157–71; and A. Rogow and P. Shore, *The Labour Government and British Industry* (Blackwell, Oxford, 1955), pp. 101–8 and 173–88.

9. By this term, I refer to a state in which the principal forms of intervention in economy and civil society are macro-economic demand management within a mixed economy together with maintenance of the external conditions of capitalist production ('Keynesian-') and which also operate a redistributive and/or insurance based welfare state oriented to the social reproduction of the 'people' via intervention at the level of the individual citizen and/or his (or her) dependants ('-welfare state'). This system underlay the British post-war settlement.

10. On the relations between financial and commercial capital in the City and industrial capital, see S. Pollard, *The Development of the British Economy 1914–67*, 2nd edn (Edward Arnold, London, 1969), pp. 14–22 and *passim*; A. H. Imlah, *Economic Elements in the Pax Britannica* (Harvard University Press, Cambridge, Mass., 1958); J. Foster, 'Imperialism and the Labour Aristocracy', in J. Skelley (ed.), *The General Strike 1926*, (Lawrence and Wishart, London, 1976), pp. 3–57 (especially pp. 5–16); E. Hobsbawm, *Industry and Empire* (Penguin, Harmondsworth, 1969), pp. 134–53 and 210–23.

11. On the general background to this period, see S. Strange, *Sterling and British Policy*, *passim*; J. Frankel, *British Foreign Policy*, pp. 255–74 and *passim*; J. C. R. Dow, *British Economic Management*, *passim*; F. Hirsch, *The Pound Sterling: a Polemic* (Gollancz, London, 1965); A. Shonfield, *British Economic Policy Since the War*, revised edn (Penguin, Harmondsworth, 1959), pp. 67–160; and S. Brittan, *Steering the Economy*, revised edn (Penguin, Harmondsworth, 1971, pp. 72–100, 419–67, and *passim*.

12. It should be emphasised that 'stop–go' cycle is unique to Britain – for, although other capitalist nations experienced business cycles, those in Britain were overdetermined and distorted by the commitment to maintaining sterling as an international reserve and means of payment.

13. Canada was part of the Dollar Area rather than the Overseas Sterling Area; Japan discouraged foreign investment through various means.

14. Military spending is unproductive in the sense that production of means of destruction creates neither new means of production nor means of consumption – it is sterile in terms of capital accumulation. It should be noted that military production was expanded particularly rapidly in response to the Korean War and resulted in the

diversion of resources and the loss of export markets to Germany, Japan, and other competitors – markets not regained at the end of the rearmaments boom.

15. Thus, whereas Britain spent 8.9 per cent of GNP on military expenditure in 1953, the comparable figure for W. Germany was 4.4 per cent; in 1960 the figures were 6.1 per cent and 5.8 per cent respectively; and in 1967, 5.8 per cent and 3.8 per cent respectively. In each of these years, Japan spent less than 1 per cent of GNP in this way. Data cited from OECD, National Accounts, in: Cambridge Political Economy Group, 'Britain's Economic Crisis: an Historical Perspective', mimeo, 1975.

16. Industrial concentration has proceeded at an uneven pace. For information on the mergers in the past 100 years, see L. Hannah, *The Rise of the Corporate Economy* (Methuen, London, 1976), *passim*. The rise of 'meso-economic' power is apparent from the fact that the top 100 companies in manufacturing held about 10 per cent of the market in the 1880s, 15 per cent in 1910, 21 per cent in 1925, 22 per cent in 1950, 46 per cent in 1970, and perhaps 66 per cent in 1980. See S. Holland, *The Socialist Challenge* (Quartet, London, 1975), pp. 49–50.

17. Cf. the influential work of bourgeois political economy, R. Bacon and W. Eltis, *Britain's Economic Problem: Too Few Producers* (Macmillan, London, 1976); and, for Marxist analyses, see I. Gough, 'State Expenditure in Advanced Capitalism', *New Left Review*, 92 (July–August 1975), pp. 53–92; B. Fine and L. Harris, 'State Expenditure in Advanced Capitalism: A Critique', *New Left Review*, 98 (July–August 1976), pp. 97–112; and J. O'Connor, *The Fiscal Crisis of the State* (St Martin's Press, London, 1973).

18. This was stressed by Peter Jay in various articles: he argued that the 'stop-go' period could not be considered a golden age even in comparison with the continuing crisis of the mid-seventies. The following table has been updated and extended to include profit data: see *The Times*, 1 July 1974.

POST-WAR CYCLES	I	II	III	IV	V	VI
Period	1952–57	1958–61	1962–65	1966–70	1971–75	1976–78
Duration	6 yrs	4 yrs	4 yrs	5 yrs	5 yrs	3 yrs
Real GNP rise (%)	16.4	12.1	13.4	11.2	7.5	8.6
Peak Unemployment (av % adult in yr)	1.8 (1952)	2.0 (1959)	2.2 (1963)	2.3 (1968)	4.4 (1975)	5.7 (1977–8)
Peak Inflation (% RPI rise in yr)	5.3 (1955)	3.4 (1961)	4.7 (1965)	6.4 (1970)	24.1 (1975)	16.1 (1977)
Peak Payments Deficit (a) (% of GDP)	0.91	1.12	1.29	†	3.6	‡
Average Pre-Tax Company Profits (av % for cycle) (b)	15.9	15.4	14.5	12.1	5.5	n.a.

† Masked by 1967 devaluation (a) current account in calendar years.
‡ Distorted by N. Sea oil (b) share of company profits in GNP.

Note: Jay's table concerned incomes policy cycles, the table above concerns 'stop–go' cycles (no longer coincident from period V onwards).

19. See the data in G. Thompson, 'The Relationship Between the Financial and Industrial Sector in the United Kingdom Economy', *Economy and Society*, vi (3) (1977), pp. 235–83 (especially pp. 254–5 and 273).

20. On the development and rôle of the Eurodollar and Eurocurrency markets, see E. W. Clendenning, *The Eurodollar Market* (Oxford University Press, London, 1972); S. Strange, 'International Monetary Relations', in *International Economic Relations in the Western World*, vol. 2, especially pp. 176–94; and F. Hirsch, *Money International* (Penguin, Harmondsworth, 1969), pp. 236–42 and *passim*.

21. Representative texts are: W. Clarke, *The City in the World Economy* (Penguin, Harmondsworth, 1967) and F. Hirsch, *The Pound Sterling*; but, for a counterview, see W. A. P. Mansur, *Britain in Balance: the Myth of Failure* (Penguin, Harmondsworth, 1973).

22. On the attitudes of unions, Conservatives, and Labour; see L. Panitch, *Social Democracy and Industrial Militancy*, pp. 48–52; J. Leruez, *Economic Planning and Politics in Britain*, pp. 81–95 and129–30; M. Shanks, *Planning and Politics: the British Experience 1960–76* (Allen and Unwin, London, 1977), pp. 53–5; N. Harris, *Competition and the Corporate Society*, pp. 235–46 and *passim*; A. Gamble, *The Conservative Nation* (Routledge & Kegan Paul, London, 1974), pp. 124–58 and *passim*; A. Budd, *The Politics of Economic Planning* (Fontana, London, 1978), pp. 82–110 and *passim*.

23. Cf. S. Pollard, *Development of the British Economy*, pp. 14–22; E. Hobsbawm, *Industry and Empire*, pp. 172–94 and 207–24; D. Purdy, 'British Capitalism Since the War', *Marxism Today* (September 1976), pp. 270–7 and *Marxism Today* (October 1976), pp. 310–18.

24. Cf. G. K. Ingham, *Strikes and Industrial Conflict* (Macmillan, London, 1974), pp. 67–88.

25. Cf. D. Purdy, 'British Capitalism Since the War', *Marxism Today* (1976), pp. 271–4; K. Coates and E. Topham, *The New Unionism* (Penguin, Harmondsworth, 1974), pp. 76–92; A. L. Friedman, *Industry and Labour* (Macmillan, London, 1977), especially pp. 50–76.

26. Cf. D. Purdy, 'British Capitalism Since the War', *Marxism Today* (1976), pp. 271–4 and 310–18.

27. On American firms in Britain, see M. Hughes, 'American Investment in Britain', in J. Urry and J. Wakeford (eds.), *Power in Britain* (Heinemann, London, 1973), pp. 157–79; and, for a major survey of inward as well as outward investment (including data on the comparative profitability of American-owned and UK-owned firms in Britain), see J. H. Dunning, 'The UK's International Direct Investment Position in the Mid-1970s', *Lloyds Bank Review* (April 1979), pp. 1–22 (especially pp. 5, 9, and 18).

28. Industry-wide collective bargaining was stimulated during the First World War and developed strongly in the interwar period when the balance of power was shifted decisively in favour of capital by high unemployment and the defeat of the General Strike; this pattern was gradually reversed after 1945. See V. L. Allen, *Militant Trade Unionism* (Merlin, London, 1966), pp. 38–40 and *passim*; *The Royal Commission on Trade Unions and Employers' Associations 1965–8*, Chairman, the Rt. Hon. Lord Donovan (HMSO, London, 1968, Cmnd. 3623), pp. 12–37; J. A. Banks, *Trade Unionism* (Collier-Macmillan, London, 1974), pp. 27–36; K. Coates and T. Topham, *The New Unionism* (Penguin, Harmondsworth, 1974), pp. 76–92 and 118–37.

29. For an analysis of strikes in Britain, see R. Hyman, *Strikes*, 2nd edn (Fontana, London, 1977), pp. 25–51; *idem*, 'Industrial Conflict and the Political Economy', *The Socialist Register 1973*, pp. 101–54; H. A. Turner, *Is Britain Really Strike-Prone?* (Cambridge University Press, London, 1969).

30. On social imperialism, see J. Foster, 'British Imperialism and the Labour Aristocracy', in J. Skelley (ed.), *The General Strike 1926*, pp. 3–57; B. Semmel, *Imperialism and Social Reform* (Allen and Unwin, London, 1960).

31. Cf. A. Glyn and B. Sutcliffe, *British Capitalism, Workers, and the Profits Squeeze* (Penguin, Harmondsworth, 1972), pp. 73 and 100–101.

32. Cf. S. H. Beer, *Modern British Politics*, pp. 339–49; S. E. Finer (ed.), *Adversary Politics and Electoral Reform* (Antony Wigram, London, 1975), pp. 99–116; W. Nordhaus, 'The Political Business Cycle', *Review of Economic Studies*, 42 (1975), pp. 169–90; and D. Hibbs, 'Political Parties and Macroeconomic Policies', *American Political Science Review*, 7 (1977), pp. 1467–87.

33. Cf. B. Reading, 'Inflation – the Social Struggle', *National Westminster Bank Quarterly Review* (August 1974), pp. 8–16.

34. Cf. H. A. Turner, D. Jackson and F. Wilkinson, *Do Trade Unions Cause Inflation?* (Cambridge University Press, London, 1972), pp. 77–94 *et seq.* on the impact of increasing taxation on net wages and union militancy; A. T. Peacock and M. Ricketts, 'The Growth of the Public Sector and Inflation', in F. Hirsch and J. H. Goldthorpe (eds.), *The Political Economy of Inflation* (Martin Robertson, London, 1978), pp. 117–36 on other aspects.

35. See the data cited in note 18 above.

36. Cf. A. Gamble, *The Conservative Nation*, p. 131.

37. Cf. S. Brittan, *Steering the Economy*, pp. 310–13.

38. Industrial capital still favoured economic planning for growth, the City was split about the need for devaluation and/or its economic costs and/or Labour's ability to make it work, the central Bank and Treasury tended to oppose devaluation but discussed all possible options, international opinion was also divided with the USA opposed because of likely threats from devaluation to the position of the dollar and the stability of the international monetary system; it is probable that, with domestic opinion finely balanced, the incoming Labour government decided against devaluation to avoid being identified as the 'party of devaluation', to reinforce the 'special relationship' with the US, and in the belief that devaluation would not solve the structural crisis or promote economic planning. See H. Brandon, *In the Red* (André Deutsch, London, 1966), pp. 39–49; S. Brittan, *Steering the Economy*, pp. 291–4 and 354.

39. Cf. Brittan, *Steering the Economy*, pp. 291–4, 303–10, 329–43; Hirsch, *The Pound Sterling*, pp. 123–36.

40. Cf. the French case study by P. Herzog, *Politique Économique et Planification en régime capitaliste* (Editions Sociales, Paris, 1972).

41. On the Federation of British Industries, see S. Blank, *Government and Industry in Britain* (Saxon House, Westmead, 1973); on the CBI, see W. P. Grant and D. Marsh, 'The Politics of the CBI: 1974 and After', *Government and Opposition*, x (1) 1975, pp. 90–104; *idem, The CBI* (Hodder and Stoughton, London, 1977); more generally, see J. E. S. Hayward, 'Employer Associations and the State in France and Britain', in S. J. Warnecke and E. N. Suleiman (eds.), *Industrial Policies in Western Europe* (Praeger, New York and London, 1976), pp. 118–51.

42. See particularly A. Jones, *The New Inflation* (Penguin, Harmondsworth, 1973), pp. 34–68; H. Clegg, *How to Run an Incomes Policy and Why We Made Such a Mess of the Last One* (Heinemann, London, 1971), pp. 47–58 and 69–78; C. Crouch, *Class Conflict and the Industrial Relations Crisis* (Heinemann, London, 1977), pp. 71–140; and R. Tarling and F. Wilkinson, 'The Inflationary Impact of Incomes Policies', *Cambridge Journal of Economics*, i (4) (1977), pp. 395–414.

43. Cf. R. Tarling and F. Wilkinson, 'The Inflationary Impact of Incomes Policies', p. 398; A. Jones, *The New Inflation*, pp. 69–217; H. Clegg, *How to Run an Incomes Policy, passim*; and J. Mitchell, *The National Board for Prices and Incomes* (Secker and Warburg, London, 1972).

44. The argument in this paragraph draws heavily on R. Tarling and F. Wilkinson, 'The Inflationary Impact of Incomes Policies', pp. 402–3 and 408–12; see also L. Panitch, *Social Democracy and Industrial Militancy*, pp. 204–34; and C. Crouch, *Class Conflict and the Industrial Relations Crisis*, pp. 203–4, 208–11, 222–6, and 259–72.

45. On the rôle of the little Neddies, see J. Leruez, *Economic Planning and Politics in Britain*, pp. 147–53, 210–13, and 271–2; M. Shanks, *Planning and Politics*, pp. 37–8, 58–60, and *passim*; T. Smith, 'Industrial Planning in Britain', in J. E. S. Hayward and M. Watson (eds.), *Planning, Politics, and Public Policy* (Cambridge University Press, London, 1975), pp. 111–27 (especially 116–20); and R. Bailey, *Managing the British Economy* (Hutchinson, London, 1968), *passim*.

46. The IRC is discussed at length in S. Young with A. V. Lowe, *Intervention in the Mixed Economy* (Croom Helm, London, 1974), pp. 39–120.

47. On the rôle of Mintech, see ibid., *passim*; Sir Richard Clarke, 'Min. Tech. in Retrospect', *Omega*, i (1 and 2) (1973); J. Leruez, *Economic Planning and Politics in Britain*, *passim*.

48. J. Leruez, *Economic Planning and Politics in Britain*, pp. 152–3 see also pp. 52–5 and 62–5.

49. Ibid., p. 231; S. Young with A. V. Lowe, *Intervention in the Mixed Economy*, pp. 121–64.

50. J. Leruez, *Economic Planning and Politics in Britain*, pp. 256–78.

51. R. Guttman, 'State Intervention and the Economic Crisis: the Labour Government's Economic Policy, 1974–5', *Kapitalistate*, 4–5 (1976), pp. 225–70; J. T. Winkler, 'The Industry Act 1975', *British Journal of Law and Society*, ii (2) (1975), pp. 103–28; S. Holland, *The Socialist Challenge*.

52. Cf. B. Fine and L. Harris, 'The British Economy: May 1975–January 1976', *Conference of Socialist Economists Bulletin* (October 1976), *passim*.

53. Cf. the important analyses proposed by J. Holloway, 'State Expenditure Cuts', mimeo, 1977; and Fine and Harris, cited in preceding note.

54. Cf. C. Crouch, *Class Conflict and the Industrial Relations Crisis*, pp. 59–66; T. Cliff, *The Employers' Offensive: Productivity Deals and How to Fight Them* (Pluto Press, London, 1970), *passim*.

55. Cf. M. Barrat-Brown, *From Labourism to Socialism* (Spokesman Books, Nottingham, 1972), pp. 91–2; T. C. May, *Trade Unions and Pressure Group Politics* (Saxon House, Westmead, 1975), *passim*; Donovan Commission, pp. 10–11 and *seriatim*.

56. Cf. M. Shanks, *Planning and Politics*, p. 21.

57. Cf. L. Panitch, 'The Development of Corporatism in Liberal Democracies', *Comparative Political Studies*, x (1) (1977), pp. 61–90; D. Marsh and W. Grant, 'Tripartism – Myth or Reality?', *Government and Opposition*, 12 (2) (1977), pp. 199–211.

58. Cf. Institute of Economic Affairs, *Inflation: Causes, Consequences, and Cures* (IEA, London, 1974); hence the increasing interest in monetarism.

59. J. W. Grove, *Government and Industry in Britain* (Longman and Green, London, 1962), *passim*; J. Leruez, *Economic Planning and Politics in Britain*, pp. 62–4 and 151–3.

60. On the Retail Consortium, see W. P. Grant and D. Marsh, 'The Representation of Retail Interests in Britain', *Political Studies*, xxii (2) (1974), pp. 168–77; on proposals for a Confederation of British Business, see W. P. Grant and D. Marsh, 'A Confederation of British Business?', *New Society*, 23 November 1972; see also references cited in note 44 above.

61. On these attempts, see C. Crouch, *Class Conflict and the Industrial Relations Crisis*, pp. 143–94 and 231–40; P. Jenkins, *The Battle of Downing Street* (Charles Knight, London, 1970); and B. Weekes *et al.*, *Industrial Relations and the Limits of the Law* (Blackwell, Oxford, 1975).

62. Cf. R. Hyman, 'British Trade Unionism in the 1970s: the Bureaucratisation of the Rank-and-File', paper presented to CSE Conference, 1978.

63. Cf. R. Tarling and F. Wilkinson, 'The Inflationary Impact of Incomes Policies', pp. 402–3.

64. Cf. A. King, *Why is Britain Becoming Harder to Govern?* (BBC Publications, London, 1975); S. Brittan, *The Economic Contradictions of Democracy* (Temple

Smith, London, 1977), pp. 247–90; R. Rose, 'Overloaded Governments', *European Studies Newsletter* (1975); and J. Douglas, 'The Overloaded Crown', *British Journal of Political Science*, vi (4) (1976), pp. 483–505.

65. On the 'Court', see L. Stone, *The Causes of the English Revolution 1529–1642* (Routledge & Kegan Paul, London, 1972), pp. 85–6.

66. For a more detailed discussion of 'parliamentary-bureaucratic' and corporatist modes of representation–intervention, see B. Jessop, 'Corporatism, Fascism, and Social Democracy', in P. Schmitter and G. Lehmbruch (eds.), *Corporatism in Liberal Democracies* (Sage, London, 1979).

67. Cf. J. P. MacIntosh, *The British Cabinet*, 2nd edn (Stevens, London, 1968); S. A. de Smith, *Constitutional and Administrative Law*, 2nd edn (Penguin, Harmondsworth, 1973), pp. 151–78 and *passim*.

68. On delegated legislation and administrative tribunals, see S. A. de Smith, *Constitutional and Administrative Law*, pp. 330–52 and 537–61.

69. Cf. J. P. MacIntosh, *The British Cabinet*, pp. 371–407; and H. Daalder, *Cabinet Reform in Britain 1914–63* (Oxford University Press, London, 1964), pp. 29–53 and *passim*.

70. Cf. F. Stacey, *British Government 1966–75: Years of Reform* (Oxford University Press, London, 1975), pp. 86–96; C. Pollitt, 'The Central Policy Review Staff 1970–4', *Public Administration* (1974), pp. 375–94.

71. Cf. Sir R. Clarke, *New Trends in British Government* (HMSO, London, 1971), pp. 1–35.

72. Ibid., pp. 42–56; M. Spiers, *Techniques and Public Administration* (Fontana, London, 1975), pp. 73–105; F. Stacey, *British Government 1966–75*, pp. 93–4.

73. Sir R. Clarke, *New Trends in British Government*, p. 51.

74. Cf. J. P. Morgan, *The House of Lords and the Labour Government 1964–70* (Oxford University Press, London, 1975), *passim*; S. A. de Smith, *Constitutional and Administrative Law*, pp. 296–313.

75. On the growth of 'quagos' and 'quangos', see C. Hood, 'The Rise and Rise of the British Quango', *New Society*, 16 March 1973; D. C. Hague *et al.* (eds.), *Public Policy and Private Interests: the Institutions of Compromise* (Macmillan, London, 1975); B. L. R. Smith (ed.), *The New Political Economy* (Macmillan, London, 1972).

76. Cf. Edinburgh CSE group, 'The Crisis of the State and the Struggle Against Bourgeois Forms', mimeo, 1978.

77. Cf. T. Bunyan, *Political Police in Britain*, pp. 76–83 and 291–3; Manchester NCCL, *The State, the Law, and Ireland* (Manchester, 1975); and B. Cox, *Civil Liberties in Britain* (Penguin, Harmondsworth, 1975), *passim*.

78. Cf. T. Bunyan, *Political Police in Britain*, pp. 93–8; 'The Atomic Police', *State Research Bulletin*, 5 (1978), pp. 76–8; 'The Anti-Terrorist Squad', *State Research Bulletin*, 8 (1978), pp. 1–3.

79. The new technologies of political control are described in C. Ackroyd *et al.*, *The Technology of Political Control* (Penguin, Harmondsworth, 1977); on contingency planning, see T. Bunyan, *Political Police in Britain*, pp. 293–9; 'Security Exercises', *State Research Bulletin*, 6 (1978), pp. 102–3; 'Civil Defense or Internal Defense', *State Research Bulletin*, 8 (1978), pp. 13–23; on strike-breaking, see 'Calling in the Troops', *State Research Bulletin*, 6 (1978), pp. 103–4.

80. Cf. A. Barnett, 'Class Struggle and the Heath Government', *New Left Review*, 77 (1973), pp. 3–41; S. Hall *et al.*, *Policing the Crisis* (Macmillan, London, 1978), pp. 260–306; see also references in note 65 above.

81. Cf. S. Hall *et al.*, *Policing the Crisis*, *passim*; A. Sivanand, 'Race, Class, and the State', *Race and Class*, xvii (4) (1976), pp. 347–68; D. Humphrey, *Police Power and Black People* (Panther, London, 1972); and G. Robertson, *Whose Conspiracy?* (NCCL, London, 1974).

82. Cf. S. Hall, 'The Great Moving Right Show', *Marxism Today* (January 1979), pp. 14–20; and S. Hall *et al.*, *Policing the Crisis*, *passim*.

83. For an extended discussion of popular incorporation, see Edinburgh CSE group, 'The Crisis of the State and the Struggle Against Bourgeois Forms', *passim.* (Cf. note 82 above.)

84. Cf. A. Briggs, 'The Welfare State in Historical Perspective', *European Journal of Sociology*, ii (2) (1961), pp. 221–58.

85. Cf. B. Jordan, *Freedom and the Welfare State* (Routledge & Kegan Paul, London, 1976), p. 122; A. Briggs, 'The Welfare State in Historical Perspective', *European Journal of Sociology*, ii (2) (1961), part IV.

86. Increasing welfare expenditure was initially financed by reduced military spending; then, after Macmillan's dismissal of the monetarist Chancellor, Thorneycroft, total spending began to rise at a faster rate (the average annual increase was 0.26 per cent from 1953 to 1957 compared with 4.18 per cent from 1957 to 1964); there was a further upward shift with the new Labour government (average 6.66 per cent between 1964 and 1967) and then a period of retrenchment (average 1.78 percent between 1967 and 1970); the next Conservative government saw a fresh upswing (average 5.02 per cent increase between 1970 and 1974). See M. Kogan, 'The Politics of Public Expenditure', *British Journal of Political Science*, vi (1977), pp. 401–32.

87. Cf. J. Kincaid, *Poverty and Equality in Britain* (Penguin, Harmondsworth, 1973), pp. 44–63; R. G. S. Brown, *The Management of Welfare* (Fontana, London, 1975), pp. 19–20.

88. Cf. Kincaid, *Poverty and Equality*, pp. 221–9; B. Jordan, *Poor Parents* (Routledge & Kegan Paul, London, 1974), pp. 46–59; and M. Meacher, *Scrounging on the Welfare* (Arrow, London, 1974), *passim.*

89. Cf. B. Jordan, *Freedom and the Welfare State*, pp. 125–78.

90. Cf. J. Westergaard and H. Resler, *Class in a Capitalist Society* (Heinemann, London, 1975), pp. 58–71; Kincaid, *Poverty and Equality*, pp. 103–63; B. Jordan, *Paupers* (Routledge & Kegan Paul, London, 1973); and *idem*, *Poor Parents*, pp. 60–97.

91. For a useful survey, see D. McKay and A. W. Cox, *Politics and Urban Change* (Croom Helm, London 1979), *passim.* See also the many studies and reports of the Community Development Programme, for example, *The Costs of Industrial Change* (CDP, London, 1978); *The Limits of the Law* (CDP, London, 1977); *Gilding the Ghetto* (CDP, London, 1977); and *Local Government Becomes Big Business* (CDP, London, 1973).

92. Cf. A. Cawson, 'Representational Crises and Corporatism in Capitalist Societies', mimeo, 1979; M. Geddes, 'Crises, Cuts, Regional Problems, Regional Policy and Planning', mimeo, 1978; and D. Massey, 'Regionalism: Some Current Issues', *Capital and Class*, 6 (1978), pp. 106–25.

93. Cf. Community Development Programme-Counter Information Service, *Cutting the Welfare State (Who Profits?)* (CDP–CIS, London, 1976); J. Holloway, 'State Expenditure Cuts' (unpublished paper); and I. Gough, *The Political Economy of the Welfare State* (Macmillan, London, 1979).

94. Cf. Edinburgh CSE, 'The Crisis of the State and the Struggle Against Bourgeois Forms', *passim.*

95. Cf. A. Gamble, *The Conservative Nation*, pp. 3–10; B. Jessop, 'Capitalism and Democracy: the Best Possible Political Shell?', in G. Littlejohn *et al.* (eds.), *Power and the State* (Croom Helm, London, 1978), pp. 10–42.

96. Cf. A. Gamble, *The Conservative Nation*, pp. 16–18; B. Jessop, *Traditionalism, Conservatism, and British Political Culture* (Allen and Unwin, London, 1974), *passim.*

97. Cf. Gamble, *The Conservative Nation*, pp. 33–7 and *passim.*

98. This is evident from initial analyses of the last general election: thus Gallup data suggest that the Conservative share of the skilled manual worker vote increased 18 per cent between October 1974 and May 1979 and reached 44 per cent compared with 45 per cent for Labour; and, even among trade unionists, there was an 8 per cent

increase, resulting in 30 per cent support for the Tories and 51 per cent for Labour; see *The Economist*, 19 May 1979.

99. 'Economic–corporate' demands are based on consciousness of the solidarity of interests among members of a class but they are restricted to demands for economic improvements, politico–juridical equality, rights to participate in legislation and administration, or even to reform them – but within the existing relations of production and domination: see A. Gramsci, *Selections from the Prison Notebooks* (Lawrence and Wishart, London, 1971), pp. 181 and 161.

100. Cf. Marx's comment on Bonapartism, namely, that 'it was the only form of government possible at a time when the bourgeoisie had already lost, and the working-class had not yet acquired, the faculty of ruling the nation': see K. Marx, 'The Civil War in France', in D. Fernbach (ed.), *The First International and After* (Penguin, Harmondsworth, 1974), p. 208. But our own analysis centres on modes of securing bourgeois domination.

101. The point is developed in D. McEarchen, *Government Action and the Power of Private Capital.*

2 The State in Contemporary France

In France there has recently been a spate of publications concerning the state. Sometimes it is seen as a totalitarian monster threatening liberties, sometimes as the social instrument of the monopolies, sometimes as the direct agent of economic modernisation, the expression of a ruling group, or the outcome of the long-term centralisation of the French political system which is resisted by the regionalists as much as by the supporters of self-determination, etc. Being an object of political change, the state itself has not stopped changing. These modifications need to be understood in terms of the specific history of the construction of the French State. Although the state's own structure has undergone fundamental change since 1945, this evolution should be interpreted as much in terms of the evolution of its rôle within present-day society as a whole and the confrontation between classes and social groups as in terms of its particular historical trajectory: indeed, the structure of any one of the states depends on the original circumstances of its creation.[1] At the present time France, Great Britain, the Netherlands, Switzerland and the German Federal Republic are all, without exception, capitalist countries in which large firms possess considerable power which they wield in quite specific ways through the state; it is nonetheless true that radical differences do exist between the actual structures and modes of action of each of these states. It is a well known fact that, in comparison with its neighbours, the state in France has for a long time had an extremely centralised form. Stage by stage in its construction, the centre in France has become endowed with an unusually powerful state, able to establish and maintain widespread control over the periphery.

In the space of this brief analysis it is obviously impossible to describe all the changes which have taken place in the French State since 1945. However, between 1945 and 1978 one can identify, somewhat schematically it is true, three main periods during which the internal structuring of the state has varied according to the ways in which it relates to the different socio-economic forces.[2]

94

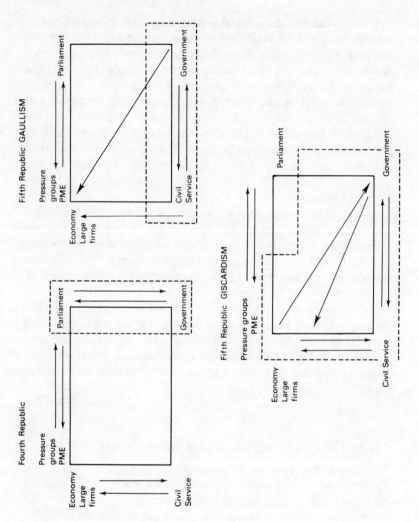

One can think of the political system of the Fourth Republic as an expression of a strict separation of the powers which go to make up the state, where the state is somewhat isolated from other sources of power. One can see the Gaullist system as the expression of a particular fusion between the civil service and government, used by the state to assert its independence. Finally, the Giscardian system can be seen as an example of a more general fusion of powers, with the state gradually seeming to abandon some of its prerogatives, allowing more power to be exercised by a ruling class, without fundamental change in its functional aspects. Thus the structure, functions and activities of the state have developed in quite fundamental ways between 1945 and 1978.

Using these three general models, we will show how the traditionally strong grip of the state has grown even tighter as the political system has changed and as new alliances have been formed, leading to the transformation of the party system. We will then analyse the reasons for and the consequences of the growth of intervention by the civil service which meets with resistance at the centre as much as at the periphery from the social groups which it tries to influence. Finally, we will examine the developments which have led to the voluntarist and 'planned' state to gradually abandon its claim to independence and revert to an economic liberalism which has since become the mode of action most favourable to the ruling class.

The New Distribution of Political-administrative Power

The Fourth Republic can be considered as a typical example of a Parliamentary or Assembly régime in which Parliament wields the whole range of powers: it determines general policy, makes law and controls the government. It exercises strict control over the executive. Overall parliamentary power thus varies according to the relative strength of the political parties. During both the 'Deputies' Republic' and the 'Professor's Republic', political power was under the control of professional political personnel. Apart from the civil service which still eluded them, politicians from the mass political parties – the SFIO, the PC and the MRP* – guided the activities of the state.

*The 'French Section of the (Second) Working-Class International', the Communist Party and the Popular Republican Movement.

What happened of course was that the alliances which were forged between the parties of the left during the Resistance and which lasted until after the eviction of General de Gaulle (tripartism) were quickly to disintegrate; under crossfire from the PC on their left and the RPF on their right, the moderate and centre parties and the SFIO were trying to govern with fragile and constantly-broken alliances.

This Parliament of forming and dissolving majorities was the expression of a broad multiparty system related to the electoral system of proportional representation. It was a place of social compromises between numerous parties with often fairly weak discipline. Despite the form of the electoral system they were made up of prominent local figures rooted in their constituencies, who had passed through the stages of a long career leading from the local council to the town hall, the general council and membership of Parliament or a senator's seat, and sometimes even to the government itself. Deputies were therefore specially attentive to local demands. France was still a rural country with a profoundly dualistic economy in which the PMEs (Small and Medium Enterprises) were largely predominant and its grass-roots interests were expressed through Parliament. The deputies – lawyers, doctors or teachers – were spokesmen whose voice was heard to the extent that they held strong local seats, belonged to local councils, accumulated a large number of mandates, many of them having been re-elected more than five times.[3]

The high-ranking officials and industrialists who had participated quite extensively in the Vichy government remained absent from the Parliament. These established links continued to exist outside Parliament: as we shall see below, the civil service was to set up specific structures designed to assist the modernisation of large firms. The multiparty state with a membership of locally-based professional figures seemed less and less capable either of ending the colonial wars of another age or of keeping up with or promoting the modernisation of the economic system.

It is well known that the political system of the Fifth Republic depends entirely on an executive which derives great benefit from the support of the civil service. It was on the basis of this partial fusion of powers that the state made its claim to independence.[4] Professional politicians were only represented in a Parliament of greatly diminished power; the middle classes and liberal professionals of the large mass parties formed 51.9 per cent of parliamentarians in the Fourth Republic and 59 per cent in the Fifth. In contrast, at the level of the executive, these categories are almost entirely eliminated, to be replaced mainly by senior officials often with backgrounds in the *Grands Corps*. Whereas this group formed only 9 per cent of the parliamentary personnel in the Fifth Republic, they formed more than 30 per cent of the members of government, compared with only 11.8 per cent in the Fourth Republic. The Gaullist ideology always stressed the independence of the state *vis-à-vis* the parties. The 1958 Constitution is entirely based on this idea: the state, which is expressed first and foremost in the executive, must be an 'arbiter' remaining 'above the parties'. From this time onwards, government originates from the elected President of the Republic, an election by universal suffrage since the 1962 reform. Benefiting from popular legitimacy, the President of the Republic is in no way responsible to Parliament; it is he who nevertheless originates a government which can be made to resign even when it has just obtained the confidence of Parliament. Thus the state seems to be embodied in the executive alone; in no sense is the decline of Parliament a myth in contemporary France. The Gaullist state's claim to independence therefore signifies the overwhelming power of the executive which recruits its ministers chiefly among senior civil servants who have often not even been elected to Parliament previously.[5] A new route is opened up which takes senior officials from ministerial and cabinet offices on to the ministerial function and finally to membership of Parliament. In the same way as in Great Britain or Italy, for example, ministers in the Third and Fourth Republics were all former parliamentarians. Today this is no longer the case in France.

This reversed route means that the executive regards itself as the expression of the general interest, which it seeks to handle in a rational and technical manner rather than in terms of local and sectional interests which it holds in suspicion.[6] Many of the civil servants are products of the ENA (École Nationale d'Administration), created after the Second World War by General de Gaulle and Michel Debré. They therefore have the advantage of a technical competence which they devote to the state in its modernising rôle and quite deliberate intervention in society at large and in the economic sector in particular, which is designed to accelerate the concentration of large firms by planning and selective aid, a theme to which we will be returning later.

The Gaullist Fifth Republic enhanced the autonomy of the state by pushing the institutionalisation of its apparatus to its farthest limit. The civil service working for the executive increased its homogeneity in terms of values, the coherence of the rules governing its activities and the meritocratic character of its recruitment. It also closed its ranks against intruders from outside, few of whom ever succeeded in joining. Of course, few would disagree that the ministers of the Fifth Republic were more inclined to *pantouflage** than those of the Fourth Republic and that senior officials, especially those from the *Grands Corps*, are less and less reluctant to resign in order to bring their various types of competence to the private sector.[7] However, this flow did nothing to alter the exclusiveness of the civil service, entry to which still remained hermetically sealed. As the specific locus of power, the civil service gave the Gaullist state the means to justify its claim to be independent from social forces as well as from political parties. With its intimate ties to political power, the civil service really did seem to fulfil the functions of the political parties.[8] Since these parties no longer occupied the commanding heights of the state as they once had done in previous Republics, it was left to the civil service to act in the name of the state, through the ministerial *cabinets*, the commissions of the plan and a whole range of *ad hoc* commissions. The strength of this fusion between the executive and the civil service can also be explained by a change in the party system. The two stage ballot reinstated in 1958 produced electoral alliances and quickly led to the bipolarisation of political forces. Thus the multiparty system of the Fourth Republic was gradually replaced by two grand coalitions, one of which, having had a majority since 1958, is closely dependent on the executive. Under the Fourth Republic, the various large parties each represented 15 per cent of the votes cast; under the Fifth Republic, Gaullism in its various guises succeeded on its own in gaining more than 30 per cent of votes and eventually reached 44 per cent of votes in 1968. In a real sense it has become a dominant mass party[9] which, since 1967, has been the most representative of the French electorate. It has managed to attract one-third of the working-class vote, gradually taking root in nearly all its constituencies including the traditional strongholds of the left, slowly taking over the local mandates which give their holders prominent status as well-established figures. Thanks to this Gaullist Party, the right has a mass party which claims several hundreds of thousands of adherents, a mass of workers who are largely subject to the wishes of the executive but who, like the parliamentarians, can do little to

*Literally, 'putting on one's slippers'. This has become a recognised French term to describe the movement from the civil service to positions in private sector firms (Translator).

control it. Given the success of the UNR (Union pour la Nouvelle République) and then the UDR (Union des Démocrates pour la République), the Gaullist state, which is hardly different from saying the executive, has an automatic majority in Parliament even though General de Gaulle and Georges Pompidou never belonged to the Gaullist Party as such. With the advantage of this practically unconditional support, the executive can govern as it were by osmosis with the civil service. In this sense, the party loses part of its representational function although it is still the medium of expression of grass-roots French interests like those of the peasants, small and medium scale firms and white collar workers, not to mention those of manual workers. But these interests are typically expressed as demands on a Parliament largely devoid of power, both because of the close subordination of the party to the executive and because of measures enshrined in the Constitution which, among other things, considerably limit the legislative power of Parliament by restricting the realm of law and allowing the executive to intervene in all other areas with the backing of regulatory measures. Parliament is thus deprived of control over its own agenda, which is one of the bases of parliamentary democracy, through the defeat of amendments by means of the block vote, the denial of any influence to parliamentary commissions, etc. Provincial France makes its voice heard in a Parliament which cannot act and which is forced to accept measures which its electorate often condemns (laws on VAT, autonomy of the Universities, abortion, etc.) whilst the close combination of the executive and civil service proceeds with quite another political and industrial project which we will return to later. With the end of Gaullism, the arrival to power of Georges Pompidou and then especially Valéry Giscard d'Estaing, the political-administrative power slowly began to abandon its claim to independence and the growing autonomy of the state was significantly reduced. The state appears increasingly like a simple function performed in a temporary manner by actors who all belong to the ruling class. The state is formed by a division of labour within the ruling class; the political-administrative fusion spreads to the economic sector itself, especially to concentrated firms and to the large banks which now play host to the senior officials who sometimes return to occupy a state post.[10] The voluntarist state gives way to the liberal state, the civil service abandons the ideology of public service and the general interest, on which its institutionalisation is based, and adopts the same perspectives as those which prevail in the private sector.

Thus the contemporary state in France claims so much the less independence that on the one hand, it no longer attempts to influence the world of business from the outside but instead co-operates with it. As we shall see, this change upsets the activities of the civil service which has long served as a pillar designed to preserve its independence. On the other hand, it is now forced to rely on an electorate which is noticeably less multi-class than it was at the time of General de Gaulle.[11]

During the sixties, and to an even greater extent since the election of Valéry Giscard d'Estaing to the Presidency of the Republic, the party system has experienced a transformation which has polarised the right and the left more sharply than at any time previously. In Valéry Giscard d'Estaing's electorate one no longer finds the large proportion of workers who rallied to General de Gaulle: whereas more than 70 per cent of workers voted for Mitterand, 72 per cent of farmers voted for Giscard, as did 67 per cent of small business owners and artisans and 56 per cent of higher management and industrialists.[12] Similarly, in the legislative elections of March 1978, close on 60 per cent of farmers, artisans and small business owners, and 54 per cent of higher management and the professions declared their support for the majority but only 25 per cent of workers did so.[13] The decline of the Gaullist Party within the majority and the rise of the coalition of Independents and various centrists marks the victory of the traditional and conservative right, or the bourgeoisie which both facilitated the departure of General de Gaulle and hastened that of the workers. The partisan character of the state becomes clearly apparent: after successfully forcing Gaullism, or the Bonapartist and nationalist right-seeking integration, into retreat, Giscardism or the new form taken by the liberal, modernist and *laissez-faire* bourgeoisie, gives birth to the new Republican Party which, like the Gaullist RPR (Rassemblement pour la République) is officially represented in the Chirac government by its national leaders.

By opposing Gaullism, Giscardism thus gives the party struggle a new impetus. In this perspective, the contradiction which we have described between policies pursued by the combination of executive-civil service and the demands expressed by a multi-class party, appears to be diminishing. The Republican Party becomes the spokesman of the executive; it is a large conservative party which openly asserts its liberal policies and aspires to follow the American model of growth which the Gaullist, nationalist and populist right continues to oppose, at least at the level of political formula. To a certain extent abandoned by the modernist grande bourgeoisie, the Gaullist right continues to receive the support of a more heterogeneous electorate, stretching from worker to small and medium scale proprietors of firms threatened by the increasing concentration which is one consequence of the prevailing liberalism.[14] In this sense, if Giscardism managed to become the generally dominant tendency within the majority (this begs the question: which electorate?) we would see a gradual reversion towards a general fusion of powers, with Parliament entering this time into the hypothetical fusion which has had only a single precedent in the July monarchy. Government would no longer be by a state but by an establishment.

The Power and Powerlessness of the Administration

The administration was already powerful under the Fourth Republic but its representatives had not scaled the commanding heights of the state as they were to do in the Fifth Republic. The strengthening of state power can be explained by a major development of the ministerial *cabinets* which have access to the executive and which also tend increasingly to control the rest of the administration. Consisting almost entirely of senior officials with backgrounds in the *Grands Corps*,[15] who agree to give a minimum of political allegiance to the majority in power, these ministerial *cabinets* are the real driving force behind the state's activities. It is through them that the senior officials educated at the ENA, who are often members of the *Grands Corps*, frame and further their careers by being subsequently appointed to head the large public and private sector corporations, to lead the parties or to manage the main media of mass information (radio, television, etc.) thus enlarging still further the partisan state's sphere of influence.

Guaranteed by the Constitution (which limits the realm of law and thus extends regulatory power because a large number of laws have a very general orientation which leaves to the administration the task of deciding upon the precise measures required) and reinforced by characteristics of the new political system, the administration's influence is simultaneously strengthened and diversified. The newly created ministries illustrate the change in the state's objectives: for example, the *Ministère de l'Équipement* (1966) and the *Ministère des Affaires Sociales* (1969), in particular.[16] These two ministries show the direction in which state regulation was moving, these being most vital for ensuring the satisfactory performance of the economic sector.

Urban planning, for instance, reveals the state's rôle in the management of social tension. Outside the traditional, vertical and segmented
administrations each acting for itself and often in opposition to one
another, the state has created a whole set of specific structures
organised separately from the traditional administration along
horizontal rather than vertical lines. They act outside the hierarchies
and they are less cumbersome, often existing for a limited period only.
In particular, one should mention those which are concerned with the
management of urban areas which provide the context for industrial
and commercial development and also influence the nature of social
relationships and the movements by which they become manifest. For
example, there was the creation in 1963 of DATAR (*Délégation
d'Aménagement du Territoire et à l'Action Régionale*)[17] which controls specific financial resources and which operates as a decision-
making apparatus directly attached to the Prime Minister and thence
to the Minister of the Interior. It has responsibility for local
collectivities and is capable of acting on behalf of the Ministries as a
whole, with the plan's modernisation commissions and regional
administrations, creating special organisations for urban affairs and
tourism, distributing credit both on its own account and through
organisations it controls like the FDES (*Fonds de Développement
Economique et Social*). It sets up committees for regional expansion,
organises the OREAM (*Organismes d'Etude d'Aménagement des
Aires Metropolitaines*) and largely controls the CODER (*Commission
de Développement Economique Régional*) which has the task of
developing, in collaboration with progressive forces outside the
traditional administrations and their respective clienteles, a politics of
modernisation, a prototype of the new influence which the state is
endeavouring to exert. Linked to these reforms, one should also stress
the rôle of the missions, like those of Languedoc–Roussilon or the
Aquitaine, which are likewise specific, provisional and horizontal,
circumventing the traditional administrations and thereby contributing
to numerous institutional conflicts at the periphery. Before we assess
this type of intervention by the administration and before we try to
show its significance, note that the state in the Fifth Republic has new,
more effective and less bureaucratic means of intervention which it
can control more firmly; these enhance still further the traditional
centralisation. Note also that the Fifth Republic sees the introduction
of new methods of management designed to improve the rationality of
administrative action – methods which are inspired by American
methods – like RCB (rationalisation of budgetary choices). It is worth

remembering that, like the centralisation of the new administrative structures, these techniques have done nothing more than limit still further the effects of attempts at decentralisation, deconcentration and participation: at best, they have led to the integration and co-optation of those on the periphery who were willing to collaborate with the administration (as was the case with the GAM, *Groupes d'Action Municipale*[18]) and they have further increased the centre's control of information.[19]. Although during the Fifth Republic the state has often entertained discussions of decentralisation, the new forms of action by the administration, including both the techniques used and its tutelage over the new regional public institutions, along with the lack of financial aid to the peripheral administrations not to mention the public institutions or even the local collectivities which cannot increase their resources or revenue, have led to the further strengthening of the power of the centre and the further weakening of tendencies which encourage segmentation in the state apparatus in France as well as in other countries.[20]

As we have already seen, the central state, in order to increase its influence and to make its actions more effective, has attempted to make other kinds of intervention in order to control, for example, regional and local planning, resource distribution, the setting up of businesses and the organisation of tourism and transport. In particular it has intervened to enhance the rôle of the large, concentrated firms which have emerged in the Fifth Republic and which require a favourable infrastructure. Hence, for example, the policy of major industrial centres which also determines the nature of regional planning and the dividing up of France into a network of nuclear power stations which perfectly symbolise the control which the centre aims to exert over the periphery.

This politics of the state tangle with the traditional administration organised vertically at the periphery which have clientele-type relationships with prominent local figures who scarcely welcome modernisation with open arms. It is true that the Prefect, who is the direct agent of central power dependent on the Minister of the Interior and who has tutelage over local collectivities, stands in a relationship of deep complicity with locally-elected representatives.[21] These representatives need the Prefect for access to the centre, for confirmation of their status, and for obtaining extra-legal credits or favours which are all the more symbolic of their personal power; in return, the Prefect needs these prominent locals to endorse the politics of the centre, to maintain the consensus and social order and to justify his own position in relation to Paris. The 'Prefects' Régime', that of the Fifth Republic, consequently reaches its limit in this traditional politics of patron and client which crushes all inclination towards the modernisation which threatens these local interests. For example, in 1964, a regional reform of great importance was attempted, partly under the impetus of DATAR, whose administrative function and economic rôle we have stressed, to outflank this solidaristic front by causing upheaval among the traditional administrations at the periphery as well as among their associated local figures. Two decrees created in each of the 21 (then 22) regions, a regional prefect to preside over a regional administrative Conference and dialogue with a CODER where it was anticipated that representatives of the progressive forces and not traditional dignitaries would come to sit. As a result, this reform threatened to destroy the circuits of solidarity formed within each of the departments, these having been integrated into the regions as Pierre Grémion has shown.[22] This reform failed because departments other than those of the Regional Prefect rejected this system of control which ought to have been the means for implementing regional planning. This reform encountered the double hostility of the departmental administrations which clung to the possibility of direct access to the centre and the local figures who were in danger of losing their direct access to their Prefect and hence to the centre, and who were also afraid of being supplanted by new socio-economic forces increasingly dedicated to modernisation and economic expansion. This defeat for the central administration, the instrument of an all-powerful executive, shows the limits to its action. At the periphery, the state encounters the grass-roots resistance of provincial France in the shape of local dignitaries, the small and medium scale proprietors and businessmen frightened by the administration's modernist policies which bring such advantages to the large scale employers. At a level where a kind of apoliticism is often prevalent[23] this resistance has rallied both the solidly established figures of the left (especially those of the *Parti Socialiste* and the *Parti Radical*) and those of the majority (the Gaullist representatives who also managed to establish themselves as prominent local figures). Thus, to all intents and purposes, the administration played the rôle of a political party at the service of modernist economic policies with the encouragement of the central state. But while it favours the major industries it typically encounters a challenge from this same centre in the form of the majority deputies who remain attentive to the diversity of local demands. As Pierre Grémion further points out 'the administrative apparatus of the state is thus heavily controlled by the periphery'. This resistance put up by local forces means the 'fragmented state and the triumph of clientelism'.[24]

Regional reform thus has the appearance of an instrument used by the centre to organise the country as a whole within a political and economic framework conducive to modernisation and the reinforcement of large firms. It is therefore no accident that the regionalist claims which are currently surfacing in France are being made most emphatically by the local interests threatened by the central state. The solid feudal systems of Brittany or Languedoc are the spokesmen of a regionalism unlike that promoted from the centre, for it would allow them, within the confines of their regions, to defend their political and economic power from the threat of state activities in support of the large firms. It follows that regionalism, apart from its strictly cultural aspects, is an expression of the clash between bourgeoisies whose interests have come into conflict.[25] By endangering the power of local interests through a deliberately modernising policy aimed at transforming the administration of the regions, the administration reveals both its strength, which comes from its close links with the executive, and its weakness. The periphery can actually withstand the centre; the mayors of the large towns who often have the gift of other national mandates (deputies, senators) act directly upon the centre in order to preserve their local equilibrium.[26] Thanks to a cabinet which comprises technical–political personnel, they are better able to defend their towns except, of course, when for political reasons the municipality simply applies locally the planning norms worked out at the centre.[27]

Threatened by an economic power with central state support, local interests likewise came to exploit the political arena: at municipal elections the various social classes sometimes formed blocs in order to bolster the power of a locally hegemonic fraction of the bourgeoisie, but sometimes they joined forces instead with the centre's policies in the hope of sharing the fruits of the new type of expansion. This was the case for example at Caen, Roanne and at Dunkerque where, on occasion, the municipality was overwhelmed by left opposition.[28] It should also be remembered that since 1977 the left has governed urban France and hence a part of the state apparatus.[29] The activities of the central administration supported by the very highest state authorities which, under the Fifth Republic wield immense power and form a homogeneous ensemble, are therefore hindered by obstacles (traditional administration, local interests, etc.) which sometimes prove difficult to surmount.[30]

From the Planned State to the Entrepreneurial State

Immediately after the Second World War, France was the only country in the Western world to endow itself with planning structures. Connecting with a long history during which the centralising state had often claimed aloofness while simultaneously intervening in economic life, France thus perpetuated the experience of Vichy which saw the development of relationships between the civil service and the large employers which were designed to guarantee the smooth functioning of the economy. Although planning had been desired just as much by the Resistance, and although the parties of the left had initially supported its implementation, it rapidly became a means of revitalising the large firms. It was very warmly welcomed by the employers who were compromised by their collaboration under Vichy and had very few ties with the parties of the left who came to power immediately after the war. This was how the relationship between the civil service and the major employers came to be established under the Fourth Republic, when Parliament was more sensitive to the interests of a whole range of pressure groups. From that time onwards, the civil service therefore played the quasi-party rôle which we have already stressed: via planning, it represents the interests of large-scale capitalism which does not have proper representation in Parliament. We shall see that under the Fifth Republic, the rôle played by the civil service in promoting the modernisation of large-scale capitalism becomes still more explicit to the extent that the relationship which binds them together comes increasingly to envelop the executive, with Parliament remaining untouched by this fusion as the place where other socio-economic interests attempt to make themselves heard.

It is very clear that from this time onwards, the actual structure of the state altered so as better to fulfil these economic functions: some institutions were modified, others were created. New institutions came into being outside the administrative structures: the *Commissariat General au Plan* (1946) and various committees instructed to report on the reforms required in the modernisation of the structure of the French economy (*Comité Rueff, Comité Rueff-Armand, Comité de Développement Industriel, Comité Nora*, etc.) which brought together senior officials and the directors of the major firms. Other examples include DATAR (1963), the ANVAR (*Agence Nationale pour la Valorisation de la Récherche*, 1967), the *Agence Nationale pour l'Emploi* (1967), the university *Instituts de Technologie*, the DGRST (*Direction Générale de la Récherche Scientifique et Technique*, 1968), the *Direction Générale de l'Industrie* and the *Ministère de l'Industrie* which is horizontally organised (1974), not to mention the various regional institutions which we have already discussed, and so on. For similar reasons, INSEE was transformed, growing from 2,700 officers to 7,200 between 1962 and 1975, like the statistical service of the *Ministère de l'Industrie* which expanded from 20 to 750 officers, involving the comprehensive reorganisation of the statistical institutions.[31] Other institutions have resulted from the remodelling and reorientation of already existing structures: the *Ministère de l'Equipement* (1966), *Ministère des Affaires Sociales* (1967), and the *Ministère de l'Industrie* which in 1969 became the *Ministère du Développement Industriel et Scientifique*. Then there are the various newly-formed or transformed *Secrétariats d'Etat*: *Secrétariat à la Condition Feminine, Secrétariat d'Etat pour la Revalorisation du Travail Manuel, Secrétariat d'Etat aux Travailleurs Immigrés*, etc. Note that a large number of these innovations took place between 1963 and 1969, or at the neo-liberal turning point at which the state became a genuine entrepreneur and gave its full backing to the strengthening, concentration and expansion of large firms. Its means for achieving this included the adjustment of its policies towards public corporations, its prices and credit policy, its subsidies, its loans to very weak interests,[32] the cartels which really only benefit a small number of firms, its diplomatic efforts designed to conquer external markets, the management of the unemployment which inevitably followed from the profound structural changes in the economy favourable to the large competitive firms and damaging to the 'lame ducks', permanent education including the training of the new technicians, etc. By being able to count on a mass party which collates demands from provincial France, local interests, small and medium size firms, the liberal professions, etc., and by channelling them rather than meeting them, as in the case of the Royer law which temporarily blocks large-scale development in order to preserve the electoral support of small businessmen, the state can instead satisfy other kinds of demand like those of the large concentrated firms dedicated to exporting – demands which rarely end in non-decisions.[33]

This is not the place to rewrite the history of French planning, which others have already written.[34] What this history teaches us is that the function of planning has been to fight against the underdevelopment of capitalism because of the profoundly dualist nature of the French economy (M. Levi-Leboyer). Thanks to 'planification' and nationalisation, the state took early charge of the reconstruction of the major economic sectors (transport, energy, etc.) which were producing limited profits.[35] It thus facilitated the reinstatement of the large firms which were the main beneficiaries of the Marshall Plan credits[36] and thereby directly threatened the small and medium size firms (which accounts for their response, from that of Gingembre in the immediate post-war period up to that of the Poujadist movement or, later, the CIDUNATI*). With its various plans, the state established a 'concerted economy' (F. Bloch-Laine) which, after the rapid departure of the trade unions, allowed close collaboration within the different state organisations, and between senior officials and the large-scale employers. This is why the planning commissions on modernisation consist mainly of senior officials and large-scale employers or directors of firms.[37] These institutionalised connections have of course allowed senior officials from the ENA with their thorough economic training to establish close links with the employers which make it all the easier to *pantoufle* on leaving the service of the state for that of large-scale, concentrated firms.[38]

In the economic realm, state activity is therefore committed to the support of the large industrial corporations. It is well known that in the early days of the Fifth Republic, the plan was described by General de Gaulle as a 'burning duty'. Even at this time the large employers were still not entirely convinced of the pressing need to face the 'American challenge', to concentrate and thoroughly modernise in order to meet competition from outside following in the wake of freer exchange. The state took a very large number of economic and fiscal measures[39] to encourage firms to rationalise. It took the initiative and set in motion a new industrial policy which the employers were not prepared to initiate, at least not on their own. In this sense, senior officials served as 'capitalism's "organic" intellectuals',[40] and forced the industrialists to take the plunge.[41]

The autonomisation of the state was enhanced when in the early 1960s it had to impose an economic policy contrary to the one recommended by an important section of the employers. The state's claim to independence was, at this time, not simply a national ideology but also a myth which made use of planning as an instrument of both development and social cohesion. It is therefore not true to say that 'the state is more than ever the political and economic class instrument of the monopolistic bourgeoisie'[42] or that, 'with de Gaulle and his government, the state is more completely than ever in the hands of the central

*Comité d'Information et de Défense–Union Nationale des Artisans et Travailleurs Independants.

bank and the monopolies',[43] that the state is 'the simple institutional translation of state monopoly capitalism',[44] or 'the instrument by which the class of owners maintains and reproduces its domination. Its forms, its structures and its organs are essentially determined by its class content'.[45] Not only has the state established an economic policy which clearly benefits the interests of the large employers, it is a political-administrative power which has taken the initiative. What is more, it must be stressed that, contrary to all the theories of the state which make it into an instrument, an abstract relation or even the simple outcome of a 'condensation' of social relations, the state is a specific entity, with particular structures which may or may not strengthen its institutionalisation, internal hierarchies, rôles, grades, corps,[46] which are often opposed to one another for reasons which have nothing to do with the power of the monopolies. It is a system of values and ideologies which accentuates and justifies its autonomy in ways which vary from period to period.

It is true that, since the 1960s, the state seems to have gradually abandoned its 'planist' ideology in favour of an 'industrial policy' which makes it more of an entrepreneur dealing closely with firms themselves,[47] acting 'in concert' with their representatives,[48] and even showing some hostility towards certain senior officials attached to the notion of the general interest.[49] As the report of the *Comité de Développement Industriel* shows, 'the search for effective competition must begin by influencing the activities of the state which condition the environment of firms – the economic environment which is the state's responsibility and the environment of laws and regulations'.[50]

From the fifth plan onwards, right up to the sixth and seventh, the state was concerned to promote the concentration of large firms, their expansion and their profits, by adapting its structures to this end and by accepting the support of the large employers who were by now convinced of the virtues of modernisation. In this liberal perspective where the laws of the market outweigh all other considerations, where even prices are being systematically de-controlled (in August 1978 the price of bread was freed for the first time since regulation began in 1791, as the symbol of a competitive economic policy), the state is abandoning some of its functions and is increasingly accepting the privatisation of a part of its activities. It is also encouraging the installation of foreign capitals which control a significant number of the leading French firms[51] and is placing a limit on national projects of vital importance (computers, nuclear power, telephones). This policy can only further aggravate the already marked contradiction between its preferential attitude towards large firms and the unsatisfied demands of numerous socio-occupational categories who, in spite of everything, continue to support the majority and attempt to make their voices heard, sometimes with a degree of success, through the parties which formulate this policy. Therefore the state in contemporary France finds itself at the nodal point of a large number of contradictions: the contradiction between the large firms which it supports and other socio-occupational categories which continue to uphold it simply because they stand to gain some benefit from its global policy, and the contradiction which finds the state opposing various types of regionalism which threaten to link up with supranational powers (both public and private) thereby calling into question its capacity for autonomous action.

Notes

1. See Charles Tilly, *The Formation of National States in Western Europe* (Princeton University Press, Princeton, 1975); R. Bendix, *State and Society* (University of California Press, Berkeley, 1973); P. Anderson, *Lineages of the Absolutist State* (New Left Books, London, 1974).

2. These schemes are derived from Stein Rokkan's suggestions in the *BPD Newsletter*, no. 23 which I used in presenting my work *Les Sommets de l'État* (Le Seuil, Paris, 1977). They have been substantially modified.

3. M. Dogan, 'Political Ascent in a Class Society: French Deputies 1870–1958' in D. Marwick (ed.), *Political Decision-makers* (Free Press, Glencoe, 1961) and 'Les Filières de la carrière politique en France', *Revue française de Sociologie*, no. 8 (1967); J. Charlot 'Les Elites politiques en France de la IIIᵉ à la Vᵉ Republique', *Archives européennes de sociologie*, 14 (1973).

4. See Birnbaum, *Les Sommets de l'Etat*, Chapters 1 and 5.

5. P. Antoni and J. D. Antoni, *Les Ministres de la Vᵉ Republique* (PNF, Paris, 1976). M. Dogan, 'Comment on devient Ministre en France, 1870–1976', Communication at the Congress of the International Association for Political Science, Edinburgh, 1976.

6. See E. Suleiman, *Les Hauts Fonctionnaires et la politique* (Le Seuil, Paris, 1976), Chapter 6.

7. Birnbaum, *Les Sommets de l'Etat*, Chapter 6; P. Bourdieu, L. Boltanski and M. de Saint-Martin, 'Les Stratégies de reconversion', *Informations sur les sciences sociales* (October 1973).

8. N. Poulantzas, *L'Etat, le pouvoir, le socialisme* (PUF, Paris, 1978), pp. 241 and 265.

9. J. Charlot, *Le Phénomène gaulliste* (Fayard, Paris, 1970), Chapter 3.

10. See P. Birnbaum, C. Barucq, M. Bellaiche and A. Marié, *La Classe dirigeante française* (PUF, Paris, 1978).

11. Elizabeth Dupoirier shows how, after 1968, Gaullism lost some of its grip on the working-class electorate in Paris and concentrated more on the affluent and traditionally conservative areas. This development meant that in the subsequent elections the Gaullist right had an electorate scarcely different from that of the moderate,

Giscardian right. In the municipal elections in 1977 the two electorates had become practically identical. 'Une ou deux droites à Paris? Les élections municipales de 1977 et la restructuration du bloc conservateur', *Revue française de science politique* (December 1977).

12. F. Borella, *Les Partis politiques dans la France d'aujourd'hui* (Le Seuil, Paris, 1974), Chapter 2. See also C. Ysmal, D. Boy, G. Grunberg and B. Moin-Roy, 'La Redistribution des électeurs de droite en Mai 1974', *Revue française de science politique* (April 1975).

13. *L'Express*, 13 March 1978.

14. Elizabeth Dupoirier shows, for example, how in Paris in the 1974 presidential elections, the electorate of Jacques Chaban Delmas 'was like a miniature of the Gaullist electorate under the presidency of General de Gaulle', whose multi-class character we have pointed out. 'Une ou deux droites à Paris?', p. 881, note 5.

15. J. Siwek-Pouydesseau, *Le Personnel de direction des Ministères* (Armand Colin, Paris, 1969); A. Darbel and D. Schnapper, *Le Système administratif* (Mouton, Paris, 1972); B. Badie and P. Birnbaum, 'L'Autonomie des institutions politico-administratives: le rôle des cabinets des Presidents de la République et des Premiers Ministres sous la Vᵉ République', *Revue française de science politique* (April 1976).

16. On the significance of state intervention in the social realm and its importance for the management of social relationships disturbed by rapid economic change, see J. Fournier and N. Questiaux, 2nd edn, *Traité du Social. Situations, luttes, politiques, institutions* (Dalloz, Paris, 1978).

17. See B. Pouget, *La Délégation à l'aménagement du territoire et à l'action régionale* (Cujas, Paris, 1968) and L. Sfez, *L'Administration prospective* (A. Colin, Paris, 1970).

18. M. Sellier, *Les Groupes d'action municipale*, Thesis, Université de Paris I, 1975.

19. J.-C. Thoenig, 'Le P.P.B.S. et l'administration publique: au-délà du changement technique', *Annuaire international de la fonction publique*, 1970/1.

20. *L'Administration des grandes villes*, Cahiers de l'IFSA, no. 14 (1977); 'Les Formes nouvelles d'Administration: le cas de la région provençale', *Revue française d'administration publique* (July–September 1977); J. Chevallier and D. Loschak, *Science administrative* (LGDJ, Paris, 1978), vol. 2.

21. C. Roig, 'L'Administration locale et les changements sociaux' in *Adminis-tration traditionalle et planification sociale* (Cujas, Paris, 1964); J.-P. Worms, 'Le Préfet et ses notables', *Sociologie de travail*, no. 3 (1966).

22. P. Grémion, *Le Pouvoir peripherique* (Le Seuil, Paris, 1976).

23. M. Kesselman, *The Ambiguous Consensus* (A. Knopf, New York, 1967).

24. P. Grémion, *Le Pouvoir peripherique*, pp. 305 and 462. Along similar lines, S. Tarrow, *Between Center and Periphery* (Yale University Press, London, 1977). The process of merging communes, which was another reform initiated by the central state to improve its control, also failed because of resistance from peripheral interests.

25. R. Dulong, *Les Régions, L'Etat et la société locale* (PUF, Paris, 1978).

26. J.-C. Thoenig, 'La Rélation entre le centre et la périphérie en France', *Bulletin de l'IIAP* (November–December 1975).

27. B. Jobert and M. Sellier, 'Les Grandes Villes: autonomie locale et innovation politique', *Revue française de science politique* (April 1977).

28. C. Soucy, *Contribution à une sociologie des centres urbains, Reconstruction et développement; les centres de Caen et du Havre* (unpublished, Paris, 1970); S. Biarez et al., *Institution communale et pouvoir politique, le cas de Roanne* (Mouton, Paris, 1973); M. Castells and F. Godard, *Monopolville* (Mouton, Paris, 1974). See also J. Lojkine, *Le Marxisme, l'Etat et la question urbaine* (PUF, Paris, 1977).

29. Since the last municipal elections in 1977 the left has held a majority of all the towns and cities: it controls 70 per cent of towns with more than 30,000 inhabitants

and 57 per cent of others. E. Dupoirier and G. Grunberg, 'Qui gouverne la France urbaine? Les elections municipales de Mars 1977 dans les communes de plus de 9,000 habitants', *Revue française de science politique* (February 1978).

30. One could also mention the opposition internal to the administration which arise from the trade union activities of some of its own members who are opposed to its policies (Syndicat de la Magistrature, police, teachers, etc.).

31. See M. Volle, *Le Métier de statisticien* (unpublished, Paris, 1978).

32. State financing for firms has obviously increased enormously. In 1974 it represented 6 per cent of gross domestic production, 28 per cent of total investment, 43 per cent of gross industrial investment and 63 per cent of gross investment by corporations, or 2.2 times the State's tax on corporations. See 'Les Transferts Etats-industrie en France et dans les pays occidentaux', in *Notes et Etudes documentaires* (Documentation Française, Paris, 1976). Conversely, the rôle of the public sector has steadily declined.

33. On this problem see P. Bachrach and M. Baratz, *Power and Poverty* (Oxford University Press, New York, 1970).

34. See, for example, S. Cohen, 2nd edn, *Modern Capitalist Planning. The French model* (University of California Press, Berkeley, 1977); J. McArthur and B. Scott, *L'Industrie française face aux plans* (Editions d'organisation, Paris, 1970); R. Catherine and P. Gousset, *L'Etat et l'essor industriel, l'Administration nouvelle* (Editions d'Epargne, Paris, 1962); L. Nizard (ed.), *Planification et société* (Presses universitaires de Grenoble, Grenoble, 1974), especially the articles by L. Nizard, G. Delange, A. Gauron and J. Hayward; C. Gruson, *Origine et espoir de la planification française* (Dunod, Paris, 1978); L. Sardais, *L'Etat et l'internationalisation du capital: un essai sur la politique industrielle de la France*, Thesis, Université de Paris X, 1978.

35. See L. Fontvielle's classic study, *Evolution et croissance de l'Etat français, 1815–1969* (Cahiers de l'ISMEA, Paris, 1976).

36. See J.-P. Scott, 'La Restauration de l'Etat: juin 1944–novembre 1945', *Cahiers d'Histoire de l'IMT* (1er trimestre 1977).

37. See P. Birnbaum, *Les Sommets de l'Etat*, Chapter 6.

38. See P. Birnbaum, C. Barucq, M. Bellaiche and A. Marié, *La Classe dirigeante française*; P. Bourdieu and M. de Saint-Martin, 'Le Patronat', *Actes de la recherche en sciences sociales* (March–April 1978).

39. A. Le Pors, *Les Béquilles du capital* (Le Seuil, Paris, 1977).

40. G. Martinet, *Le Système Pompidou* (Le Seuil, Paris, 1973), p. 44.

41. As Stanley Hoffman puts it 'since it was dealing with swimmers noted for their lack of enthusiasm, the state heated the water to remove any fears the swimmers may have had of catching cold, and produced all sorts of arguments to convince them that swimming was not simply harmless but profitable as well'. *Sur la France* (Editions du Seuil, Paris, 1976), p. 104.

42. *Traité marxiste d'économie politique* (Editions Sociales, Paris, 1971), vol. I, p. 84.

43. Theses of the XVth Congress of the PCF, para 3, June 1959.

44. A. Demichel, F. Demichel and M. Piquemal, *Institutions et pouvoirs en France* (Editions Sociales, Paris, 1975).

45. L. Fabre, F. Hincker and L. Seve, *Les Communistes et l'Etat* (Editions Sociales, Paris, 1977), p. 13.

46. A. Darbel and D. Schnapper, *Morphologie de la haute administration française* (Mouton, Paris, 1969–72) 2 vols; J.-C. Thoenig, *L'Ère des technocrates* (Editions d'organisation, Paris, 1973).

47. E. Friedberg, 'Administration et entreprises', in M. Crozier, E. Friedberg, P. Grémion, J.-C. Thoenig and J.-P. Worms (eds.), *Où va l'administration française?* (Editions d'organisation, Paris, 1974).

48. P. Grémion, 'La Concertation', in *Où va l'administration française?*

49. J. Chevallier, 'L'intérêt général dans l'administration française', *Revue internationale des sciences administratives* (1975); J. Sallois and M. Cretin, 'Le rôle social des hauts fonctionnaires et la crise de l'Etat', in N. Poulantzas (ed.), *La Crise de l'Etat* (PUF, Paris, 1976).

50. Report of the CDI, p. 59.

51. See M. Delapierre and C. A. Michalet, *Les Implantations étrangères en France* (Calmann-Levy, Paris, 1976).

3 Developments in the Political System of West Germany Since 1945

JOACHIM HIRSCH

West German Marxists are observing with concern the political development of the Federal Republic of Germany. In the light of mounting economic interventions in various parts of the world (for example, in Portugal and in Africa), the significance of the catch-word, the 'German model', becomes increasingly evident; that is, the close connection between the imperialist rôle of West Germany and authoritarian political developments within the FRG itself. Indeed, changes within the political relations that have taken place since the mid-sixties are disturbing. However, the reference here is not only to the well-known practice of professional and occupational proscription (*Berufsverbote*) and the accelerated abolition of constitutional guarantees on the pretext of fighting terrorism. On the contrary, considerable transformations which indicate fundamental changes in state and political structures, and which result in changed forms in the political handling of crises, are to be noted.

On the face of it, the traditional institutions of the bourgeois democratic system appear to be largely unaffected. Moreover, a relevant rightist or fascist mass movement does not currently exist in the Federal Republic. Because of the novelty of this development, for which there are no unequivocal prototypes or parallels, discussions of the character and the development of the West German system of political domination are marked by conspicuous theoretical and political uncertainties. It remains hotly disputed whether the development of political repression involves an 'undemocratic' deviation – rooted in the historical tradition of Germany – from the 'normal' form of a bourgeois, liberal–democratic state, or a 'new form of fascism', or the expression of a tendency towards an 'authoritarian state', or a 'state of emergency' ('*Ausnahmestaat*'). The problem would appear to result from the fact that the political and theoretical categories are lacking that would enable there to be an adequate understanding of the more recent political and economic developments of advanced capitalist states. This chapter makes use of a very provisional theory of the state which, however, cannot be explicated here.[1]

The Economic Development of the FGR

Until the middle of the 1960s, the socio-economic development of the FRG was characterised by an extremely rapid pace of capital accumulation (average growth rates 1950–60: 8 per cent; 1960–5: 5.1 per cent; 1965–70: 4.7 per cent; 1970–5: 1.7 per cent).[2] This initial, relatively stable and strong growth process was, nevertheless, bound up with several specific historical conditions. At the beginning of the 1950s, this included not only the presence of a relatively technologically advanced production apparatus that had generally escaped the destruction of the war, but also the extraordinary weakness of the working-class and its organisations after their devastation by fascism. This weakness was increased even more by the particular political and economic conditions of the post-war period (refugee immigration and unemployment; the intervention by the allied occupation powers for the benefit of capital, and so on). The demoralised working-class could be somewhat pacified, over the years, by a comparatively modest improvement in the originally catastrophic material living conditions, and integrated into the re-established bourgeois system. This was the essential basis for the relative political and economic stability against crises exhibited by the Federal Republic during the so-called 'Period of Reconstruction'.[3]

The Federal Republic's relatively low level of wages ensured high rates of profit and assured West German capital of important competitive advantages on the world market (the net wage rate declined from 66.7 per cent to 59.8 per cent between 1950 and 1960). At the same time, the political and economic weakness of the working-class was an essential prerequisite for fundamental transformations in the economic structure and in social relationships during this period. Characteristic of this were radical changes in the structure of industrial sectors (the predominance of export-oriented 'heavy' manufacturing industries), the general capitalisation of agriculture, and reforms in regional administrative structures (amalgamations). The percentage of industrial production accounted for by manufacturing industries rose from 53 per cent in 1950 to 68 per cent in 1970, while the share of consumer goods industries fell from 33 per cent to 28 per cent as a result of the relatively stagnatory buying-power of the masses. In the same period, the percentage contributed by the 'new', technologically advanced industries in the value of industrial production (chemicals, electrical engineering, petroleum processing, synthetics, and automobile construction) increased from 17 per cent to 38 per cent. The percentage of foreign industrial turnover rose from 8 per cent to 20 per cent from 1950 to 1972, while in several important branches it amounted to over 50 per cent.[4] From these figures it can be concluded that several fundamental fractional displacements of capital occurred that were brought about by the growing dominance of technologically advanced and export-oriented capital. At the same time, this process of economic transformation resulted in a significant reduction in the agricultural sector. The percentage of those employed in this branch declined from 23 per cent to 7 per cent from 1950 to 1975.[5] Simultaneously, a strong monopolising process occurred which was related to a significant expansion of the 'tertiary' sector. As a result of this, the proportion of the working population who were self-employed decreased; falling from 13 per cent to 9 per cent between 1961 and 1975. At the same time, 86 per cent of all those employed were wage-earners, whether as state employees, office workers or labourers. The percentage of wage earners employed as office workers and state employees increased considerably; from 36 per cent in 1961 to over 50 per cent in 1975.[6]

On the whole, therefore, a displacement in class structure can be noted, characterised by intensive monopolisation, sweeping shifts between economic branches to the benefit of the technologically advanced and export-oriented industries, the decimation of the 'old' petite bourgeoisie and the increasing numerical significance of 'white collar' wage earners. Furthermore, the rapid development of industrial production was accompanied by growing ecological destruction, while the 'social infrastructure' exhibited serious deficiencies; for example, poor educational facilities, public health services, etc.[7] This meant, in general, a relative lowering in the standard of reproduction of the working-class and this had a stabilising effect on the rate of profit and created, thereby, favourable conditions for the process of capital accumulation. However, the comparatively grave deterioration of the material living conditions in the 'reproduction sector', still did not lead to political conflicts – primarily because of the power relations sketched above.

Accelerated capital accumulation in the fifties gradually led to the reintegration of the extremely large industrial reserve army that characterised the immediate post-war period. From 1950 to 1960 the official unemployment rate decreased to 1.3 per cent after being more than 10 per cent.[8] With this development, the conditions for the valorisation of capital also began to change fundamentally. A further expansion of production was possible only by means of a substantial intensification of the means of production in proportion to living labour-power. Simultaneously, wages rose as a result of the more favourable market position of the worker. The large-scale recruitment of foreign workers – their numbers increased from 329,000 in 1960 to 2.4 million in 1972[9] – was able to slow this development but not to stop it.

Intense involvement in the world market by West German industry – a consequence of the specific power relations and conditions of accumulation that existed during the 'Period of Reconstruction' – meant that the economic reproduction process had, at the same time, become extremely dependent upon the competitive position of West German capital on the world market. This position had been dependent upon a comparatively low level of wages and, during the 1950s, rather sluggish technological change. It then began to deteriorate rapidly because of an increase in the organic composition of capital and a high level of wage increases. This problematic situation, indicating an urgent need during the 1960s to restructure the labour process, was ideologically reflected in a catchword – the 'technological gap' – between West German industry and competing capitalist countries. The result of this constellation was a fall in the rate of profit, and it finally culminated in the crisis of 1966/7.[10]

It was, however, rather easy to overcome this crisis from an economic point of view. Decisive in this was the wage restraint practised by unions and the consistent application of the Keynesian maxim of state control. In addition, an international heterogeneous trade cycle granted West German capital the option of seeking foreign markets as soon as wage-cost conditions improved. However, with this, the accentuation of exports in the West German economic system increased.[11] Yet the crisis of 1966/7 marks a decisive turning point in the economic and political development of West Germany. It impressed upon capital the necessity for a rapid transformation of the techniques of production and the development of new forms for disciplining the working-class. This was reinforced after 1966 when the unions succeeded in taking advantage of the beginnings of an economic boom, and spurred by spontaneous strikes in various industries, obtained large wage increases. Capital reacted to this development by accelerating the process of structural rationalisation and by an intensification of foreign investments. The unemployment rate, that reached a low point at the end of the sixties, climbed from 0.7 per cent in 1970 to 4.8 per cent in 1975, to persist at a high level until the present.[12] At first, however, wage earners still succeeded in protecting the (relatively) high level of wages that had been attained.[13] Simultaneously, it can be assumed that the process of accelerated rationalisation and automation, while not further increasing the organic composition of capital, in any case, did not reduce it. The consequence was continuing pressure on the rate of profit, the effect of which was reinforced by other influences in the world market (international decline of trade and the oil crisis). This process culminated in the second economic crisis of 1974/5, and introduced an economic phase of relative stagnation, which could not be offset by a slight reduction in real wages to which workers had to submit once again when their market position subsequently weakened.

The current economic situation appears to be characterised by the fact that difficulties of capital-valorisation, resulting from the attained value structure (organic composition) and the subsequently changed market structures (advanced monopolisation and international capital involvement) can hardly be solved by the traditional means of Keynesian trade cycle control and a 'restrained' wage policy by the unions. The leeway for concessions by the unions for a valorisation-stabilising wage policy was significantly narrowed by crisis and declining economic growth. This was shown, at least in part, by the massive resistance of the union rank-and-file to the low wage settlements after the beginning of the crisis. The unions are thereby under strong pressure at least to defend the material standard of reproduction of wage earners that they had attained. Present relations of class power are generally characterised by the comparatively strong defensive position of the working-class which, despite several losses, could resist a massive reduction of its reproduction standard, both of wage income as well as of state services. This indicates a certain degree of lability of class relations of power; capital continues to be compelled to improve valorisation conditions extensively. In the light of existing power positions, this cannot follow from a frontal attack on the 'wage' front but only from forced economic and technological restructuring. However, such changes must be politically and ideologically secured because of their explosive social consequences.

But the crisis of 1966/7 also marks the point at which political resistance began to increase against the deterioration and exacerbation of living conditions and against established political power relations; spontaneous strikes, the student movement, struggles in the cities, and various 'grass-roots' interest groups (*Bürgerinitiativen*) began to influence the political process. It is also against this background that the changes within the political system, taking place since 1966, must be seen.

Summarising, one should note the following: the unique economic development of West Germany during the post-war period and the specific form of 'crisis solution' since 1966/7 have resulted in the consequence that today the guarantee of capital-valorisation is very closely related to the protection and expansion of the hegemonious imperialist position of the FRG. This means that pronounced involvement in the world market of the West German economy which was, on the one hand, the basis of relative economic stability and prosperity, creates, on the other, intensified pressure for economic and social adaptation to changed conditions of competition on the world market level. However, this adaptation has its prerequisite in the possibility of continuing to carry out the socio-economic restructuring processes with a minimum of friction, despite their increasingly incisive effects on the conditions of living and working for the population. The consequences which present themselves for the political and economic 'stability' of the FRG, can be sketched as follows. First, the protection of West Germany's competitive position on the world market and the capital profit that is dependent upon this position – when seen from the 'wage-perspective' – requires that conflicts over distribution between entrepreneurs and unions are not inflationarily exaggerated. Rather, for capital, this means that a falling rate of profit engenders the ever more urgent assault on the position of workers' real wages which, until now, has been carried out through strategies of organisational discipline. This means it must be able to repress unconceded forms of advocating economic interests as well as incalculable disturbances in the production process (due, for example, to spontaneous strikes).

Secondly, the intensified implementation of an imperialist 'division of labour' (the displacement of labour-intensive and technologically simple production processes to foreign countries), as well as the continual introduction of rationalisation processes means the spread of structural unemployment, increasing the degree of exploitation, increasing the processes of massive dequalification and degradation, and an increase in the tendency to marginalise entire social groups (youth, women, old and unskilled workers). With this, grows the potential of social conflict and more and more societal realms and social groups become problem areas that must be (repressively) regulated.

Thirdly, such a 'structural transformation' (*Strukturwandel*) in production means that the tendency for the destruction of the natural basis of reproduction will increase, through the building and expansion of industries that threaten life itself, as well as processes of 'internal colonialisation', and the exacerbation of natural and social conditions for living (the destruction of the environment and the cities). Therefore, there is no reason to expect that the vehemence of conflicts in this sphere (for example, in the question of atomic power) will abate in the future.

The Organisation and Function of the State

The state institutional system of the FRG is characterised by the fact that – in contrast to other large West European countries – *no economic administrative planning apparatus* was erected after the Second World War. This does not mean, however, that there have not been far-reaching planning and long-term interventions by the state.[14] The formation of a state planning bureaucracy proved to be superfluous because of the extraordinary degree of concentration and involvement of capital, making organised interventions by the state in the structure of capital unnecessary.[15] In comparison with Great Britain and France, for example, the high degree of monopolisation of industrial and finance capital and the close involvement of industrial monopolies with large banks allowed the latter, to some extent, to take up encroaching positions as clearing houses for capital assuring, furthermore, a 'tight' structure of alliance. From this it follows that West German capital itself, to a large degree, has an organisational structure at its disposal which enables it to co-ordinate and implement processes of adaptation brought about by changed competitive conditions on the world market. The state, then, is assigned the task of supporting these processes, legislatively and financially, and with providing legitimation; in other words, of providing 'general production conditions'.[16] The more important state enterprises that arose as the product of the fascist war economy were, for the most part, returned to private owners. The 'planning activity' of the state could thereby be accomplished by the ministerial bureaucracy that had been taken over, making a separate administrative basis unnecessary. The 'economic' state apparatus, in essence, the Ministries of Finance and Economics, and the Ministry of Research and Technology that was added in the mid-sixties can be fairly efficiently co-ordinated by the Office of the Federal Chancellor because of its extensive authority. (This, of course, does not preclude the influences of capital fractions nor departmental conflicts.) Nevertheless, as a consequence of the crisis-like and changed conditions of capital valorisation since the mid-sixties which reinforced the necessity for intervention by the state in the social reproduction process, there have been several essential modifications in the structure of the state apparatus. Consequently, there has been an increase in the extent of administrative centralisation and the growing detachment of structural, political planning and decision-making from representative parliamentary bodies. At the same time, corporate elements have become drawn into state structures and there has been a considerable expansion of the repressive apparatuses for the regulation of zones and social conflict.

Such changes in the administrative structure of the state correspond to the predominance of technologically advanced sectors of monopoly capital (electro-technical industry, chemical and machine-making industries), which were conclusively consolidated as a result of the changed conditions of valorisation of capital with regard to the world market in the second half of the 1960s. Such a change in the function of the state found its economic and political expression in the increasing significance of the concept of 'active structural politics' (*aktive Strukturpolitik*) which generally dislodged the Keynesian programme of global control. (The latter did not become the official guideline for state economic policy until the crisis of 1966/7 with the entrance of the Social Democrats as the ruling government party. However, this programme already suffered its first defeat with the development of 'stagflation' in the beginning of the 1970s having, therefore, a comparatively short life-span in the Federal Republic.) Examples of this new economic and political orientation include an 'active labour-market policy' – although this was very strongly and repressively modified as a consequence of the crisis – the implementation of new labour-power qualifications and the enhancement of the 'mobility' of labour-power; attempts to adapt regional structures to changed conditions of production (determined by the world market); selective subsidising of investments; but, above all, through intensive organisation and subsidising by the state of industrial research and development and, thereby, the technological transformation of industrial structures and of labour processes.

At first, the crisis of 1966/7 led to the introduction and expansion of the Keynesian model of state control (the law of economic stability) whose actual effectiveness, however, remained limited. Yet, more crucial was the expansion of 'structural political' units, started at this time on a centralised level (Ministries of Science, Education, Technology, Federal and State Commission for Educational Planning, etc.)[17], the extension and broadening of the jurisdiction of centralised state apparatuses for control and surveillance (Federal Criminal Office, Office for the Protection of the Constitution, Federal Border Control Police – organised as a militarily equipped Federal police),[18] and the taut centralisation of an originally federal system. Involved with this was the extension of the central authoritative jurisdiction of the federal government (curtailment of the fiscal autonomy of the individual German states, and especially, the municipalities; the widening of federal legislative and administrative authority), and 'regional reform', whose purpose was to incorporate small, local political units (counties, municipalities) into larger units of broader regional planning and administration. From 1967 to 1978 the number of municipalities has decreased from 24,357 to 8,518. This has also meant the creation of 'intermediate' administrative organs (Financial Planning Councils, Trade Councils, regional planning associations) which are no longer effectively accountable to the diverse levels of parliament. The tendency that these changes indicate, is one of creating political planning and decision-making bodies that are insulated against 'disturbing' regional and local influences. In that way, it becomes possible to circumvent resistance articulated at the local level to political institutions responsible for the processes of restructuring.

This new form of state economic activity becomes particularly evident in the area of research and technology. Total state expenditures for research and development rose from 4.2 to 12.75 billion Deutsche Marks in the period from 1967 to 1974. Since 1972 these state expenditures have surpassed those of the private economic sector.[19] Essential elements for the development of technology are located, in the meantime, in a tightly-woven state-industry complex in which the institutional interrelationship between state administration and the leading technological industrial monopolies has expanded to a remarkable degree. From this, of course, one could hardly infer the presence of an 'autonomous' economic–technological control capacity of the state. Rather, what is actually manifested here, is the technologically dominating monopolies claiming the financial and organisational capacities of the state for the strategies of development and investment that are determined by world market competition. To be sure, this has the consequence that the state must increasingly appear as the supporter and executor of industrial investment strategies. This direct involvement of the state apparatus in the processes of economic and social restructuring, determined by the valorisation of capital, modifies its relationship not only to the dominated classes but also to the various fractions of capital. Its 'relatively autonomous' position in relation to the classes of bourgeois society becomes more problematic. This posits changed conditions for the integration of the masses, and for the making of compromises among the various sectors of capital. In addition, it creates new forms of political conflict and crisis. The case of the state nuclear energy policy especially underscores this point because the economic interests of the atomic power industry have been directly enforced by the repressive state apparatus against the massive resistance to it by large sectors of the population.

It becomes clear that, within the context of the state or the state-supported implementation of socio-economic restructuring processes which are conforming to conditions of capital-valorisation, the state apparatus cannot seriously obstruct the economic processes determined by the competitive conditions of capital on the world market; to do so would call into question the accumulation process of capital and thereby, the very basis of bourgeois society (and, hence, of itself). Rather, it is forced to support, promote, and increasingly, to execute such processes. Simultaneously, with the declining pace of accumulation, the material leeway for state intervention to alleviate and to compensate for the social effects of such economic restructuring becomes increasingly limited. In this manner, a kind of structural dilemma develops: on the one hand, social marginalisation (permanent unemployment, etc.), the deterioration of the cities and countryside, uneven regional development; and, on the other, an ever more constricted margin of possibilities for the state to provide material compensation. With decreasing growth rates, the growing demands for state subsidies of private capital, and 'structural politics' (consonant with the conditions of valorisation of capital), as well as the flood of social problems resulting from capital accumulation and restructuring create a fiscal crisis of the state which has become a permanent manifestation.[20] It appears as the specific expression of the political crisis once a particular phase of capitalist societalisation (*Vergesellschaftung*) has been reached.[21] Objectively, this general process involves the perspective of an ever-growing potential for diverse social and political conflicts.

The Crisis of Integration of the Masses

It is important to note that in the Federal Republic – and this distinguishes it from otherwise comparable countries – organisations of mass integration hardly exist that can assimilate the conflicts, interests, and movements mobilised by these developments, mediating them into the apparatus of the political system where they could, at least for a time, be absorbed. The dominant political parties have developed into aloof bureaucratic apparatuses ('People's Parties' – *Volkspartei*), which limit themselves to tactical mobilisation for elections, without being anchored in actual societal milieus and fields of conflict.[22] The unions, on the other hand, oriented to permanent economic growth and the conception of wage politics as 'social partners' are helpless to face the problems of an imperialist 'structural transformation' that include permanent unemployment, massive dequalification and marginalisation. This leads the established mass parties to appear ever more clearly as appendages and transmission belts of state administration. This development finds its expression in the growing dependence of parties on state finance, the dominance of the 'party in government' over the ordinary 'party membership', and the decreasing activity of party members at the lower level. This applies particularly to the SDP, which has considerably changed its structure since the 1950s, not only in terms of party programmes, but rather more specifically in terms of the composition of its membership and organisational structure. Although largely forfeiting its image as the 'party of the working-class', it has at the same time, remained the primary 'voting address' of the workers. The socio-economic reasons for this development are rather complex. Particularly decisive for this, of course, was the defeat of the labour movement by fascism and the prevention of its revitalisation by the political and economic conditions of the 'Restoration Period' after 1945. This created points of intrusion for bourgeois ideology (anti-communism, 'the economic miracle', and ideologies of equal opportunity), as well as preparing the ground for the phenomenon of the 'People's Party – without ideology'. Contributing to this, however, was the dissolution of class-determined social milieus (the destruction of community and communication contexts, the differentiation and mixing of social circumstances, and forced residential mobility), set in motion by the reorganising process of capital which, at first, met little organised resistance. There was also an increase in the size of the 'middle class' and the 'negative societalisation' (*negative Vergesellschaftung*) process, characterised by the exclusion of large social groups from the context of economic reproduction, and by social marginalisation.[23] With these developments, stable social contexts, milieus for living, and the political and organisational structures that have their bases within them are thereby undermined, abruptly transforming the socially disintegrated subjects into objects of administrative 'welfare' and control. On the other hand, the wave of initiatives by special-interest and 'grass-roots' groups (*Bürger-initiativen*) that came into being towards the end of the 1960s as a consequence of the deterioration of living conditions in the 'sphere of reproduction', but which were especially directed against desolation in the educational system and the destruction of cities and living space did not, at first, seriously impair the functioning of the established organisations of mass integration. It was neither possible for the parties to integrate and neutralise these movements, nor was it possible for them to politicise, in the sense of generalisable goals, so that they could elevate themselves beyond their limited issue-orientation and organisational weaknesses. The most important movement politically, namely, the student movement, did not fail solely because of its internal contradictions but also because of the massive use of state force against it; just as the wave of spontaneous strikes, originating after 1969, was broken by the effects of the economic crisis.

Such a disengagement of apparatuses of mass integration from social contexts and concrete spheres of interest, and the comparative weakness of extra-institutional grass-roots movements was and is an essential prerequisite so that the socio-economic 'structural transformation' could and still can be implemented to the advantage of imperialist West German capital without significant resistance. At the same time this means that a frontal attack on the organisations of the working-class or massive political repression by capital remains, at least for the time being, superfluous. The state's intervening manipulation of the crisis (for example, by displacing crisis manifestations into the so-called 'infrastructural sphere' and the selective reduction of social–political services) is only one means by which the political unification of detached and mutually isolated social realms of conflict is made more difficult; conflicts and interests can still be fragmented by the traditional means of integration, canalisation, and the occasional use of repression. The fact that the cautious reform strategy of the Social Democratic and the Liberal government after 1969, nevertheless, gave impetus to social movements which threatened to destroy the framework of system conformity of these 'reform programmes', clearly indicates the increasing and dangerous (for those who rule) possibility that 'dammed-up' conflict potential can become manifest in forms and practices that can no longer be institutionally assimilated.

One can assume that it is particularly characteristic of Germany that bureaucratised, quasi-federal political party apparatuses have developed that are unspecified with regard to class, and that this is closely related to the transformation of functions of the state. In effect, this means that the increasing involvement of the state in the social spheres of production and reproduction is related to this development and is, thereby, the expression of a more general tendency. In any case, it is this form of mass integration system that facilitates, for example, the separation of parliamentary decision-making processes from the politics of state administration (this is especially evident in the entire sphere of Research and Development policy); the technocratisation of politics (for instance, the ostensibly 'class-neutral' concepts of 'modernisation', 'growth', 'stability'); and the tactical handling of systematically fragmented interests which are, at this level, susceptible of being played off mutually against each other. However, it cannot be overlooked that it is precisely this system of mass integration that is confronted with crucial risks of crisis, that will be aggravated even more to the extent that it loses its original economic basis – namely, continuous economic growth. Combined with this is the successfully established 'end of ideology' of the fifties and particularly, the increasingly 'instrumental' attitude of the population towards the apparatuses of political parties and of unions. The Social Democratic Party, as the ruling party was, and is, especially faced with the dilemma of stimulating concrete material 'reform expectations' and, at the same time, constantly having to disappoint them. It becomes more and more difficult to absorb this contradiction by the mobilisation of traditional bonds and loyalties.

At the same time, a further development causes the established system of mass integration partially to lose its function: the anarchy of the capitalist societalisation process must be compensated for to an ever-increasing extent by the direct administrative incorporation of those social spheres threatened with crisis (for example, the educational sector as a reservoir for the potentially unemployed, the broadened functions of 'social administration', etc.), while the material preconditions are not even approximately present for the resolution of its pressing problems. The capitalist process of development has the effect that relevant social groups are omitted from the immediate context of economic reproduction (the permanently unemployed, young and old people, the physically and psychologically ill, and the deterioration of familial and neighbourhood relations). This means the progressive dissipation of the relationship between the spheres of production and reproduction, to such an extent that it is no longer mediated by wage-labour and commodity exchange, but rather must be established through state regulation. In this new and quite contradictory way, the state becomes a moment that must guarantee makeshift solutions in the unplanned and fortuitous context of reproduction in a society whose cohesion increasingly disintegrates. It follows from this that the realm of state administration must be increasingly and further extended into social spheres, thereby, becoming a more immediate field of social conflict. The mediating and canalising effect of 'integrating' special-interest organisations is rescinded, so that the confrontation becomes ever more direct with a state bureaucracy that can control its problem areas only by increasing regulation. It certainly does not follow from these developments that a political consciousness is evolving that has a mass basis and is capable of organisation. Rather, the prevailing outcomes are diffuse protest postures, apathy, and 'being fed up with the state' (*Staatsverdrossenheit*). In other words, despite probable economic developments that objectively widen the fields of social conflict, this does not mean that a revolutionary situation is imminent. The growing inability of bureaucratic political party and union apparatuses to absorb crucial social conflicts, and the increasing brittleness of formerly functioning legitimation ideologies ('prosperity for all') lead to the basic structural *lability* of the entire system of domination, the consequences of which are not predictable. Paradoxically, it is precisely the disjuncture of mechanisms of mass integration from the fundamental structures of class and interest-representation which accounts for the depolitisation of political party conflicts, despite the occasionally staged ideological fireworks. With this, the possibility is enhanced that politisation takes place *outside* the political apparatuses of bourgeois society.

Currently, the *mode of integration of the masses* prevailing in the FRG centres on the participation of the SDP in the government, thereby permitting the assimilation of the union bureaucracy in state decision-making processes. The inducement for the creation of this mode of integration was the crisis of 1966/7, when the existing 'bourgeois' ruling coalition disintegrated and was replaced by the 'Great Coalition' of CDU/CSU and the SDP, and then by the 'Social–Liberal Coalition' of the SDP and FDP after the 1969 elections. This change in the mode of mass integration did not, however, have its immediate causes solely in the crisis; rather, it also had more fundamental structural origins. These were the fundamentally changed conditions of capital valorisation after the end of the 'Period of Reconstruction', the related pressure for accelerated reorganisation of socio-economic relationships and changes in the class structure brought about by the processes of post-war capital accumulation. The significance of the SDP in the government must be considered from two angles. On the one hand, it was a precondition for the 'responsible' inclusion of unions in the central contexts of economic and political decision-making. This was in keeping with the general economic rationality of capital since it induced them to accept policies of wage restraint and to tolerate technological changes that have grave consequences for the working-class. It was this constellation that was *the* crucial basis for the 'solution' of the crisis of 1966/7, and also a central moment in the crisis politics after 1974. Institutionally it meant the creation of 'corporatist' structures with a tripartite character ('concerted action'). This is certainly one of the most essential characteristics of structural changes in the state apparatuses in the FRG since 1945.[24] On the other hand, it was the SDP that was more likely than the Christian Democratic Union/Christian Socialist Union (which were directly involved with small and middle-sized fractions of capital), to be in a position to implement the impending measures of socio-economic restructuring for the advantage of technologically-advanced and internationally operating monopoly capital. Indeed, it was essentially those state strategies for 'modernisation' ushered in by the Social Democratic and Liberal coalition (1969) that affected, above all, technological policies, the educational system, and city and regional development. It is also within this context that one must take into account the important revision of the Federal Republic's policy towards East Germany and the Eastern Bloc countries, based upon considerations of foreign trade and strategies of investment.

As to class relations, the Social Democratic and Liberal government represented a kind of unstable compromise between the dominant political groups of monopoly capital, union-organised skilled workers and, above all, the quantitatively and politically ever more important 'new middle classes', consisting of clerks and state civil servants. It was they who could be hopeful of material improvements resulting from a state strategy for modernisation; particularly through the expansion of the state sector. Excluded were the unqualified mass labourers, especially foreign workers whose spontaneous strike actions in 1973 were characteristically and violently repressed with the help of the unions.

The fundamental basis of this 'compromise' was, therefore, changed

class structures that had been considerably altered after the 'Reconstruction Period', especially in the sphere of wage-labourers (the
appearance of the 'new middle classes', the tendency for a division
between domestic 'skilled' and foreign 'mass workers'), and the
displacement of power among fractions of capital to the advantage of
those fractions that were technologically advanced and export-
oriented. These transformed class constellations found expression
after 1966 in important conflicts and schisms within the party system.
There was a sweeping re-orientation by the FDP; this was formerly
anchored within the 'old petite bourgeoisie' and the farmers, but after
1969 it generally changed its electoral basis, finding its main point of
reference in the 'new petite bourgeoisie' of state employees and office
workers. In addition there were serious battles within the CDU, and
between the CDU and CSU that bordered, at times, on destructive
tests of strength. The contents of the reform policies introduced after
1969 clearly reflected this 'class compromise' although within the
context of measures acceptable to capital.[25] This programme of
reform had continuous economic growth as its prerequisite, and it was
on this that the state's margin of movement depended in the realms of
capital subsidisation, economic restructuring, as well as in the partial
material concessions made to the dominated classes. Consequently,
the development of economic 'stagflation' and the crisis of 1974
brought the mode of mass integration, that had existed since 1966,
into an open crisis situation.

Digression: Some Remarks about the Relation between 'Political' and Economic Crises

What can be designated, at any given moment of time, as the *mode of
mass integration* refers to the concrete constellation of the institutional
system of domination in bourgeois society that constitutes
respectively, the 'repressive', the 'ideological', and the 'mass integrative' apparatuses, by which the integration of the exploited and
dominated classes is established and stabilised, as well as the related
fractional compromises within power structures.[26] Each concretely
existing mode of mass integration corresponds to a specific situation
of the class relations of power. Changes in these class relations of
power, of the related movements of classes, and the conditions of
economic reproduction of capital must have as a consequence,
changes in the modes of mass integration and, thereby, changes in the
interdependent constellation and function of the political apparatuses.

Because of the institutional rigidity of the political apparatus, the entanglement of interests of its personnel and of their existing class relations, it can be assumed that such a transformation in the mode of integration must tend to take the form of disruptive breaks and institutional crises. When changed economic conditions, class relations of power, and class movements force specific modifications in the institutional system of integration, we can speak of a *'political crisis'*. The 'adaptation' of the system of mass integration can follow by a simple 're-adjustment' of the existing apparatuses (for example, by the inclusion of the SDP/unions in the government apparatus in 1966), but also in the form of a radical break with existing political institutions (for instance, fascism). The manner in which political crises develop and are 'resolved' depends on the concrete conditions of economic reproduction and class relations of power; the establishment of a 'State of Emergency (*Ausnahmestaat*) is completely consistent with the historical normalcy of bourgeois society.

Hence, if we consider political crises as vehicles for the adaptation of the institutional system of integration to changed class conditions, then we can define the relation between 'political' and 'economic' crises more precisely: economic crises, that is, disturbances of capital reproduction become politically critical only if they lead to class movements and to modifications in the class relations of power. On the other hand, crises in the political apparatus are always an effect of changed class reproduction conditions, without having necessarily to appear in the form of cyclical disruptions of reproduction. It follows from this that the usual distinction between 'economic' and 'political' crises is absurd. Thus, crises in advanced capitalist states must be understood as crises of the social formation as a whole, that is, as the unity of political, ideological and economic crises. However, there can always occur displacements in time and form between these levels as a consequence of the 'relative autonomy' of the political system.

Reinforced by the economic crisis, the political process in the Federal Republic during the 1970s can be characterised, in essence, as an attempt to secure, by more repressive means, a mode of mass integration after the 'reformist' mode was brought into crisis by the loss of its economic supports. The government is forced to provide capital with a series of 'reorganisation' and 'modernisation' policies particularly in terms of curtailing infrastructural and social services, and the relaxation of existent ecological protection standards. These developments inevitably create new areas of conflict and moments of instability. One essential constituent of these policies is the reduction of state expenditure and the implementation of measures which are 'growth-oriented'; in other words, those that subsidise profits.[27] For example, the economic crisis of 1974/5 led to policies which violated every tenet of 'Keynesian' economics. On the one hand, there were 'tax reforms' (1974, 1979) which narrowed the state's financial base but which gave considerable advantages to business enterprises, while on the other, state subsidies to industry were expanded and social services curtailed.[28]

The reasons for this restrictive economic strategy are closely connected with the position of West German capital on the world market.[29] After 1969, the reform programme of the Social Democratic–Liberal government was largely based on the premise that, in periods of high economic growth, a surplus could be created which would provide material concessions to large sectors of the working and middle classes, by means of expanding the state's share of the social product without interfering with the profitability of capital.[30] The crisis that was beginning to manifest itself put an end to this strategy; the consequences of the 'politics of reform' – expansion of state credit, monetary policy oriented towards full employment – had begun seriously to impair the general position of West German capital which, in any case, was in some difficulties. The transition to a more restrictive deflationary policy became a major need for capital since it helped to contain wage demands and increased the general level of unemployment. The political logic of this state budgetary policy, which stands in direct opposition to the SDP's original reform programme, is to reduce the state's material surplus available for coping with politically-articulated demands; this entails a reduction in the operational field of the 'reformist' mass integration apparatuses (for example, the political parties and the unions). The scope available to the dominant 'Peoples'' parties is decisively narrowed, the logic of which had previously been to pursue a policy of tactically avoiding conflict by selectively distributing material concessions on the basis of relative continuous (and nominal) economic growth. The usefulness of the SDP as the ruling party for the dominant fractions of capital depends upon whether it can succeed in implementing such a policy since it necessarily undermines its own political basis. This was why the Social Democratic–Liberal Government could not easily switch to a tough 'austerity policy' but, rather, was forced to reduce expenditure upon 'excludable' social groups such as the unemployed, the young, women and those receiving pensions. Thus, until now, the standard of the material reproduction of the working-class *as a whole* has not been seriously affected; instead, several of the gains attained towards the end of the 1960s have been revoked with the costs falling upon 'marginal', economically and politically weak groups.

This change in policies led to shifts of power within the SDP and to considerable conflicts (fortifying the party bureaucracy against the membership base, the suppression of dissenting party wings, and forcing the Young Socialist organisation into conformity with the party). With this, the party robbed itself of an essential anchorage in the younger generation. The abrupt replacement of Chancellor Brandt by Herr Schmidt in 1974 was merely symptomatic of this development.[31] Parallel to this has been the intensification of conflicts between the union bureaucracy and its basis; an indication of the limited flexibility of union policies that are integrationist, loyal to the government, and where government and unions are defined as social partners in a situation of crisis and unemployment.[32] This forces the union leadership to distance itself, at least, symbolically, from the government. A distinct signal of this is the (provisional) withdrawal of the unions from the 'concerted action' programme, that indicates the possible failure of this 'neo-corporatist' institution.

All of this points to the fact that the class compromise on which the 'social democratic and reformist' mode of mass integration is founded, is threatened. This is confirmed by a larger proportion of SDP voters abstaining in elections, sections of the petite bourgeoisie turning to the CDU/CSU and hence throwing the FDP into an existential crisis, the calling into question of the ruling government coalition, and the increasing divisive tendencies and ruptures within the established parties. To some extent, the changing conditions of capital valorisation within the context of the world market, have made the type of mode of integration, founded upon 'economic growth' incompatible with capitalist strategies necessary to sustain the rate of profit. Capital has been compelled to withdraw from its initial policies of tolerating concessions and to attack the reproduction standard of the working-class at various levels; for example, the toughening of wage-settlement policies, increasing technical rationalisation, the introduction of extensive processes of degradation and the reorganisation of labour, and the curtailment of state mediated reproduction funds (broadly speaking, 'social policy'). On the other hand, the defensive position of the working-class, which is still evident, is related to the participation of the Social Democrats in the government. Despite many disappointments, this helps to explain the essential and persistent, even if more distanced, loyalty of large portions of wage-labourers to this party. When considered from the class relations of power, this suggests a situation of instability that forms the basis for a kind of permanent political crisis. Characteristic of this are the conflicts, schisms, and divisions within the mass integrative apparatuses, growing conflicts between the SDP and the unions, a visible 'lack of confidence' in the ruling party in general, and the emergence of ideological battles that are becoming more pronounced.

However, it can be argued that this 'crisis' of the West German political system cannot be resolved by change within the ruling coalition in accordance with the established procedure of a bourgeois parliamentary system for dealing with conflict; namely the periodic change of government and governing coalition. In fact, the relevant political and social fronts of conflict are located *contrary* to these mechanisms. The actual explosiveness of future developments could lie in the potential spread of autonomous and extra-institutional 'grass-roots movements', and alternative forms for the direct expression of interests within both the realms of 'production' and 'reproduction'. The basis for this development is, on the one hand, the obdurate structure of the mass integration system itself and, on the other, the socio-economic reorganisational process with its accompanying destruction of material living conditions, social contexts, and traditional norms and values. As a consequence of this process, the cohesion and reproduction of society must be mediated by means of (repressive) state regulation. This, in turn, results in a specific redrawing of the fronts of social conflict. These now tend to be found between the integrated complex of the political apparatus as a whole, and the objects of various state mechanisms of 'welfare' and 'repression'. The resentment of the bourgeoisie and the proletariat appears in terms of social movements which are forming, although assuming a very mediated, displaced and broken form. Specifically 'middle-class movements' are beginning to arise, ranging from the student movement to the numerous 'grass-roots' movements (*Bürgerinitiativen*) – which indicate that this class – or, rather, certain parts of it, can no longer be considered as a 'residual' of the two 'main classes', but is beginning to influence the level of class conflict in a relevant manner.[33] This structure of conflict, located partially across class lines, rests upon penetrating socio-economic reorganisational processes that are not class specific, and upon tendencies towards massive dequalification and proletarisation of members of the 'new' middle classes; for example, the de-valuation of academic degrees and high unemployment among managerial, professional and technical workers. This means that the field of social conflicts will, as a whole, become more complex and that, to a growing extent and in diverse spheres, this will increase with the autonomous pursuit of interests and with the collective re-appropriation of practical living contexts. This also suggests that it will become more difficult to 'play off' the production and reproduction interests of individuals against each other, increasing the probability that incidental social conflicts will spill over into other realms. Proof of this can be found in the question of nuclear energy that has become the focus of innumerable conflicts and interests.

Since the system of mass integration is characterised by an absence of parties that are anchored in stable social milieus and living contexts, and by the predominance of a bureaucratic party of integration (the 'Peoples' Party') and by unions that are – by nature of their functional logic – committed to the capitalist process of accumulation, the West German bourgeoisie must waive the opportunity to enter into an 'historical compromise' with a reformist working-class party (that is firmly anchored within the working-class) for the purposes of undertaking the restructuring processes necessary for capital realisation. What, for a long time, was considered to be the warranty of West Germany's political stability, namely, the structural avoidance of themes of class conflicts at the level of central political decision-making processes, and the subsequent and related 'neutralisation of ideological politics', increasingly becomes a moment of lability of mass integration. This probably designates a significant distinction in the political structure of the FRG, compared with other Western European countries, and is an essential cause for the development of an authoritarian police-state *within* parliamentary and democratic forms. It is probably the possible break-down of mechanisms of mass integration which explains the development of political repression within the FRG; these mechanisms still function, but on a more narrow basis. The manifestation of such factors as student protest, spontaneous strike movements, and the spread and radicalisation of 'grass-roots' political movements are distinctive warnings to those who rule. Political terrorism in West Germany may also be considered as an expression of this development: it is the appearance form (*Erscheinungsform*) of the dissolution of mass integrative and ideological structures and serves, at the same time, as a legitimation for attempts to repressively maintain stability.

Measures of state repression, introduced after 1969 and reinforced since the outbreak of the economic crisis of 1974 are, therefore, primarily directed at protecting the existing institutional system of mass integration from 'disturbances' and from preventing the dissolution of established forms and institutions of 'political decision-making' (*politische Willensbildung*). In addition, they are directed towards keeping the state authoritative apparatus intact as a reserve against crises. It is no coincidence that political repression is a correlate of social democratic 'reform politics' which, from the beginning, involved the risk of creating 'areas' for movements and processes that are 'dysfunctional for the system'; both inside and outside the established political apparatuses. Repression which, under current conditions, must not yet assume the form of open violence against the masses – and especially not against the established organisations of the working-class – must, therefore, be directed at potential supporters of radical goals within both the apparatuses of mass integration and those parts of state administration concerned directly with the control of realms of potential social conflict; potential propagators of ideological 'deviations' within ideological apparatuses who could prevent or disturb the difficult process of adapting the dominant ideology to changed societal relationships; 'autonomous' movements – that is, those not integrated within the existing institutional system of mass integration – and those various unconceded forms of unmediated political and economic pursuit of interest. The particularly severe reaction of state authorities to these movements indicates their potential and politically explosive character. They undermine institutionalised forms of political decision-making and articulation of interests which function to filter and canalise the demands of the masses into forms conforming to the system (e.g., particularisation, rules of competency, representation, delegated representation of interests, bureaucracy). In other words, they call into question the central principles that are fundamental for the success of political mass integration.

It is within this process that the repressive state apparatus (police, law administration, intelligence services) gains its double-edged centrality: as an instance to ensure ideological mass integration within the existing system through repressive actions (the curtailment of the 'autonomy of institutions of higher learning', censorship of the media, surveillance and intelligence operations, suppression of economic struggles that are independent of the unions, and autonomous forms for the pursuit of specific interests), as well as a reservoir of authoritative violence if mass integration should become too unstable and finally collapse. It is no coincidence that an essential moment in the changes of administrative structures since 1966 has been the centralisation of the police apparatus ('Federal Criminal Bureau' – '*Bundeskriminalamt*', the extension of the duties of the Federal Border Control Police – '*Bundesgrenzschutz*' – to a Federal Police force with training for civil war) and the diffusion of police and intelligence services within the state administrative authorities.

Nevertheless, the particularity of the present political relations in the FRG consists in the fact that the existing mass integration system shows signs of comparative constancy despite its character of repressively-supported instability. This is primarily because the extra-institutional 'grass-roots' movements are still comparatively weak, divided, and fragmented into various groups. To be sure, the established institutions are faced with a significant 'lack of confidence', but they are not seriously threatened in terms of their formal functions. At the same time, it is possible that the Social Democratic and corporatist solution to the problem of mass integration is appropriate to the present stage of development in the forces of production and to the position of West German capital on the world market. However, this is contingent upon the willingness of the union bureaucracy to co-operate in guaranteeing that the technologically advanced production process remains free of disruptions, and that the necessary socio-economic processes of restructuring can be carried out with comparatively little friction. The 'reformist' mode of mass integration that is dependent upon the co-operation of the union bureaucracy will probably continue to function so long as a massive attack upon the living conditions of the core of the working-class does not become necessary, and providing that the deterioration of living conditions can be shifted to politically and economically marginal groups, as well as to ecologically insignificant realms. The hidden existential logic of current relations of domination and control is based upon the possibility of displacing the costs of accelerated structural adaptation to these social groups and spheres of life.

At the same time, this makes possible – although to a reduced degree – material concessions to the working-class *core* and to parts of the petite bourgeoisie. Nevertheless, a worsening of the economic crisis could force the technologically advanced part of monopoly capital into a course of open collision with the entire working-class. Assuming that the leadership of the SDP (and even less that of the unions) cannot completely disengage itself from the interests of its members and voters, then this would mean the end of the mode of mass integration that has existed since 1966. The transition to an even more reactionary mode of integration (for example, based on support by the CSU and the right wing of the CDU) would mean several changes within the current political party system as its prerequisite. In fact, such processes are already in motion; the separation of the CSU from the CDU, attempts to form a rightist, conservative 'fourth party', the erosion of the electoral base of the FDP, and the formation of dissenting parties. A further precondition for this would be a new comprehensive ideological organisation which would create a durable basis of consensus, especially within the petite bourgeoisie, and that is no longer grounded upon 'reformist' expectations of the mass integration apparatus. These processes have, for some time, manifested themselves in terms of increasing ideological surveillance by the police and the intelligence service, censorship, intensified attacks on the mass media, professional proscription, and the curtailment of the autonomy of institutions of higher education. In a paradoxical way, it is the present government that is carrying out, or at least supporting, the very developments that threaten its existence. The necessity of attempting to protect the existing mode of mass integration by means of increasing repression shows itself, simultaneously, as the precondition for its future elimination.

However, such an alteration in the mode of mass integration would not only imply a rearrangement of existing political apparatuses and not only fundamentally call into question the form of the integrative political parties, but also the homogeneous union organisation operating under the principle of being social partners with the government. One possible consequence of this would be a 're-politicising' of political processes in a way that class struggle would again be more directly expressed within bourgeois political apparatuses; alternatively, increasing political and social conflicts could only be prevented by massive and open repression. Both of these consequences, however, would threaten internal socio-economic structural transformation and hence, the position of West German capital on the world market. It is probably this risk that still causes relevant sections of the bourgeoisie to favour the existing mode of mass integration.

Notes

1. Joachim Hirsch, 'Bemerkungen zum theoretischen Ansatz einer Analyse des bürgerlichen Staates' in *Gesellschaft. Beiträge zur Marx'schen Theorie 8/9* (Suhrkamp, Frankfurt, 1976), pp. 99–149.

2. Kommission für wirtschaftlichen und sozialen Wandel, *Wirtschaftlicher und sozialer Wandel in der Bundesrepublik Deutschland* (Schwarz, Göttingen, 1977), p. 45.

3. E. M. Huster *et al., Determinanten der westdeutschen Restauration* (Suhrkamp, Frankfurt, 1975); Eberhard Schmidt, *Die verhinderte Neuordnung 1945–1952* (Europäische Verlagsanstalt, Frankfurt, 1970); U. Schmidt and T. Fichter, *Der erzwungene Kapitalismus* (Wagenbach, Berlin, 1971); Peter Brückner, *Versuch, sich und anderen die Bundesrepublik zu erklären* (Wagenbach, Berlin, 1978).

4. Joachim Hirsch, *Staatsapparat und Reproduktion des Kapitals* (Suhrkamp, Frankfurt, 1976), pp. 119–72; Kommission für wirtschaftlichen und sozialen Wandel, *Wirtschaftlicher und sozialer Wandel in der Bundesrepublik Deutschland* (1977), p. 76.

5. Kommission für wirtschaflichen und sozialen Wandel, p. 60.

6. Presse- und Informationsamt der Bundesregierung, *Gesellschaftliche Daten 1977* (Bonn, 1978), pp. 109–21; Statistisches Bundesamt, *Statistisches Jahrbuch für die Bundesrepublik Deutschland 1977* (Kohlhammer, Stuttgart–Mainz, 1978), p. 98; J. Huffschmid and H. Schui (eds.), *Gesellschaft im Konkurs?* (Pahl-Rugenstein, Köln, 1976).

7. Kommission für wirtschaftlichen und sozialen Wandel; J. Huffschmid and H. Schui (eds.), *Gesellschaft im Konkurs?*; Institut für marxistische Studien und Forschungen (ed.), *Wirtschaftskrise und Wirtschaftspolitik* (Marxistische Blätter, Frankfurt, 1976).

8. Sachverständigenrat zur Begutachtung der gesamtwirtschaftlichen Entwicklung, *Jahresgutachten 1977/8* (Parliament Print, 8/1221), p. 29.

9. Elmar Altvater *et al.,* 'Entwicklungsphasen und -tendenzen des Kapitalismus in Westdeutschland', Parts 1, 2 in *Probleme des Klassenkampfs*, Nr. 13, 16/1974.

10. On developments in the rate of profit in West Germany see E. Altvater *et al.,* supra.
Changes in the rate of profit brought about by the shift in the organic composition of capital are decisive for economic development and the constellation of class struggles in West Germany because of the comparatively low autonomous potential for struggle shown by the working-class for so many years. Because of this, struggles for wages appear as the *reaction* to conditions that are determined by the quasi 'objective' course of the process of capital accumulation. Simultaneously, developments in the sphere of wages, even if as a reaction, still represent essential determinants of profit and forces capital to take defensive measures. This has become especially apparent since 1970, when the working-class first succeeded in defending its wage position attained towards the end of the 1960s as a result of the economic boom. There are several indications that, in future, wage struggles will represent an independent determining factor on the development of the rate of profit without, however, bringing about changes in the fundamental value relations necessary (organic composition, exploitation rate, etc.).

At this point, it is perhaps appropriate to comment upon the theoretical status of the 'law of the tendency for the rate of profit to fall'. This law designates the objective reference point for strategies of capital and class struggle, represented in categories of value, that are always expressed only in mediated and inverted forms on the 'surface of society' and in the consciousness of the agents of production, the results of which do not find direct expression at the level of empirical, economic variables (composition of capital, wage rates, profit). This law designates the objective and structural basis for actual class action to the extent that capital in order to exist, must mobilise 'counter-reactions' in the form of intensified exploitation in its struggle for the rate and proportion of profit. As long as the social context of the actors cannot, or only imperfectly, be identified under the conditions of the domination of the law of value, it is only the formulation of this context in terms of the theory of value that allows the actions of the struggling classes to be defined as 'strategies'. In my opinion, the fundamental meaning of this theorem, therefore, lies in its making possible the consistent connection of the theory of structure and the theory of action in the

Marxist analysis of capitalism. The success of class strategies and the consequences of struggles determine whether, and how, the tendency of the rate of profit to fall will prevail. The effectiveness of the same regularities comes to light with the development of an open crisis that would otherwise remain hidden over a long period of time by the effectiveness of 'counter-tendencies'.

The law of the tendency of the rate of profit to fall, then, formulates the objective context of reference of class struggle, with the 'counter-acting causes' signifying the results and conditions that assume the form of complex social relations. In other words, 'the law' cannot, in itself, explain the empirical course of development of capitalist societies; it is the formulation of its contradictory driving forces that finds expression in class struggles, strategies of capital, and the course of crises – always modified by innumerable empirical situations and historical particularities. It is my opinion that a consistent theory of class movement, and thereby, of political processes, can hardly be formulated without reference to this theorem. For an elaborated statement of this see J. Hirsch, *Staatsapparat*, and J. Hirsch, *Bemerkungen*.

11. See H. G. Hoffschen, E. Ott and H. K. Rupp, *SPD im Widerspruch* (Pahl-Rugenstein, Köln, 1975); Jörg Huffschmid, 'Karl Schillers konzentrierte Aktion', in *Blätter für deutsche und internationale Politik* (Pahl-Rugenstein, Köln, 1967), p. 442.

12. Sachverständigenrat zur Begutachtung der gesamtwirtschaftlichen Entwicklung, *Jahresgutachten 1977/8*, p. 29.

13. O. Jacobi, W. Müller-Jentsch and E. Schmidt (eds.), *Gewerkschaftspolitik in der Krise. Kritisches Gewerkschaftsjahrbuch 1977/8* (Rotbuch, Berlin, 1978).

14. See Andrew Schonfield, *Modern Capitalism* (Oxford University Press, London–New York–Toronto, 1965); Joachim Hirsch, *Wissenschaftlich-technischer Fortschritt und politisches System* (Suhrkamp, Frankfurt, 1970).

15. Except the Aerospace industry, which was to a large extent, organised by the state.

16. Joachim Hirsch, *Staatsapparat und Reproduktion des Kapitals*.

17. Joachim Hirsch, *Wissenschaftlich-technischer Fortschritt und politisches System*.

18. Peter Koch and Reimar Oltmans, *SOS. Freiheit in Deutschland* (Gruner & Jahr, Hamburg, 1978).

19. See Kommission für wirtschaftlichen und sozialen Wandel, *Wirtschaftlicher und sozialer Wandel in der Bundesrepublik Deutschland*, p. 241; Institut für marxistische Studien und Forschungen, *Wirtschaftskrise und Wirtschaftspolitik*, p. 157.

20. The public debt increased between 1966 and 1977 by 328 per cent. During the same period, the nominal social product raised only by 246 per cent. See Sachverständigenrat zur Begutachtung der gesamtwirtschaftlichen Entwicklung, *Jahresgutachten 1978/9* (Parliament Print 8/2313), pp. 240, 265.

21. Rolf-Richard Grauhan and Rudolf Hickel, *Krise des Steuerstaats*, Leviathan-Sonderband 1/1978 (Westdeutscher Verlag, Köln und Opladen, 1978).

22. J. Dittberner and R. Ebbighausen (eds.), *Parteiensystem in der Legitimationskrise* (Westdeutscher Verlag, Köln und Opladen, 1973); Joachim Raschke, *Innerparteiliche Opposition* (Hoffmann und Campe, Hamburg, 1974); R. Deppe, R. Herding and D. Hoss, *Sozialdemokratie und Klassenkonflikte* (Campus, Frankfurt/New York, 1978); J. Bergman, O. Jacobi and W. Müller-Jentsch, *Gewerkschaften in der BRD* (Europäische Verlagsanstalt, Frankfurt/Köln, 1975); A. Funk and Chr. Neusüss, 'Wirtschaftskrise, und Krise der Gewerkschaftspolitik' in *Probleme des Klassenkampfs*, Nr. 19/20/21 (1975), p. 171.

23. Claus Koch and Wolf-Dieter Narr, 'Krise – oder das falsche Prinzip Hoffnung', in *Leviathan*, Nr. 3 (1976), p. 291; Peter Brückner, *Versuch*.

24. Cf. J. Bergmann, O. Jacobi and W. Müller-Jentsch, *Gewerkschaften in der BRD*; Hermann Adam, *Die konzertierte Aktion in der Bundesrepublik* (1972);

Werner Meissner and Lutz Unterseher (eds.), *Verteilungskampf und Stabilitätspolitik* (Kohlhammer, Stuttgart/Mainz, 1972); Eberhard Schmidt, *Ordnungsfaktor oder Gegenmacht, Zur politischen Rolle der Gewerkschaften* (Suhrkampf, Frankfurt, 1971); New contributions to the 'corporatism-debate' are Bob Jessop, 'Corporatism, Fascism and Social Democracy', Congress Paper, 1978 and Leo Panich, 'Recent Theoretisations of Corporatism: Reflections on a Growth Industry', Congress Paper, 1978.

25. Manfred G. Schmidt, 'Die "Politik der inneren Reformen" in der Bundesrepublik 1969–76', *Politische Vierteljahresschrift*, vol. 19 (1978), p. 201.

26. Joachim Hirsch, *Bemerkungen zum theoretischen Ansatz einer Analyse des Bürgerlichen Staates.*

27. See several remarks of the 'Sachverständigenrat' in the *Jahresgutachten.*

28. J. Huffschmid and H. Schui (eds.), *Gesellschaft im Konkurs?*

29. E. Altvater and Chr. Neusüss, 'Wirtschaftskrise, Konjunkturprogramm und die Entwicklung der Klassengegensätze', *Links*, Nr. 70 (1975), p. 1.

30. Sozialdemokratische Partei Deutschlands, *Langzeitprogramm 1. Texte* (Neue Gesellschaft, Bonn/Bad Godesberg, 1973).

31. Cf. Deppe, Herding and Hoss, *Sozialdemokratie und Klassenkonflikte*; Wolf-Dieter Narr, Hermann Scheer and Dieter Spöri, *SPD – Staatspartei oder Reformpartei?* (Piper, München, 1976); Horst W. Schmollinger and Richard Stöss, 'Bundestagswahlen und soziale Basis der politischen Parteien in der Bundesrepublik' in *Probleme des Klassenkampfs*, Nr. 26 (1977), p. 111.

32. Jacobi, Müller-Jentsch and Schmidt (eds.), *Gewerkschaftspolitik in der Krise. Kritisches Gewerkschaftsjahrbuch 1977/8.*

33. Nicos Poulantzas, *L'Etat, le pouvoir et le socialisme* (Presses Universitaires, Paris, 1978).

4 Swedish Welfare Capitalism: The Role of the State

CASTEN VON OTTER

Introduction

The welfare state, as it exists in Sweden and a number of other countries, represents an economically 'rational' order for the reproduction of labour and the support of the productive system in all sectors of social life.[1] Economic considerations now enter into almost all spheres, including those in which moral, religious and social traditions formerly played a decisive rôle. Since the state mobilises the nation in the pursuit of economic growth, it takes on an increasingly active rôle in the economy. For instance, in the historical process of transforming a country from agrarianism to an urbanised, secular, industrial society, the state might, by intervention, accelerate development. Furthermore, in a highly developed international economy, it may promote the competitiveness of a country's industries by monetary policy, economic planning, social programmes, and so on.

However, a serious contradiction – in terms of social integration and stability – stems from a disparity between the political and economic systems for the *articulation of needs* and the productive means available for *their satisfaction*. The major threat to the stability of a country, in both political and economic terms, is posed by an imbalance between political (in the 'pure' sense of the term) and economic resources. Although needs may be expressed by both the political vote and in the market, the productive system responsible for the satisfaction of needs under traditional Western liberal capitalism, however, responds only to those expressed in the market. Political powerholders, therefore, have to look for alternative means in order to satisfy those needs which are not met in the market.

A socio-political system must therefore be developed in which the exercise of power is representative of that found within both the political and the economic spheres. The outcome is normally some kind of *corporatist* arrangement in which different groups are

142

represented not according to head counts but in terms of their ability to apply sanctions and exercise various forms of veto. It might be expected that social democratic governments might be more inclined toward corporatism than their bourgeois counterparts because of the greater discrepancy between the *real* distribution of power, including the economic, and the distribution of electoral votes in Parliament.[2]

Another tension – equivalent to class conflict – which has to be brought under control is in the labour market between wage labour and capital. In modern society these have developed institutions for the purpose of bargaining and thereby transformed conflicts of interest into disputes of civil law. In most cases this process of institutionalisation has been initiated by the state, although its character has been largely shaped by the conjuncture of class forces. The nature of conflict, however, calls not only for the creation of 'bargaining' institutions but also additional reforms characteristic of the welfare state. This is because the market tends to be ill equipped to provide the *basic necessities* of life. People are not prepared – as voters or as workers – to accept a distribution of income that accurately reflects their earning power in the labour market since they would be forced to settle for economic resources far below the socially-determined level of subsistence. A system of redistribution therefore seems to be an almost inevitable feature of the liberal democratic state. Furthermore, since the market tends to be an inefficient producer and distributor of various necessities which people demand through the political system, state programmes are created in order to determine the allocation of housing, food, and other similar necessities.

The welfare state, then, fulfils several functions. First, it has to resolve various conflicts from contradictions between liberal democracy and the capitalist mode of production. Thus, it guarantees political control through the integration of the masses by partly satisfying the material needs of the majority of the population. This is often achieved by a policy of redistribution and the public provision of certain necessities. Secondly, political institutions have to be supplemented by various corporatist controls. Within this context, the development of class-based organisations is a prerequisite for the institutionalisation of class conflict. Thirdly, the state promotes economic 'rationality' in the organisation of a country's affairs: for example, the allocation of productive resources, the utilisation of labour, and the protection of national interests in different areas of international relations. Through these means, then, the welfare state integrates society, particularly the 'economic' and the 'political' and the relationship between wage labour and capital. I will now concentrate on these three points with reference to Sweden, giving due regard to the institutional specificity of the Swedish system.

Some Notes on Sweden

In order to understand the specificity of the state in a particular country, it is necessary to take into account the society's particular features; its population, cultural forms, historical traditions, and so on. Sweden is one of the largest countries in Western Europe with abundant natural resources including minerals, forests and water power. The eight million inhabitants are largely homogeneous in terms of religion, language and culture. Its demographic structure is typical of that of most advanced industrial nations with a low birth rate and a large proportion of the population in non-productive age groups: approximately one million are over seventy years old. Recently, there has been an increase in the proportion of immigrants who now constitute about 5 per cent of the population. Some 250,000 are from Finland, 100,000 from other Scandinavian countries, 34,000 from Yugoslavia, and about 90,000 from other countries. Sweden has a common labour market with the other Nordic countries, enabling workers to move freely between them. The rate of participation in the labour force is high: 87 per cent of all men and 70 per cent of all women between the ages of sixteen and sixty-four. In terms of its labour force, Sweden might be considered a post-industrial society since more than one-half of its labour force is engaged in non-industrial employment. This is illustrated in Figure 4.1 which shows the remarkable growth that has occurred in the public sector.

A Brief History

Sweden gradually changed from a relatively poor, agrarian country into a liberal-democratic state during the latter part of the nineteenth century, although a first step in this direction had already been taken as early as 1809 when the constitutional monarchy was established.[4] Through reforms in 1866, parliament – consisting of four estates – was succeeded by the *riksdag*, with two elected chambers. But property and income qualifications were retained and only in 1909 was suffrage extended to all adult men and then, a decade later, to women.

The Social Democratic Party (SAP) was formed in 1889, the Trade Union Confederation (LO) in 1898 and a few years later, the

Employers' Confederation (SAF). The right of workers to organise into trade unions and to bargain collectively was first acknowledged by employers in 1906 in exchange for labour's acceptance of the employers' prerogative to hire and fire, and to organise work. This principle prevailed until the 1970s when new labour laws were introduced. The LO is mainly an organisation of blue-collar workers; salaried employees have separate organisations which developed in their modern form during the 1940s. The high level of unionisation in Sweden is well known, but what is equally as important for an understanding of contemporary industrial relations is the organisation

Figure 4.1: Employment in Various Sectors of the Swedish Economy[3]

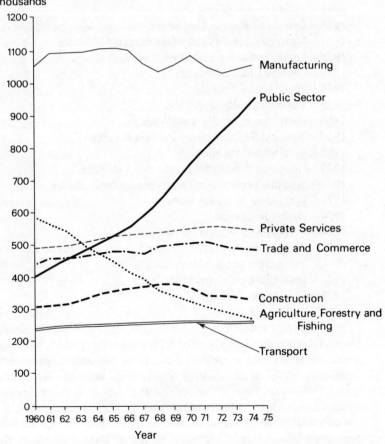

of employers. Since the 1950s the opposing parties in the labour market have developed a highly centralised system of wage and salary negotiations; today, both white- and blue-collar workers are included in the same centralised negotiations. The first Social Democratic government took office in 1920 and remained for only a short period, but in 1932 it returned to stay in power for more than forty years. The more outstanding reforms in Sweden this century may be summarised as follows:

1909 – Introduction of Male Suffrage.
1912 – Law on Industrial Safety.
1913 – General Pension Insurance (the first old-age pension).
1918 – Universal Suffrage (women obtain the vote).
1919 – Eight-Hour Working Day.
1928 – Law on Collective Bargaining.
1937 – Maternity Benefits and Maintenance Allowances.
1938 – Legal right to have holidays (two weeks).
1948 – General Child Allowance.
1953 – Three weeks' vacation.
1955 – National Health Insurance.
1960 – Forty-five Hour Working Week.
1960 – National Supplementary Pension Scheme.
1963 – Four weeks' vacation.
1969 – Housing subsidies for families with children.
1970 – Simplified compensation scheme for medical care.
1971 – Forty-hour Working Week.
1974 – Dental Insurance.
1974 – Employment Protection Act.
1976 – Flexible Pension Age (reduced from sixty-seven to sixty-five; partial pensions introduced).
1977 – Industrial Co-determination Act.
1978 – Five Weeks' Vacation.

Since Sweden did not enter the Second World War, the Social Democratic government approached the post-war period with high hopes for developing a welfare state, given the international competitiveness of an intact industrial structure. At the same time, many Social Democrats were of the opinion that private economic power could be regarded in the same manner as the monarchy and the church; just as the power and privileges of the king and clergy have been gradually reduced, according to the official ideology, so too could the power exercised by private economic interests through the expansion of state regulations over the economy.

The Mode of Political and Economic Incorporation

In the first part of this chapter I mentioned the contradiction between a liberal market economy and a political system based on the equality of individuals. Thus, forms of incorporation are necessary even if this implies a certain 'corruption' of the idea of a free market economy and a liberal-democratic polity. This is primarily achieved through corporatist representation in the political system, and the introduction of state in the 'free' market.

The Political

As a parliamentary democracy, Sweden largely resembles many other small Western states. One distinguishing feature, based upon historical tradition, is the provision for representation of civil and corporate interests in public administration.[5] This allows for the articulation of different interests within the political process as well as for the integration of corporate organisations and mass movements within this process. Besides this, there are a number of informal avenues of contact between the government, its bureaucracy, and various interest groups.

Today, the *riksdag* (or parliament) consists of one chamber with 349 elected members. Elections are held every three years, simultaneously for the *riksdag* and for the county and municipal councils. The *riksdag* determines the level of state taxes and the national budget. While the regional and local councils also have the right to levy taxes, this is restricted in practice through 'voluntary' agreements with the government. The government relies on public agencies or authorities, as distinct from ministries, for the purposes of much of its administration. Thus, while the ministries have less than 2,000 employees, public authorities have about 250,000. In all, there are some 80 government authorities; for example, the National Labour Market Board, the Social Welfare Board, the Board for Consumer Protection, and so on. At the same time, there are seven large state business agencies (e.g., the Post Office, Telecommunications, and the State Railways), and 24 regional authorities. These authorities are controlled through laws and regulations issued by the *riksdag* and the government. However, the authorities do have some independence and this is reinforced by boards of directors – often with 'corporatist' compositions – and minority representations for employees. There are also a large number of government commissions that are organised on an *ad hoc* basis in order to investigate various problems and to draft proposals for new legislation and reforms. These serve as channels through which different interest groups can influence government, and also to achieve reconciliation and consensus around specific issues. Often there are some 300 such commissions at work.

In several respects the municipalities are independent of the national government. The tradition of local self-government and a right to levy local taxes are key considerations in Swedish politics in spite of the fact that the government keeps a close watch on them. The government is anxious to encourage certain local activities, and there has been a characteristic trend toward developing these through economic incentives rather than by legislation. Accordingly, only about one-half of the municipal budget is accounted for by local taxes. The national government covers 25 per cent of the budget with contributions earmarked for regional equalisation; that is, for compensation for differences in revenue sources and for the stimulation of various types of services. The main items of expenditure are social services and welfare (32 per cent of total net costs) and education (30 per cent). Since 1974 there are 270 municipalities compared with 2,500 in the 1940s and 1,000 after the reforms of 1952. This 'rationalisation' has been significant for the development of the welfare state as we know it today, since the new municipalities have the financial strength to support expanding production within the public sector. They provide a competent and highly-organised local base that is needed for the implementation of social legislation. At the same time, however, the reform of local administration reflects a drastic weakening of popular government; economic efficiency is assigned high priority, to the neglect of concerns for broader popular participation in, and more democratic control of, government.[6] Despite this, an important reform – with positive democratic implications – was introduced in 1976 when aliens who are permanent residents in Sweden were given the right to vote and to be candidates in elections for the municipal and county councils.

The principles of local self-government and taxation give the municipal and county councils some power in their relationships with national government. This is reinforced by the fact that local interests are organised on a national basis in two major associations, the *Kommunförbundet* and the *Landstingsförbundet*. These semi-autonomous political institutions have become very powerful in reconciling local and national interests. They enable the organisation of interests which safeguard 'the periphery' from 'the centre'.

The Economic

Given the market system, it is impossible to regulate terms of employment according to politically expressed demands. Consequently, the state has, in several respects, declined responsibility in this area. In recent years, however, certain modifications have occurred with important implications for the relationship between politics and economic control.[7]

The system of industrial relations, based on the 'Saltsjöbaden Agreement' of 1938, places a great deal of emphasis on the independent position of trade unions and the employers' confederation from the state. Thus, the prospect of a state-controlled incomes policy is still less likely in Sweden than in many other countries. But the 1938 agreement also confirmed the principle that the organisation of work was solely the responsibility of the employer. In the middle of the 1960s, however, the trade unions tried to get this principle changed and because of resistance by employers they altered their attitude toward state intervention in certain areas of industrial relations. Consequently, they demanded new or revised legislation concerning industrial democracy, work safety, and job security.[8] During the early seventies legislation concerning these issues was passed; the Industrial Co-determination Act of 1977, although a framework for further bargaining between the parties, deprived employers of their former prerogative to organise work without consultation with unions but it did not give employees any new substantial, formal rights except to negotiate and to acquire information.

Prior to this legislation had been passed, which gave unions the right to two seats on the boards of companies.

The Safety At Work Act and the Employment Protection Act were more affirmative in giving employees specific rights. The regulations concerning work safety and employers' liability for infringing rules were drastically tightened. Resources for work safety inspections were increased, and an official authority was authorised to instruct employers to implement various improvements in the work environment. Union safety officers were given the authority to stop production if conditions became hazardous. This has since been extended so that, if particular health risks exist, employees can stop work while awaiting official inspection. The Employment Protection Act assures every worker who has been employed for at least six months the right to his or her job while there is work to be done. Dismissals on the grounds of poor work or behaviour have been made more difficult. It is estimated that, as a result of the law, industries have retained employees during the present economic slump at a level several percentage points higher than that during earlier recessions.[9] However, the law has been sharply criticised by some economists and employers for restricting mobility in the labour market.

The essential effect of the laws has been to change patterns of conflict behaviour; in terms of Hirschman's well-known categories, there has been a shift from 'exit' to 'voice' behaviour.[10] In other words, the rôle of market mechanisms as a regulator has diminished, while the span of political processes has extended. Furthermore, competition among employees has, to some extent, ended. While this is a major achievement of the reforms of the early seventies, many employers have blamed these laws for the present economic difficulties, particularly in relation to the decline in labour mobility and the costs of improving work safety and preventing pollution.

The Public Sector

A very significant factor in an analysis of the Swedish social structure is the rôle of public employment. The labour force participation rate has increased in Sweden throughout the post-war period, even during the recent recession. In this, it is the municipalities which have been responsible for the major share of the expansion; from 1950 to 1960, and from then until 1974 public employment has increased from 8 per cent to 12 per cent and then to 25 per cent. In 1974, 7 per cent of the labour force was employed by the central state and 18 per cent by local government. With increasing employment in the public sector, interest in employer–employee relations has grown. Long after the parties in the private sector had established a system for collective bargaining, government employees were prevented by law from similar patterns of negotiation. But in 1966 they were given this right and, ever since, the policy has been one of 'equalisation' in terms of the industrial relations systems in the different sectors (mainly by the adoption of private practices in the public sector). The 1977 Industrial Co-determination Act made few exceptions for public employees in terms of their rights to negotiate on the organisation of work and this has led some critics to claim that co-determination in this sector is incompatible with political democracy and constitutes a move towards an even more corporatist state. However, a different threat to political democracy is more likely. Increasingly, for a growing proportion of employees, it is the case that politicians are not only seen as 'the guardians' of the national interest, the political authority, but also as their employers and prime adversaries in matters of crucial concern in their lives. This is likely to jeopardise the legitimacy of the governmental system, as was demonstrated in 1971. In that year, a major conflict arose in the public sector, primarily among professional groups organised in SACO and SR (two trade unions dominated by public employees and civil servants). Negotiations between the parties proved unsuccessful as one group after another stopped work in a series of strikes and lockouts. Consequently, the government did not hesitate to lock out its employees, including officers in the military. With no solution in sight, the government then took the unprecedented step of asking Parliament for a six-week suspension of the right to strike. This ended the conflict but the situation clearly demonstrated the peculiar circumstances of industrial relations in the public sector and the politicians' double rôle as employers as well as legislators; as rule makers as well as players in the game.[11]

Mobilisation and Mass Integration

In the above discussion I have tried to describe the various means whereby various interests are represented in the economic and political systems. I have also pointed out ways in which administrative praxis is often at odds with a formal view of liberal democracy. However, the legitimacy of a political system also depends, at least to some extent, on the representativeness of a society's mass organisations since central to the workings of a liberal-democratic society are pluralism and integrity; their presence is necessary not only in the political system but in the mass media, education and other systems that exist for the analysis, criticism and direction of social development. If a welfare state lacks these qualities, it is more or less tautological to claim that a government can be responsive to the wishes and demands of the population.

Sweden has an old and very strong tradition of *popular movements* based upon different social classes. The high degree of organisation among employers and employees has already been mentioned. Associations rooted in the labour movement include a national tenants' union and a co-operative movement that is the largest commercial enterprise in Scandinavia. The temperance movement, nonconformist churches, and adult education associations also play an important rôle. To some extent, all these organisations have been integrated into the public sphere of production: for example, the tenants' union participates in the negotiation of rents and the adult education associations arrange government educational programmes for immigrants. Providing a public base for their activities, they are more open to popular influence and control than government authorities; each has a democratic constitution and forms a type of guild, not altogether different from that conceived by the early guild socialists. Yet they have not escaped the influence of 'the iron law of oligarchy', and often it is claimed that they have been co-opted into the governmental web of administration. Thus, dependent as they are upon financial support from a variety of public sources, these associations probably do more to legitimate official policies than to question them; they are part of what might be described as an 'institutionalised opposition'.

Since the mid-1960s the state has supported the press. Grants are usually channelled through the political parties with the purpose of keeping the press pluralistic, competing at both the national and local levels. However, the ownership of popular magazines and intellectual journals remains heavily concentrated in the hands of a few families. Thus, a plan for the state to support publication of quality periodicals and books has been put into effect. Radio and television broadcasting is controlled by a state monopoly, the Swedish Broadcasting Corporation. Guidelines for its general policy are stipulated by law and the board of directors consists of representatives of the popular movements and of the political parties.

In general, the institutional prerequisites for open, pluralistic debate in Sweden have been improved; the advantages enjoyed by private capital in disseminating information have, at least, been partially counterbalanced. However, the *present* influence of the state is much less than that of private capital in the 'free' enterprise press media.

Political Penetration in the Economic Sphere

Not only has capital been able – through a variety of corporatist arrangements – to influence political decision-making, but to an increasing extent the economic system has been affected by political decisions. Therefore, in this section I will discuss examples of political planning as it has affected the economy. In this, I will make a distinction between 'market-conforming' and 'market-directing' policies.

Traditions and Goals of Planning

Swedish governments have applied a variety of measures in attempting to encourage industry, trade and commerce, and the trade unions to comply with official policies. To a considerable degree, economic planning during the Second World War was based on binding regulations;[12] the parties concerned were represented on commissions that issued regulations which were then stipulated under the law. For example, the war economy provided the necessary stimulus for centralised systems of wage bargaining which developed during the fifties. This form of incomes policy – without *formal* state intervention – has been in practice ever since. However, in terms of economic management, few of the wartime planning procedures remained; on the contrary, the subsequent period was characterised by a return to liberalism. At most the government held informal talks with big industry and sanctions always took the form of positive stimuli. This coincided with a harmonious period of economic development since industrial investments were high, industry was internationally competitive, and – of major significance – the drive to expand productive capacity in industry was strong.

However, since the late 1960s the quest for economic growth has led to large-scale structural rationalisation in the economy in terms of an increase in the level of mergers, monopolisation, and the development of labour-saving technology. International competition has become more intense and all this has reduced the level of industrial harmony. Consequently, this phase has been accompanied by a greater use of legislation in order to cope with problems of economic policy and industrial relations. This has primarily been related to *direct* state intervention in terms of full employment, economic growth, regional balance and an equitable distribution of economic resources. One set of state activities may be seen as reinforcing free market forces while others are more concerned to modify these forces. There are several areas in which the state, in the last two decades, has extended its normative and mediating function. These are economic planning, the labour market, and consumer protection. I will briefly comment on each of these.

Economic Policy and Industry

During the 1960s Sweden was one of the leading countries in Europe in terms of its economic development; productivity increased at an unprecedented rate. This is in sharp contrast to the present when the international economic recession has affected Sweden more than many other Western countries; during the past few years its share of world trade has been declining. As a result, during the past two years, six branches of heavy industry (iron ore, steel, textiles, shipbuilding, shipping and forestry) have received almost Sw. Kr 10,000 million in direct subsidies, Sw. Kr 7,000 million in loans, and Sw. Kr 12,000

million in credit guarantees; this is equivalent to Sw. Kr 8,500 per
employed Swede. Another Sw. Kr 16,000 million has been earmarked
for the shipbuilding industry.

Up until the mid-sixties government policy depended more or less
exclusively upon general macro-economic management (except for the
selective labour market policy). But in 1967 the Social Democratic
government took the first steps to alter this when they established a
larger and more aggressive nationalised sector of industry, created
new institutions in order to promote investment in private industry,
and formed a Ministry of Industry. On the whole, these policies have
achieved little; a number of problems – the low level of economic
growth, unemployment, and the desire for regional balance – have
accentuated the need for an active, selective, industrial policy.
However, it is clear that what has been done so far has been dictated
by a short-term need to reduce the level of unemployment rather than
bring about a structural regeneration of Swedish industry.

Analysis would suggest that Swedish industry's difficulties are
grounded in several somewhat related circumstances, generally
situated beyond the scope of national policies. The oil crisis and the
ensuing economic stagnation for Sweden's main trading partners are
part of the picture. Another factor is the investment boom in Far
Eastern countries which, to a certain degree, has altered the competitive advantages of a high cost and technologically advanced industrial
system. But whatever the cause, the solution is to be found in increasing the level of industrial investment. Swedish industry seems unable
to do this, reflecting not only a lower level of savings but also negative
expectations for the future of the economy. (At the same time,
however, investments by Swedish companies in other countries have
continuously increased, from 7 per cent of domestic investment in
1962 to 15 per cent in 1977.) Since 1955 the level of corporate savings
has declined while savings in the sector of social in-
surances – especially the funds of the state supplementary pension
scheme – have shown notable increases. In 1950 private savings were
90 per cent of total gross savings, in 1960 they were 75 per cent, and
in 1970 they were less than 55 per cent. In keeping with this trend,
several new channels have been opened in order to allow for the
investment of public capital as venture capital. Since the late 1960s the
state has become the owner of two banks: one operates as a full-
service commercial bank and the other as an investment institution. A
new state pension fund has also been created in order to invest in
stock on the open market. The large number of state concessions and

direct subsidies to industry reflect various efforts to persuade industry to comply with government's intentions; there are loans and grants, many provided to achieve regional balance and others intended for energy, transportation, on-the-job training, and job creation.

One important political issue following this trend is the proposal for a collectively-owned savings and investment fund. This began in 1976 when Meidner proposed to the Confederation of Trade Unions (LO) the creation of a fund which, by investment in private industry, would try to bring about a more equal system of wage differentials, counteracting the concentration of wealth and power, and supporting industrial democracy through co-ownership of the means of production.[13] Thus, a portion of corporate profits would be appropriated by wage earners with the long-term effect that employees would control a majority share in a large sector of Swedish industry. However, there is still much discussion within the labour movement and specific plans have yet to be formulated. Even so, the idea has been planted among rank-and-file Social Democratic and trade union members and there is likely to be vociferous protest if the proposals are not implemented, albeit in the long-term.

The Labour Market

The state's active rôle in the economy is compatible with Social Democratic ideology. However, the trade unions have always been keen to maintain their freedom of action and to preserve their autonomy. Nevertheless, economic growth requires restraint on the part of the unions in terms of an incomes policy. As a means of resolving this dilemma, LO have pursued a *solidarity wage policy* or *active labour market policy*.[14] According to this theory, wage increases should be based on solidarity; that is, equal increases for all irrespective of differences in profitability within the various companies and branches of industry. In theory, companies which could not afford the increases would have to either become more competitive or close down. On the other hand, there would be profits remaining in the better companies for further investment and expansion. Labour that is redundant in the declining sectors would be absorbed in the expanding areas of the economy with the result that there would be a better appropriation of both capital and labour. However, there is a need for a guiding hand since workers would be laid off in one part of the country and new jobs would be created in another. Similarly, discharged employees would have different skills to those needed in the expanding sectors. Thus the state has given a labour market board the authority to intervene actively not by *general* means of economic stimulus and restraint – as suggested by Keynes – but by direct selective measures.

As it happened, reality was somewhat less than obedient to the theory; people were not keen to be treated as mere units of mobile labour. Many resented being 'forced' to go to job retraining centres and having to move to the expanding urban areas of southern Sweden. But among the merits of the policy have been a sustained level of high employment throughout the post-war period, a more equitable distribution of income than in many other countries and a decline in wage differentials. However, the policy has tended to increase the concentration of capital and critics have shown that, in a number of cases, profits have risen higher than could be either tolerated or justified. Thus, what is needed in the view of some trade unionists, is a plan for the collective ownership of capital funds and a share in 'excess profits'; hence, as stated above, Meidner's proposals for a collective wage earners' fund. Indeed, one of the major problems with an active and selective labour market policy is that, by and large, it still depends on private capital to invest and function as the expansive force in the economy. There were few difficulties during the 1960s when investments were fairly buoyant but with 'stagnation' in the 1970s the problems have become acute; a national economic crisis has superseded structural 'imperfections'. Consequently, attempts by the government to combine an active labour market policy with an active industrial policy have met with limited success.

Consumer Protection

Compared with many countries Sweden's anti-trust legislation is very weak. Furthermore, until recently, people's rights as consumers were largely unprotected by law. But now there are a number of laws which determine practices for conducting 'fair' business while the first consumers' ombudsman was appointed in 1971. There is also a special court to which the ombudsman may bring complaints filed against businesses. Finally, a Board for Consumer Protection was assigned (in 1973) to examine and evaluate goods and services available on the market, to protect the interests of 'weak' consumer groups, and to promote high standards of accuracy in labelling merchandise. These new laws and institutions have been rather successful in raising the level of conduct in commerce, but have lacked the resources to cope with economic malpractices. What is perhaps the most significant is that consumer protection has become part-and-parcel of the political system and not simply a feature of the market-place.

Production and Consumption in the Public Sector

The functions of the family are becoming increasingly problematical, in terms of their adaptation to changing economic and social circumstances. Thus, the public sector provides people with many of the services previously performed by the family. This has given them greater freedoms but at the same time, it has paved the way for a higher level of industrial production.

The Public Sector

Relatively speaking, the public sector in Sweden is larger than in any other Western country; including transfer and subsidies, it accounts for approximately 60 per cent of the GNP. One-third of total consumption is determined by political decisions and about a quarter of the GNP consists of goods and services which are free (or almost free) for specific groups and individuals. Average full-time working Swedes pay about 50 per cent tax on their earnings and a 20 per cent sales tax on consumer goods. The sum of social insurance payments, transfers, and subsidies is equal to 21 per cent of the GNP. The public sector

Table 4.1: The Development of Public Consumption in Sweden (at 1968 prices)

Sector	1975 (in millions of crowns)	Percentage of Annual Growth in Volume		
		1965–70	1970–5	1975–80 Basic Estimate
Collective Services				
Defence	5,350	−0.3	1.1	0.2
Judicial System	2,020	3.5	2.8	1.5
Social Services				
Education	9,660	7.3	2.4	1.6
Health Care	8,340	8.6	4.0	1.7
Welfare	5,170	14.0	6.4	4.6
Other				
Roads and Highways	1,440	2.7	4.4	1.3
Other Services	6,610	3.9	3.5	1.6
Total public consumption	38,590	5.7	3.3	1.6
Gross National consumption	180,600	4.0	2.9	(3.0)

Source: The Swedish Economy (1975)[15]

has increased at a very rapid rate; in spite of the fact that between 1970 and 1978 the Swedish economy expanded by only 12 per cent, the public sector grew by roughly 25 per cent. The increase in those services controlled by local government was particularly rapid, standing at 33 per cent. By 1980 the public sector will probably account for 65 per cent of the gross national product.

Of special interest when describing the state and its relationships with various interest groups in society is production in the public sector. Of course, there is no direct correlation between public consumption and production, as indicated by the various arrangements that exist in different countries for such things as communications, medical services, education and so on. A number of justifications can be found for production within the public sector in both economic theory and political practice.[16] For example, there are often advantages of scale (telecommunications, public transportation, etc.), the need for collective commodities and services (in other words, production that cannot be consumed individually – i.e., military defence) and because of imperfections in the market. The organisation of production in the private and public sectors is often a consequence of historical circumstances in which differing ideological concepts as well as notions of a more empirical economic nature are important. Thus, in Sweden there are some state monopolies (for example, in telecommunications, postal services, liquor distribution, radio and TV broadcasting) while in the industrial infrastructure, the state electricity board and the nuclear energy authority operate in competition with private capital. Although the state railway is not protected by law from competition, it is the sole supplier of this form of transportation. To the pragmatist, it is very much a question of interpreting the empirical evidence to discover whether or not there are advantages of scale or imperfections in the market that ought to be corrected by public intervention in the productive sphere. Social Democrats have often cited these sorts of reasons in order to justify intervention in the market.

Nationalised corporations comprise a rather small segment of industry; during the Social Democratic era (1932–76) they increased slightly to about 5 per cent of the total industrial sector. In recent years – as a result of recession – the state has also obtained a major interest in several industries, particularly shipbuilding, steel and textiles. Most state-owned industries are controlled by a single holding company whose statutes dictate that it is to operate under the same conditions as private industry except that it is also to maximise employment as well as yield an interest on invested capital that is acceptable from a financial point of view.

The municipalities provide the usual services of supplying water and electricity but they are prohibited by law from operating industries. They are forbidden from making a profit on any of their activities, especially in housing, with the result that their ownership of about one-half of the stock of apartment buildings is on a non-profit basis.

The costs of social welfare, subsidies, and transfers amount to one-fifth of the GNP. The major welfare schemes are the National Supplementary Pension, Health Insurance and Unemployment Insurance. Economic security for the aged is provided by a National Pension Scheme and the costs of child rearing are subsidised by a general

Table 4.2: The Cost of Social Welfare

Estimated Costs for 1977 (in millions of crowns)	Insured Person's contribution	Employers' contribution	Municipal subsidy	Government subsidy	Total
Basic Pension, Supplementary Pensions, and Partial Pensions	–	30,470	2,200	4,600	37,340
Health Insurance, Parents' Insurance Dental Insurance, and Administrative Costs	–	14,210	–	2,870	18,570
Voluntary Health Insurance	16	–	–	4	20
Disability Insurance	175	365	–	–	510
Unemployment Insurance	230	300	–	700	1,230
(Labour Market Cash Grant)	–	47	–	33	80
Welfare	–	–	650	–	650

Source: *Vår Trygghet* (Our Social Security)[17]

system of allowances. Housing is subsidised on the basis of a means test and allowances are received by a majority of tenants in multiple residence apartment buildings. While some transfers are of a general nature (pensions) others attempt to specifically raise standards; for example, housing allowances are granted only for a certain size and quality that conforms to the official stipulations. This is particularly reflected in government payments to the municipalities; of a total of 69 subsidies (in 1976/7), 63 had a specific purpose – for instance, to promote the provision of day-care centres and various kinds of social services.

Care and Maintenance

The public sector has accepted the responsibility for providing an increasing number of people with means for their basic care and maintenance. Among others, children and students (young and old), childbearing mothers and fathers of newborn children, the disabled, the unemployed, and the sick, can receive a substantial share of their upkeep through different allowances. There are also a wide range of economic subsidies including those for medicine, hospitalisation, dental care, housing, recreation, cultural and political activities, publishing, and municipal transportation. Despite the different purposes of these programmes, the general effect has been an increasingly widespread acceptance that people's basic living expenses are primarily the responsibility of the state, irrespective of the market demand for their productive capacity. An increasing number of people not employed on the open labour market are provided with temporary or permanent jobs in 'sheltered' workplaces subsidised by the labour market authorities. People over sixty years of age are offered the opportunity to retire on a part-time basis under a special pension scheme while more and more Swedes, at an earlier age, are being provided with disability insurance and early retirement. Whereas at the beginning of the 1960s less than 150,000 were dependent upon disability pensions, today the number is above 300,000.

Increasingly, people are employed in a 'sheltered' labour market. At present there are almost as many unemployed Swedes undertaking 'relief' work and undergoing special programmes in occupational training as there are those who are openly unemployed. Approximately 10–15,000 have special 'relief' work of a rather permanent nature; people in these jobs are usually 'disabled' either physically or socially. The number occupied in general 'relief' jobs varies, from 20,000 in a recession to below 5,000. Occupational training schemes also vary according to economic trends but during the 1970s they have averaged between 30,000 and 40,000.

One notable development of the last twenty years is the diminishing rôle of the family in the socialisation of children accompanied by the expanding rôle of public agencies in this process. This is also the case for the care of the elderly. In 1960 there were facilities for approximately 16 out of every 1,000 pre-school children but by 1976 the number had multiplied seven-fold. Access to recreation centres for children aged between seven and fourteen has also expanded while compulsory nursery schools for pre-school six-year-olds were introduced in the beginning of the 1970s. Care for the aged has also rapidly improved so that today nearly 25 per cent of all those over the age of 67 receive 'at home' services. At the same time, while in 1960 there were 42,000 places in homes for the aged – 56 places available for every 1,000 citizens over the age of 67 – by a decade later the number had increased by 50 per cent. As far as material conditions are concerned, such social services function rather well but in the matter of psychological and social needs of the aged there are lingering doubts. For example, the question has been raised of whether this aid should be regarded as a service to the young families who are relieved of responsibility for their elders rather than as assistance to the aged themselves. Certainly, such services are necessary pre-conditions for the entry of women into the labour market.

Attitudes Toward the Public Sector

In spite of many doubts, there is little evidence in Sweden of demands to reduce the rôle of the public sector. All the political parties, by and large, support the system. Even the Conservative Party – regardless of its resistance to high taxes – is reluctant to propose any drastic cutbacks in social programmes. In fact, one of the main ambitions of the centre-rightist coalition government elected in 1976, was to prove to voters that Social Democratic accusations were false: they *could* be entrusted not to permit the depreciation of collective social welfare services.

The general public also seems to support the ongoing trend. In one opinion survey, in which people were asked to express their preferences in the allocation of a hypothetical amount of national income derived from future growth, there was a pronounced support for expanding the social services.[18] People from all social classes were in favour of further expenditure and production in the public sector. According to the survey, out of every Sw. Kr 100 of any future increase in resources, Sw. Kr 26 should be spent on social services, Sw. Kr 14 on leisure facilities, and an equal amount on environmental protection services. According to the respondents, slightly less should be appropriated to education and transportation. Overall there was a definite preference for *more* rather than less government.

Conclusion

Sweden represents an interesting instance of welfare capitalism for several reasons. Few, if any, countries have developed the system as far; the change of government in 1976 has led to few attempts to alter the general course of development. This, of course, may be indicative of an 'inner logic' of the system under present economic circumstances. Sweden remains a capitalist state after more than forty years of welfare politics although there have been some attempts to transcend these limits; for example, the wage earners' fund. The integration of the masses in present-day Sweden is probably not the result of repressive measures so much as a consequence of the ideological hegemony of the capitalist-welfare structure. Indeed, the repressive character of governments in the neighbouring East European countries reduces the credibility of a socialist strategy for solving the current problems.

Among the so-called welfare capitalist states, which are generally oriented towards the creation of equitable affluence for their populations, two conflicting tendencies often appear. On the one hand, there is the *technocratic*, the main objective of which is to maximise economic growth and to give little priority to the collective provision of various services and facilities. Indeed, the latter are often regarded as inefficient for the purposes of the allocation of resources. On the other hand, there is the *ideological* which proceeds from a more clear-cut conception of welfare rights. While in the first case the institutions of the market economy are considered basic for determining the direction of social development, the *ideological* attempts to replace market choice by a process of political decision-making. Thus, the conflict between these two approaches seems to be inherent within welfare capitalism. Consequently, it seems evident that the sheer size of the public sector and the disparity between political democracy and a free market economy, in themselves, bear the seeds of a post-capitalist social order, albeit not necessarily *socialist* in character.

Notes

1. For a critical analysis of the welfare state in Sweden see the various articles in *Acta Sociologica*, vol. 2 (1978), Special Supplement, 'The Nordic Welfare States'.
2. For a discussion of corporatism in Sweden see R. Huntford, *The New Totalitarians* (Allen Lane, London, 1971); and R. Scase, 'Social Democracy in Sweden', in W. Paterson and A. Thomas (eds.), *Social Democratic Parties in Western Europe* (Croom Helm, London, 1977).
3. Central Statistical Bureau, *Arbetsmarknsadstatistik Årsbok* (The Annual Year-book of Labour Statistics) (Sveriges Officiella Statistik, Stockholm, 1977).
4. For a brief historical account of political developments in Sweden see K. Samuelsson, *From Great Power to Welfare State* (Allen and Unwin, London, 1968).
5. N. Elvander, *Intresseorganisationerna i Dagens Sverige* (Pressure Groups in Contemporary Sweden) (Gleerup, Lund, 1969).
6. This is discussed by H. Lindström, *Kommunen och Medborgarna* (Local Government and Citizens) (Licförlag, Helsingborg, 1978).
7. A review of these is provided by C. von Otter, 'Sweden: Labour Reformism Reshapes the System', in S. Barkin (ed.), *Worker Militancy and its Consequences* (Praeger, New York, 1975).
8. See, for example, W. Korpi, *The Working Class in Welfare Capitalism; Work, Union and Politics in Sweden* (Routledge & Kegan Paul, London, 1978); and R. Scase, *Social Democracy in Capitalist Society; Working-class Politics in England and Sweden* (Croom Helm, London, 1977).
9. Evaluations of labour market policies and social programmes have been undertaken by various government commissions. See, for example, SOU (Statens Offentliga Utredningar), no. 39 (Liber, Stockholm, 1974); SOU, no. 90 (Liber, Stockholm, 1975); and SOU, no. 60 (Liber, Stockholm, 1978).
10. A. Hirschman, *Exit, Voice and Loyalty* (Harvard University Press, Cambridge, Mass., 1970).
11. A brief account of this development can be found in von Otter, 'Sweden: Labour Reformism Reshapes the System'.
12. The development of economic planning and its rôle in Sweden has been described by L. Lewin, *Planhushållningsdebatten* (The Debate on the Planned Economy) (Almqvist & Wiksell, Stockholm, 1967).
13. R. Meidner, A. Hedborg and G. Fond, *Löntagarfonder* (Wage Earners' Funds) (Tiden, Stockholm, 1975). A revised edition is available in English, *Employee Investment Funds: An Approach to Capital Formation* (Allen and Unwin, London, 1977).
14. R. Meidner and B. Öhman, *Fifteen Years of Wage Policy* (Landsorganisationen, Stockholm, 1972).
15. SOU (Statens Offentliga Utredningar), *The Swedish Economy* (Liber, Stockholm, 1975).
16. I. Ståhl, *Den Offentliga Sektorns Expansion* (The Growth of the Public Sector) (SAF, Stockholm, 1977).
17. Bureau for Social Information, *Vår Trygghet* (Our Social Security) (Folksams Sociala Råd, Stockholm, 1977).
18. H. Zetterberg, 'Allmänhetens Prioritering Av Offentlig Och Privat Konsumtion' (People's Priorities in Public and Private Consumption), in D. Tarschys (ed.), *Offentlig Tillväxt* (Public Sector Growth) (SNS, Stockholm, 1975).

5 Social Change and Transformation of the State in Italy

CARLO DONOLO

The Model

The object of this chapter is to provide some basic information and data helpful in making a type of analysis which, though partly speculative, commands considerable support among sociologists and political thinkers in Italy at the present time. To begin with I would emphasise three points which I believe to be central to the issue.

First, Italian society has all the characteristics typical of latterday capitalist development and this can be seen at the level of state institutions. The connections and analogies between what is happening in the more advanced capitalist countries and the dynamics of Italian society are very strong despite the undeniable importance of specifically national features. (These particularly concern the historical process by which national unification was attained and then politically administered within a context of uneven internal development; the manner in which, after much delay, the political integration of the subordinate masses was achieved; and finally, the specific characteristics of the two major political parties, the Christian Democrats (DC) and the Italian Communist Party (PCI).)

Secondly, the crucial historic break with the past represented by the forming of the Republic. Only after this event was democracy practised on a mass scale and socio-political pluralism fully developed. Nevertheless, the intimate reality of the state institutions, of public bureaucracy and the very way in which the political parties relate to the state testifies to the heavy legacy of the past, in particular to the institutions and regulations of the age of Giolitti and of fascism. It is especially important to understand the origins within fascism of many of the structures and instruments of state intervention in the economy and in society, instruments which the Christian Democrats have refined and perfected.

Finally, in speaking of the relationship between state and society in

Italy it is difficult to restrict oneself to an examination of the public institutions. The truth is that despite the material dimensions, the resources absorbed, and the political weight of the state apparatuses, the state cannot be viewed as a unit. Its essential configuration might be better represented as that of an *archipelago*. It is a 'pluralistic' phenomenon, a federation of institutions, a field in which different institutional strategies are exercised and developed. Especially since the advent of mass democracy the state has been transforming itself into a political system. There is a sense in which this development is obvious and indeed common to other countries where political parties and mass organisations which express a plurality of interests tend to assume the rôle of the state in public life. But there is something specifically Italian in the symbiotic relationship established by political parties and, more recently, trade unions, with state institutions which have expanded into a political system. The identification is made concrete in terms of policies and personnel exchanged. The Christian Democratic Party in particular has consistently developed this line and has 'occupied' the state, transforming itself into the state party. This has had the effect of inspiring in the other parties similar aspirations towards a fusion between their own political organisation and the organisation of the state (in terms of exchanges between the two spheres and some degree of reciprocal supplementation). This process was encouraged by the fact that initially the two major parties projected themselves as the heirs of two great political subcultures based respectively in the regions of Emilia, which was largely communist and the Veneto, a stronghold of Christian Democracy; regions where local political systems, institutions and political organisations share the same structures. The occupation of the state by the Christian Democratic Party has been followed by what may be termed as a 'quota distribution of spoils'. To sum up, one can only analyse the state by performing a logical reconstruction of the development of its institutions within the context of the transformation of the Italian political system.

Some other characteristics of the Italian situation follow from these facts. The uneven historical processes of unification and capitalist development have between them produced a heterogeneity in the dominant block, and also in the composition of the subordinate classes, which broadly expresses itself in the polarity between landowners and capitalist entrepreneurs on the one hand and the agricultural and urban working-class on the other. These historical circumstances have had important consequences for the structure and form of the state. The workings of the institutions are seen to be conditioned by the need for compromise between the two fractions of the dominant bloc and the need to tap the potential support offered by the subordinate mass of agricultural workers whose position is one of isolation and lack of political status by comparison with that of the urban working class. It is no accident that the strategies of the working-class movement have always tried to end the above mentioned compromise (but with little success except in brief moments of collective enthusiasm and explosions of social activity). Within the state this has favoured the development of attitudes geared to compromise and mediation (for example: liberal overtures towards industry but postponement of agrarian reform). Not only do the institutions of representative democracy – before and after fascism – specialise in this work of mediation but a part, at least, of the state apparatus actively joins the game as partner to particular interests and then as mediator between these and other power groups and interests. In this situation the pluralistic, *archipelago* configuration of the system of institutions is reinforced in the sense that each institutional area tends to follow its own power logic. Furthermore, the executive distinguishes itself in this context not by its command of the situation and initiative but as a universal mediator which often manages – even at the level of governmental formulae – to hold together incompatible elements. The tendency is exemplified among certain heads of government or statesmen such as De Gasperi and Moro and in the political culture of the governing groups, now shared by all other political groups, anxious above all to avoid the dangers of fragmentation in the corporatist structures. For the main part the executive acts autonomously only on those occasions when it manages to clear the way for the strategies of high finance (and here success depends upon the alliance between the executive and the major technical structures of the state such as the Bank of Italy) or where it manages to secure for itself resources which it may then distribute to elements or to important sections of the dominant bloc (a clear example of this is seen in the policy of incentives for industrial investment in southern Italy).

To avoid confusion, however, it should be said that the state or in particular the executive, is by no means, even in this rôle, the instrument of monopolistic capital. The dominant element, even here, is that of the transaction (for example, the investment of capital in exchange for material advantages offered to men linked with the government or respectively to the political faction represented by the head of government). This procedure of exchange of resources between the executive or, more generally speaking, the apparatuses of state and interest groups is a precise characteristic of a pluralistic system dominated by a network of particular interests. This, however, does not diminish the importance of the other activity which is that of mediation. This, although obviously centred on the interests to be satisfied, is first and foremost a 'political' matter. It often entails exchanges between different and opposing parties. It is within this context that the executive – linked as it is with the leaders of representative democracy – acquires a sort of autonomy in the political sphere (not in a decision-making capacity but as the ability to shape situations, even those involving adversaries). We might say that the primacy of politics in Italian social life – leaving aside recent mass politicisation which is a different thing – depends basically on the fundamental importance of the function of mediation. It is not so much a question of the state projecting itself as the ideal capitalist entrepreneur, as of the rôle assumed by the mass parties and the governmental formulae which they manage to express. This primacy of politics is synonymous with total inability to take decisions on vital questions; witness the feeble attempts at reform within capital, the strength of paternalist Christian Democratic populism and the absorption of the work of the political system in the satisfaction of particular interests.

Essentially the matter may be summarised as follows. While there is no doubt that the separate organs of the state all follow their own logic of development, with the accumulation of institutional procedures which produce, on the one hand, resources to be traded with outsiders and, on the other, limitations on the freedom of action of the institutions themselves, the entity of the state is chiefly distinguished by its plural dimension. The significance of this emerges in a comparative analysis *vis-à-vis* the bureaucratic and administrative experience of countries like France and Germany where the bureaucracy and the authority exercised by the state apparatus is substantially different. By contrast, organised political forces in Italy – the parties of mass democracy, the fascist experience, Catholic organisations and trade unions – have made a weightier contribution to the development of state institutions and, conversely, have themselves taken on a more institutional quality. The Italian experience is thus significant in as much as it demonstrates the expansion of the state into a political system and the immersion of the state apparatuses in civil society.

A further aspect of the situation which stems from the heterogeneity present in the dominant bloc and in the dominant classes is the balancing of particular interests and the general interest; that is, the production of consensus and the political integration of the masses with the dictates of the capitalist model of development. This has had to be entrusted to moderate parties of mass support, a fair measure of which comes from non-capitalist interests; the Christian Democratic Party is the prototype here but not the only example. The bourgeoisie has no party of its own and it uses a moderate party of mass support as the centre of the power system. In this necessity lies the historical reason for the conversion of the Christian Democratic Party (known first as the *Partito Popolare*) from a political party outside the system to the very vehicle of the capitalist state. Mediation between government and the masses is exercised in populist and paternalistic relations or via financial supports. The point to stress is this: the model described here tends to impose itself on any other party which might wish to accede to that power centre.

To conclude this preliminary outline of the problem it is worth noting the form that the crisis in Italy takes. The *archipelago* state, 'occupied' as it is by the dominant party, consumes a large quantity of resources at a very low level of efficiency. The poor performance of its structures is counter-balanced by various socio-political mechanisms. For the dominant capitalist groups it is possible to 'use' sections of the state or to exchange resources directly with it and in particular with the executive. For the lesser capitalist groups, satisfaction of interests is mainly achieved through arrangement and illicit practices at the level of local institutions and via direct alliances with elements or sectors of the local political class. For the remainder of the middle class, private solutions are left open whereby interests may be satisfied particularly by means of fiscal evasion. In general, for all the above mentioned groups the best guarantee offered by the state is that of non-interference or direct support, *laissez-faire* or subsidy according to the circumstances. In a context of economic growth and social mobility such devices are usually sufficient to bind these groups to the dominant party and at the same time to convince them of the greater effectiveness of the private use of the institutions, as opposed to the social effectiveness of the institutions themselves. Almost all these groups in any case can exercise a veto power (as demonstrated with text book clarity by the failure to reform the laws which govern agriculture and the history of the so-called 'fair' rents law for private dwellings).

As private interests make use of it, the state is further degraded in terms of efficiency, planning and decision-making. At the same time these 'bourgeois' social groups, with the exception of their slender liberal, radical or progressive elements, offer only a support which is external and outside the law. This the more so because mediation between these groups and the state is undertaken by the Christian Democrats, a moderate Catholic party (often decidedly clerical in its point of view and attitude towards the state). It is a party which tends to identify itself with state institutions, thus investing itself with an authority properly that of the state. It is no accident that in common parlance *la democrazia* often means *la Democrazia Cristiana*. The relationship between capitalist groups, the intermediate classes and the Christian Democrats as a state party is, in general, one of political delegation and the privilege of private access to the state. In this sector of society there is little wish to investigate the latent breakdown of rational order in the state apparatus or the shaky legitimacy of the institutional structures; even by reference to the letter of the written Constitution.

In addition, however, the Christian Democratic Party acts as mediator between the state and those large sections of the subordinate classes who are outside the organisation of the working-class movement. Chief among these are the agricultural workers. In this case the relationship between the masses and the Christian Democrats is a more intrinsic one based on a vaguely social ideology, broadly populist and moderate (but in some matters decidedly reactionary). The relationship of these masses with the state, particularly in the early stages of development of the political system, say up until about 1960, is not based therefore on legitimate procedures designed to confirm constitutional democracy but on confidence in the protection offered by the dominant party. This relationship is maintained by the distribution of favours (jobs) and subsidies, especially in the country areas of the South. In this way, private relations are developed with the state (and primarily the dominant party) which subsequently develop into more or less organised, more or less political forms of clientelism, culminating in the more complex present day phenomena of corporatist group clientelism. Faith in the Christian Democrats is confidence placed in the party which remains dominant, 'central', immovable, indispensable. Legitimacy is given to the institutions only indirectly. Until the beginning of the seventies the constitutional legitimacy and the performance of public offices went unchallenged.

Throughout the sixties a crisis over these questions remained latent; the fact that it wasn't found necessary to implement the reform policies announced by the Centre-left government demonstrates on the one hand that these problems were objectively there, and on the other, that they could be shelved simply by broadening the political bases of the system to bring in the Italian Socialist Party.

It is left to the workers' movement, in particular the General Federation of Labour (CGIL) and the Communist Party, to insist on the necessity for state institutions to be made legitimate in terms of the criteria contained in the Constitution and to call for more democratic and efficient institutions. But these demands were voiced by forces considered to be outside the system, outside the narrow confines of the democratic area centred on the Christian Democratic Party. For this reason they remained unable to play a more active rôle in bringing the crisis to a head. Not before 1968 did the growth of mass movements and the general shift of power to the left bring about an explosive twofold crisis in the institutions. But for reasons already mentioned, the two questions, legitimacy and rational organisation of the institutions, are closely connected in Italy with the crisis of the Christian Democratic régime and thus with the growing problems in the symbiotic link between this party and the state.

The Apparatuses of State

Turning our attention to the state apparatuses, the first feature to note is the pluralistic character of the system of institutions which is historically stratified and markedly diversified in its forms. The state is a conglomerate of scattered, regional elements, synthesised and condensed in very few of its institutions. We might briefly trace the genealogy of the elements which make up the state system.

In formal terms the centre of the nebulous state is occupied by the bureaucracy and the traditional 'ministerial' structures with their central and peripheral offices. These provide employment for more than 600,000 people to whom may be added the million or so working in schools and the armed forces. State employees in the narrow sense, then, number close to two million. In addition there are workers in local administration – the communes and provinces and more recently the regions and districts – constituencies, and other decentralised administrative areas. These structures together with the semi-official state offices ('*parastato*') employ approximately 10 per cent of the national workforce. The semi-official state network is made up of institutions and organisations which have grown around the original nucleus, which with time has obviously expanded and diversified by, for example, increasing the number of ministries and the different levels of autonomy in regional administration. Most prominent in this semi-official administration is the public banking system which includes all the major banks with the Bank of Italy occupying the dominant position, even with regard to other institutions in which the power of the state is vested. After this may be listed the various institutions and bodies of the state welfare system inherited from the period of Giolitti and more particularly fascism, and then further proliferated in the reign of the Christian Democrats. The number of these bodies is unknown but they certainly run into many tens of thousands especially in the fields of social and health services. Through these bodies, which for the most part are uncontrolled by any central co-ordinating agency, not to say financial accountability, the state intervenes in all aspects of social life. Such intervention is not 'active', however, but usually takes the form of direct or indirect distribution of income. This flow of funds – rather than the provision of material assistance – is the means by which the Christian Democratic Party binds together the social bloc it dominates. Beyond the universe of the semi-official bodies there lies a series of autonomous enterprises governed by the state which in practice are enterprises not tied to the logic of profit. The same holds for the RAI-TV, the national broadcasting corporation, which is a public company. This brings us to the question of *'partecipazioni statali'* by which is meant, apart from the banking system, the public sector of a mixed economy. This is composed of various financial corporations which are linked with institutions such as the Institute for the Reconstruction of Industry (IRI) and that for steel and mining (EGAM). These are joint stock companies managed according to capitalist criteria but at the same time expected to keep in step with government strategy. Strictly speaking these corporations are not part of the state in as much as their rôle is not political or public but solely economic. Nevertheless they are of great importance to the state for they may be politically aligned and they certainly represent opportunities to govern by the distribution of spoils, having vested in them political and financial resources. The public sector of the economy has grown around a nucleus which took shape during fascist policies developed after the crisis of 1929. To this, however, have been added many new elements, primarily the National Petroleum Corporation (ENI). The

Christian Democrats have exploited this situation in order to create a power base characterised by more autonomy than it enjoys in its relations with the Confederation of Private Industries (*Confindustria*). The populist and technocrat components of Catholic political culture have thus found an outlet and made significant contributions to the modernisation of both political institutions and the network of economic enterprises. Following this, the system of *partecipasioni statali*, together with the welfare institutions of the state, have become the foundation of the Christian Democratic régime. The political functions of the system of public enterprises have steadily grown in importance, both with respect to private capital and the political system, particularly as a means of political clientelism. Finally, one must remember that the national broadcasting corporation (RAI) is also part of this system and that with the Christian Democratic monopoly within its directorship, unbroken until the present day, this ideological instrument has played an important rôle in bringing the masses into a sociocultural order as subordinates.

In practice there has been, admittedly in highly particular forms, an expansion of the public institutions, of state administration and of state participation in the management of the economy. Thus, in Italy, the term 'parallel administration' is used to describe the various administrative structures, both economic and ideological, which have been added to the nucleus of the centralised state. In more recent times, however, other sorts of institutions have acquired importance which, though they are clearly of a public nature often enjoy special statutes and, in some cases, private rights. These are the various joint stock companies to which public functions have been delegated – for example, certain technical activities undertaken by the ministries – and also private associations which depend upon public bodies for the realisation of particular objectives. Likewise there are public finance companies whose authority is restricted to regional areas and regional funds, industrial syndicates and various other intermediate organisations between the public and the private sector.

The crucial problem in this plurality of public bodies and institutions is that of the co-ordination of the different activities *vis-à-vis* the general aims of government policies. As has been stated this co-ordination has proved almost impossible and of no logical use in terms of the socio-political interests expressed by the dominant party and its allies. The result has been the emergence of a 'feudal' structure with many and relatively separate centres of power and influence. These provide the material base for the formation of factions within the

Christian Democrats and act almost as pressure groups within the party. An extreme case in point is the Federation of Agricultural Syndicates, a Christian Democratic fief which on many occasions has acted like a party within the party. The *archipelago* formation of the political, state system illustrates the fact that the interests of various social groups are always found to have a political organisation either in 'feudal' dependence upon a party or in unions and associations tied to a party, often in competition with other associations tied to other parties, or even in specially created party organisations. The pluralism of the institutions does indeed reflect the activities of the interventionist state, with the stratification of its parallel administrations but it is itself the very substance of interests in political form. There is no external connection between institutions and interests since a large part of the system of institutions *is* the political, state organisation of interests. This, a peculiar form of latent corporatism – owing much to fascism, as mentioned – has been built up by the Christian Democratic Party which during years of its steady monopoly of the state has progressively constructed the system of institutionalised interests and an expression of the political system, legitimising them as it cornered for itself the privilege of representing them. An extreme case of this process by which interests are made a political quantity is still furnished by the situation of small farmers. The class of the small farmer finds its identity in terms of the Farmers' Federation (*Coldiretti*), a public institution, the Association of Agricultural Unions (*Federconsorzi*) which operates within this sector as an agent of the interventionist state, and other financial institutions like the Agricultural Welfare Agencies (*casse rurali*) and the party identity it assumes as a fraction of the Christian Democratic Party. Without these measures of political and institutional mediation agricultural workers would have no more status than 'a sack of potatoes'. To this petty political organisation of the countryside may of course be opposed the classic union organisation of farm workers within the ambit of the workers' movement.

It is important to stress the pluralism of the system of institutions and the manner in which interests are given political substance within it. This helps to explain much about the growth of political awareness, decision-making and other processes which characterise the life of the government and of Parliament. Furthermore, this omnivorous state has its clearly identifiable command centres and in this sense it is certainly not unstructured. Originally located in the Ministry of the Interior, the command centre of the system of public institutions later moved to the ministries in control of economic and monetary policies. Since economic reconstruction the Treasury, working in close collaboration with the Bank of Italy, has been the major command centre.

Another institution which enjoys great 'technical' power is the General Accounting Office, a kind of filter through which all public finance flows. In the past, economic and financial policies were drawn up and decided upon essentially by the Treasury and the Bank of Italy. This latter, incidentally, is perhaps the sole great technical instrument of the state, endowed with the highest prestige and competence in all areas of the economy where decisions must be taken. Indeed, during the presidency of Guido Carli economic policy was entirely conducted by the Bank of Italy (in particular the deflationary credit squeezes which were quite frequent during the 1960s).

More recently other important centres have emerged such as the Ministry of Industry and the Ministry of Public Enterprises, which is more important as a political rather than as an economic power centre. This shift which gives new weight to the 'technical' ministries responsible for particular activities is due to the changing nature of state intervention in the economy. From a Keynesian type of global direction the state has tended to turn to direct intervention concentrating on precise areas where the economic crisis is most keenly felt (at present, the chemical and steel industries). The pyramid of authority thus has at its summit the centres of financial and monetary control. Below these are the area ministries appointed to administer development schemes and to contain the crisis in specific sectors. Among the strictly political ministries, the Ministry of the Interior holds the central position since it is at the head of state repression. Modernised by the Christian Democrats it has been able to take a violent hand in class conflict and in the last few years played an active rôle in the political tension strategy. Following this, it has become a battleground for inter-bureaucratic rivalries.

Essentially the ministries which in various capacities control the collection and investment of public money are the ones which count, for the extensive public system of semi-official and official corporations and all the enterprises in which the state participates depend upon them for funding. The central position of these ministries and institutions does not, however, mean that they are capable of any real direction of the economy, with the one exception of the Bank of Italy which does in fact play the rôle of ideal capitalist. On the whole these centres operate primarily as transfer stations where financial resources pass between parties within the economic system in proportions and according to priorities which very clearly reflect the economic and political importance of various interest groups. So, for example, the abundant resources made available for the development of southern Italy have always been subdivided into three quotas: to support private investments by large concerns in the chemical and metallurgical industries (the fixing of prices, the provision of free infrastructures and capital grants, etc.); to support investment by businesses which involve state participation (steel), and finally for diffused resource distribution in terms of financial aid to maintain client relations within the local structures. In all three cases public money is spent not to implement the development projects formally announced but for the purpose of accumulation *and* to recruit support from the subordinate masses. In other words it is precisely those measures designed to implement progressive economic policies which have been used to further development, at a socio-political as well as economic level, of the capitalist economic model already operative. Naturally the lack of economic success, as well as the failure of various planning ventures both at national and sectorial level has had consequences. More and more funds have been allocated in pursuit of the stated objectives and there have been further ramifications in the system of institutions which finance, or direct, or otherwise intervene in various aspects of economic and social development. The result, then, has been the growth of a welfare state (*stato assistenziale*) which offers financial encouragement to both capital and the underprivileged masses and is identified with an even greater degree of patronage made possible by its control of fiscal revenue. This activity is highly congenial with the manner in which power is exercised by the Christian Democratic régime. Furthermore, the other branches of public administration, rather than looking after interests via institutional procedures, have progressively assumed the rôle of representatives of outside interests within the state and by their close relations both with external pressure groups and certain state structures, serve as a fifth column for those interests within the state. This tendency is more rife in certain sectors than in others and most notable in the case of the Ministry of Agriculture. Such processes reinforce the feudal aspects of the structure of public administration so that it becomes a series of unco-ordinated islands each devoted to the satisfaction of particular interests. In this way the transition has been made from traditional clientelism to that of a political and bureaucratic nature, internalised within the state apparatus and connected with the parallel transformation of the mass parties into catch-all parties (though partial exception must be made for the PCI), whose different factions are the political reflection of clientelism. Once again, the intimate connection between the system of interests, the political model and the characteristics of the administrative apparatus emerges clearly.

On many occasions, and especially during the period of the Centre-left administration, when economic planning at national level was attempted, efforts have been made to overcome the 'feudal' organisation of particular interests and to promote higher standards in decision-making by the co-ordination and even the fusion of different administrative authorities. By and large the attempts have failed as is illustrated by what happened to the Budget Department (*Ministero del Bilancio*) and the abortive plan to constitute a central Ministry of the Economy. Other efforts have been made to reduce the ever-increasing number of ministries but again without success. Decision-making in the conditions prevailing is always very slow, not only in terms of legislation but even with regard to normal procedures and implementation, especially where the decisions taken affect a number of different and not strictly personal interests. To put it simply the present state of public institutions in Italy is one of stalemate, or one where innovations are extremely difficult to envisage. This situation which halts the development of the institutions (without curbing the intense cultivation of interests within them), culminates in the complete arrest of socio-political progress within the party system where the central position of the Christian Democratic Party in all government formulae remains unshakeable. The centrality of this party and the power of the moderate bloc which it stands for, are closely connected with the way the state apparatus functions. The power of this association between state and party and between state and organised interests is such as to impose constraints even on the political forces of the workers' movement. The alternative way to unite interests and govern public affairs which they still propose tends either to come to an understanding with the Christian Democratic régime in the manner of the associations described above or to take over from the Christian Democrats their interclass mediatory rôle and their occupation of the administrative apparatus.

The Bureaucracy

Another link between society and state is provided by political and bureaucratic personnel. Sixty-three per cent of all state bureaucrats come from southern Italy and 10 per cent from the area of Rome alone. This fact brings together the Southern question and the question of administration. The phenomenon is explained by the lack of other job opportunities, apart from agriculture, in the South and, more systematically, by the mediation between regions whose uneven development has been a characteristic of social progress since the unification of Italy with the corresponding mediation between different categories of bourgeois society. The flood of southerners into state employment is a result of the relationship between economic liberalism and the 'occupation' of the state which has been practised in various forms over the last 100 years. Like emigration it has provided a 'solution' to the problem of the South while at the same time offering a social basis within the state for the policies of moderation so wholeheartedly pursued by the Christian Democrats. The relationship between the upper layers of the state bureaucracy and the political élite was, in the early days of national unity, one of identification on account of the greater similarity at that time between their rôles and a closely shared sense of class. Later, with the advent of the mass parties the apparatus of state administration expanded and the political and bureaucratic classes grew apart. From then, there were tensions between different sections of the bureaucracy and between bureaucracy and the system of representation. (During fascism, for example, there was antagonism between the traditional bureaucracy and the institutions of the régime.) Nevertheless, bureaucratic concerns for status and the aims pursued by the political class continued to reach compromises. A new element was introduced by fascism in the form of institutions like the IRI (Industrial Reconstruction) and the system of public banks. Within these institutions there developed a select class of technocratic personnel which was to be partly inherited by the Christian Democrats.

The important features of the period after the Second World War are as follows: from 1948 onwards the interests of capital pass, for the first time, under the direction of a 'popular' party held together by Catholic ideology. In the Christian Democratic Party, a protective or paternalistic kind of populism is mixed with anti-capitalist, anti-modernist elements. This creates a dualism between the bourgeois economic leadership – which is secular and liberal – and the Catholic political leadership. By delegation and division of labour, however, a working relationship is developed which proves quite satisfactory for about ten years. The Christian Democrats can claim to be a party of the dominant class and at the same time of mass support, in so far as it defends the interests of capital while offering ideological reassurance and some material encouragement to the subordinate masses. Popular reaction to the Christian Democratic Party is enhanced by the influence of the Church and by some degree of state intervention in such cases as the reform of property law. Furthermore, as regards the state, the Christian Democrats claim a legacy consisting of elements from both the liberal and the fascist periods and guarantee the bureaucracy against the threat of purges, reform or updating which come from the secular forces and from the left. However, this political phase draws to an end as the Christian Democrats begin to create for themselves an autonomous basis of economic power through the expansion of the state participation system and of state welfare facilities. With this begins what in the mass media is referred to as the 'Christian Democratic occupation of the state', that is to say, the ever-close symbiosis between the party and the state apparatuses in terms of political and bureaucratic personnel and in the system of power. Few strongholds resist or impede this ongoing march and today perhaps only the Bank of Italy is situated outside the Christian Democratic system as an organ of the general interests of capital. In this process the sociological and political differences between the old and the new layers of bureaucracy disappear since jobs in the enlarged public sector tend to assume ever greater similarity within the pervasive political and administrative culture of the Christian Democratic régime. This situation remains perfectly acceptable to the various branches of capital until the crisis of the system causes a general demand for rationalisation and for limits to state spending of revenue. At this point progressive forces within capital even begin to ask for the support of the left in order to clear the way for a reform of the state which might reduce the cost in resources lost to the accumulation process and by increasing welfare services, promote a fuller degree of co-operation with the masses. This reforming drive, however, lacked real impetus and once again, as when economic planning was previously attempted, it would seem that capital preferred to settle with the power structure centred on the Christian Democrats which, at least, guarantees a degree of political stability.

For all this, two notable tendencies have become apparent which partly modify the situation described. On the one hand certain technical structures which are efficient and characteristic of a more modern administrative culture are emerging from the morass of state apparatuses. In some cases these are functions of technical importance to capital which are extracted, so to speak, from the traditional ministerial system and entrusted to more active bodies who are free of constant involvement in mediation. On the other, the politicisation of all sections of the bureaucracy continues, in terms of party alignments and clientelist systems, but also partly as an internal resource of the state played off by one party against the other. This naturally makes for a close connection between administrations and political directions for in the case of a change of direction the bureaucratic body is not always disposed to 'serve' the new guide. This has been experienced particularly at the level of local administration where the politico-clientelist inertia of the bureaucracy has often paralysed left-wing administrations. In general, a public bureaucracy of this nature is little inclined to tolerate changes in leadership.

To sum up: the level of autonomy of state bureaucracy *vis-à-vis* political power is very low. On the other hand, it is highly efficient in negotiations which involve its own status, in imposing non-decisions, in exercising vetos and generally in obstructing any power system which could achieve efficiency. The desire for rationalisation is at best half-hearted and produces nothing more than a modest degree of self-discipline to adapt to new situations. The complexity of the administration, with its historical stratification and feudal structure, is perfectly consistent with the politics and the interests of the Christian Democratic system. This certainly conflicts with any strategy based on 'the general interest' or on broad political coalitions. It also conflicts with the interest of capital but here, in the long-term, the advantages of a state which subsidises capital outweigh the cost of a state which also subsidises the Christian Democratic electoral bloc. In response to the present crisis there has been a growing tendency to further centralise political control over economic, fiscal, financial and industrial policy in order to attempt more aggressive economic and political solutions. This is reflected in dealings with the workers' movement and with fringe elements in the middle class and in the power bloc itself. At the same time, there is a drive to strengthen the machinery of repression within the state, in tune with high and persistent levels of social conflict. Finally, it would seem necessary to speak of the state welfare system (*stato assistenziale*) in terms of the 'protection' it offers in ever more numerous forms not as part of any reform plan, drawn up either for capital or labour, but only as an expansion of the power structure centred on the symbiosis between a dominant party and the state. This reflects political and institutional mediation in a situation of uneven development and division within both the dominant and the subordinate classes. Unification of the former and the integration of the latter is brought about via the activity of the welfare state.

The 'Social' and 'Fiscal' State

The classic North–South dualism has been replaced by an accumulation–consensus dichotomy. The economic and social sectors in which accumulation is paramount and which operate according to international standards are quite different from those whose basic function is to integrate the masses and thereby recruit support for institutions so that political and institutional stability is guaranteed. This illustrates the relationship between accumulation (which is practised on an international scale) and the continuing necessity for capitalism to base itself upon national, political systems. Within this context the welfare state is the product of the limitations which affect the process of accumulation and the relative extensiveness of the sectors left behind by development. It deals only with the social conse-quences of insufficient development, due to the manner in which national industrialisation has been achieved and to Italy's position in the international division of labour. Furthermore, it consumes resources which otherwise would be available for accumulation. Thus, it endorses and institutionalises uneven development and the relative limitations of productive structure. The new dualism, however, can-not be described merely in terms of advanced and backward sectors because many sectors which are advanced nevertheless demand state aid – for example, price fixing, and free or partly free capital allocations – whereas some of those whose function is to engineer 'consensus' are technologically highly advanced. There again, whereas the classic dualism was territorially defined (the South and certain depressed areas in the North), the present one is more 'analytic', that is to say, it can be deduced by analysis of the direction followed by different social and institutional spheres and in each sector of produc-tion. The symbiosis between the Christian Democratic Party and the state is the keystone in this arc-like span once territorial but now increasingly a social and institutional matter. The symbiosis has, to date, preserved and guaranteed the general social make-up threatened by this dualism. Today even the traditional difference between southern landowners and northern capitalists has been replaced by differences between fractions of the ruling class and of its ruling group. On the one hand we have those whose interests are always tied to the success of the processes of accumulation, and on the other those who defend their own status while absolving within the system the specific functions of socio-political integration. Since the state has expanded into a political system it has itself become an organised segment of society. Within it are reproduced millions of individuals, while 50 per cent of the GNP circulates in its channels.

To clarify what has been put forward, it would be useful at this point to consider certain aspects of public spending and the relationship between the state and the economy. First, recent analyses have attempted to move from a consideration of the official state budget to that of the extended public system, because only in this way can one gain an idea of the extent and real nature of revenue and public spending. In looking at public spending overall it will be seen that with regard to revenue the level of direct taxation is falling compared with that of indirect taxation and the all important social security contributions. In other words tax is mainly levied on prices which provokes further inflation. Another structural feature which explains no small part of the quantitative fiscal crisis is systematic evasion of VAT and tax payment on personal income which is thought to amount to something like 20 per cent of the total revenue. It may be deduced from what has already been said that the problem of tax evasion is not a question of ethics or of a failure to espouse the values of representative democracy, but is born of the 'opportunist' semi-involved attitudes of large sectors, especially the middle classes, as well as of the Christian Democratic tolerance of the private satisfaction of interests in exchange for political support. On the other hand, since the Christian Democratic Party largely depends on the wealth of resources available to the welfare state, one might think it had an interest in an efficient taxation system. In reality it is the tax paid by the working classes and indirect taxation (of which they bear the brunt) which guarantee the state income while the middle classes benefit from arrangements such as the tolerance of tax evasion, on which the régime is based.

As regards public spending, the most prominent items are the salaries for state personnel and subsidies and allowances inherent within the welfare system. These items are strictly controlled when they affect the lower echelons but elsewhere they tend to follow a pattern of automatic incrementation and in recent times have grown to meet the wage claims coming in from the public sector. Investments on the other hand are less of an item and diminishing in relation to rising current expenditure. These features are typical of a state through which money flows only to be rechannelled according to the different demands made upon it (whether private, family, or to subsidise investments). Other aspects of the budget, however, are equally revealing of the way the state works in relation to various interests; especially those of 'residual liabilities'. These are funds allocated but not spent during specific budgetary periods. The amount of these has been increasing, largely as a result of the inability to implement decisions because of the excessive degree of bureaucracy at all stages of the route taken by money from the moment it is funded to its actual transfer to the recipient. These residual liabilities, furthermore, constitute considerable financial resources over which the executive in charge of public spending has more direct control.

There is no doubt that until the procedures for making funds available are speeded up it will not be possible to carry out reforms and implement state aid programmes such as those demanded, for example, by the situation in southern Italy. But it is obvious that this is an area where inter-bureaucratic interests and the interests of the executive come together so, here too, we find an alliance which works in support of the régime. It should be noted also that the state budget deficit has been increasing in recent years and, though estimates as to the extent of this vary, the deficit must amount to something like one-third of the total figure and is rising inexorably. This is the nature of the Italian fiscal crisis; limited levels of revenue (given the tax system and the level of fiscal evasion, which recent efforts have only slightly reduced) and automatic incrementation of public expenditure. If one considers the extended public sector, that is to say the global budget of public offices, one notes that the financial requirements of this system, that is the sum of the current expenditure deficit plus the debt run up with the banks are swiftly rising and likewise there is a growing connection between the financial requirement and the GNP (from 12.5 per cent to 18.2 per cent in recent years).

This tendency of the state to corner savings and credit has in recent years been attacked by the representatives of capital who have asked for a cut in public spending and for policies of 'austerity' (especially in the area of family allowances) but with little success. The aim here would be to reduce the current expenditure deficit and the overall financial requirement in order to release more credit for investment directly geared to accumulation. This has not happened but, in general, measures to support capitalism have been increased; for example, rescue operations, temporary unemployment benefit, financial back-up for public enterprises, funds for modernising industry. The precedence of funding over direct public investment means the abandoning of public direction of the economy in favour of the strengthening of 'market forces'. This is the latest phase of the 'free-trade interventionism' always practised by the Italian State. The fiscal crisis in Italy can be summed up in the following figures; in 1977 tax due but never collected amounted to 30,000 billion lire; funded money totalling 45,000 billion lire (residual liabilities) was not spent; while tax evasion accounted for something like 20 per cent of the total due. According to some projections the absolute deficit could reach 60,000 billion lire by 1981. One must add that, in the meantime, with the setting up of regional structures and the decentralised administrative system, local offices throughout the national territory have been given various functions but have lost much of their fiscal autonomy. The debts that they inevitably run up (principally in terms of interest to be paid on monies borrowed) are one more symptom of the fiscal crisis. The restrictions which have been imposed as a result of this have often provoked angry reactions from citizens whose life-style they threaten, especially in central and northern Italy.

It would appear in fact that public expenditure seems to have little effect on internal demand (it concerns consumer goods more than investments) and it is not a supple instrument in the sense that it cannot be easily manoeuvred in response to economic trends (few cuts can be made in public spending and it is now extremely difficult to get public investments going). Public spending, however, with its financial requirements conditions the whole credit system. Again the appropriation of resources by the state is essential to maintain a sufficient level of compliance in the social bloc directed by the Christian Democratic Party even if this manner of producing consensus has its cost in terms of accumulation. For this reason too large a part of the economic system finds it profitable to use means such as undeclared labour and 'clandestine economics', that is to say, means of production which are barely legal and beyond the control of public institutions (which enables the non-payment of employers' contributions and of VAT and the disregard of labour legislation).

In summing up the characteristics of the relationship between the state and the economy in Italy the following points need to be made. To begin with, the state is 'social' in the sense that it mediates between economic imperatives and the interests of the dominant classes. As ideal capitalist, however, it plays a very restrictive even if decisive part while the inner life of the state is ordered by mediation between particular interests and between various and often disparate components of the social bloc which supports the régime. From this all-important mediatory function, developed in response to the internal dualism and its subsequent transformation, sprang the social state, organised in its political and institutional structures as a 'political system'. Many of the features and problems of the state budget, indeed the need to turn the state budget into an extended public sector budget, have their origin in the process by which social cohesion is achieved in Italy. Mediation and the primacy of the function of income transfer are closely connected. Furthermore, the state participates as capitalist, directly involved with its own system of industries, present in all sectors and dominant in some. Together with the technical structures of the various sectors and the system of public banks this amounts to a very powerful public presence in the economy. Obviously, this public sector has never entered into real conflict with private capitalism, although there have been sharp disagreements on occasion. The two parties are simply different fractions of capitalism, often competing for support from public finance. Again the state, as the extended public sector, is a highly important labour market giving work to perhaps 20 per cent of those employed, governed by its own rules and now, powerfully unionised. In this manner, the state which has transformed itself into a sector of society adopts the modes of conflict inherent within it. More specifically, the social base cultivated and expanded by the Christian Democratic-state symbiosis is now sufficiently developed as to hold to ransom, from within and via its own institutions, the political context which has used it. Here again one meets the mechanism which arrests the evolution of the Italian political system.

The Crisis

In 1967 there began a cycle of social conflict which, though less intense and certainly less widespread, continues even today. The contradictions which had built up in the previous phase of development became an explicit political problem creating a need for change in the political system itself. Conflicts on specific themes and in specific areas soon expanded to generalised social conflict and the calling into question of the institutions and the governing class. The crisis is social in as much as it is a crisis of the processes by which the masses are integrated in the state and it is a positive phenomenon for it calls for profound transformations of the social structure; for example, in the conditions of employment, the position of women in the family, the relation of schools to the labour market, etc. At the same time it is a political crisis because these demands on behalf of a broad spectrum of society and by no means limited to the working-class, cannot be entertained by the existing institutions, shaped as they are by the Christian Democratic régime.

The crisis takes the form of a confrontation between collective demands and the state's capacity to meet them. Herein consists the crisis of legitimacy. The economic crisis is first and foremost a political reaction of the dominant class; for example, the suspension of investments. Although certain sectors are attracted by the idea of different parties alternating in government, the power structure which links capital and the Christian Democratic régime remains as strong as ever. Collective demands even for reforms of a social-democratic nature are not met and the working-class is kept away from the levers of political power (by the veto on inclusion of the PCI in government). The new levels of social conflict have increased the strength of the working-class and although the elections of 1976 produced a shift to the left these changes have not been sufficient to open up any real possibility of transformation. On the contrary, a position of stalemate has been reached both in class and party relations especially as a result of the compromise strategy generally adopted by the working-class movement. The crisis has therefore entered a phase of uncertainty and become endemic. It manifests itself at a social level while political developments show a return to moderate positions with the Christian Democratic Party once more at the centre of things. The fluctuating economic crisis which forms the background to this era has never been the determining factor. On the one hand it has been exploited at the expense of the working-class, on the other it has manifested itself principally as a fiscal crisis, as a crisis of the fiscal state under pressure from two different directions: popular pressure for more and better planned policies of social spending and capitalist pressure for a reduction of these with more attention directed to the accumulation process. But, as we have seen, the fiscal crisis does not admit drastic solutions, not even in the interests of capital and thus tends to become an endemic crisis of the institutions, bereft of legitimacy and inefficient. Meanwhile, the forces of capital seek to restore a private dimension to functions already made public, and individuals and groups attempt to appropriate what they can by such means as nepotism, clientelism and corporatist systems.

The most prominent aspects of the crisis, therefore, concern the disposition of the political system. It is a crisis of the state party and its régime. Again, it manifests itself as a social crisis, the struggle to reorganise a society both from the viewpoint of labour and that of the individual citizen, the attempt to cast off traditional rôles of subordination and passive acceptance. It is a social crisis aggravated by the ever more precarious status of formative social processes, following rapid changes in the institution of the family and the permanent crisis of the educational institutions. The pattern of the crisis in society is one of disintegration and dislocation, the breakdown of social norms, widespread apathy, lack of motivation and the growing alienation of young people. Collective dissatisfaction with the political system has caused a crisis in the régime. The strategies evolved to contain the social crisis – a mixture of repression and various compensations to different sectors of the population – have weakened the drive to transform society and have attempted to stabilise the political situation wherever possible. All the same no proper equilibrium has been attained, even if there are several indications that the sharpest confrontations are over and Italy is moving into a phase dominated by forces moderate, both social and political.

The social and political crises come together over the question of the state institutions. They are undergoing a profound crisis in terms of legitimacy and the rationality of structure. In response to the first problem the dominant bloc seeks to reduce the question of legitimacy to one of 'compliance', stimulating defensive and regressive reactions of identification with the state as it presently exists. Compensation for the social inefficiency of the institutions, on the other hand, is provided by ease of access and the private use of them. The strategy of the workers' movement operates, in the main, to produce broadly-based solidarity and collective demands which would imply a transformation of the institutions, but so far with little success. The question of legitimacy is complicated by the confusion between legitimacy in democratic-constitutional terms and legitimacy resulting from the identification of the Christian Democratic Party with the state to the point where that part, and no other, becomes the real vehicle of the state. More progressive political formulae which aim to reduce the Christian Democratic domination of the state are under discussion, but the rediscovery of the Constitution is proving to be a slow and laborious business. Furthermore, the collective demands which have emerged out of social unrest look forward to a more highly evolved and emancipated society than that adumbrated by the 1948 Constitution (though the Constitution in no way obstructs evolution in that direction).

It must also be recognised that the new ideas and social demands require an authorisation no longer contained within the limits of the

Constitution and would imply a new constituent phase. Government by the united left would represent a caesura in the life of the Constitution, a break with the continuity of the Christian Democratic régime. This is what makes it so difficult to achieve. More specifically, it is the problem of the old, internal structures of the institutions, their traditional authoritarianism, their bureaucratic excesses and their resultant failure to meet social needs, and their impenetrability to democratic rules of management. An attack upon the centralised state is being proposed. Protests are being voiced against 'Rome'. Regional and even local autonomy is cultivated; social control and even social management of a variety of services which most immediately affect the population and are widely distributed across the country, is suggested. The drive to realise participatory democracy has brought pressure to bear on institutions more used to treating 'deferential' citizens than 'sovereign' citizens. There is a widespread awareness of these aspects of the state and in general it can be said that state authority has been badly eroded.

The state institutions show very little ability to reform themselves even under persistent and pervasive social pressure. Self-scrutiny is something for which the state has little inclination, preferring as it does to adapt to circumstances and employ delaying tactics against institutional innovation in order to survive the most critical moments and the sharpest attacks. The causes of institutional stagnation are to be found not only in the recalcitrant bureaucratic network but in the lack of decision-making at a political level which results in mediation and compromise; the circumstances of reforms like those of the health service well illustrate the progressive dilution of innovatory impetus coupled with the salvaging of particular interests within the official framework. The nature of relations between political power groups and the conservative nature of state institutions make important innovatory decisions difficult to undertake, but a further obstruction is caused by the links between political forces and social interests. Social life – what used to be called civil society – is transformed by the processes of politicisation and integration within the state apparatuses. These refer to two distinct processes: politicisation 'from below', that is through collective mobilisation in terms of social relationships and behaviour previously neutralised politically. Alternatively it refers to the political organisation 'from above' of interests and loyalties by mass organisations. This is a measure designed to prevent any alternative alignment of interests on new loyalties at odds with the thinking which dominates the political system, or simply to enhance the importance of interests organised within the political market. The politicisation of society from above produces intermediate formations between the trade unions and the traditional pressure groups, defined by political affiliations and serving to represent associated interests within the parties, or parliament or the bureaucracy. It is a form of collateral, providing not so much ideological as political and organisational back-up. Examples of this are *Coldiretti* (federation of small farmers), and the traders' and artisans' organisations. The point is that the political parties actively promote these collateral organisations, which may even be commercial enterprises like the co-operatives, each organised according to a distinct political orientation. Thus, there develops within the area between the political system and civil society, party businesses and organised interests which the parties promote and influence but which in turn act as fifth columns and factions within the parties. It is this politicisation of society, the expansion of the political system into the organisation of many spheres of social life, that creates the material situations within which, under certain conditions, the other potentially antagonistic processes of politicisation, that is, from below, may take place. This mixture of politicising and socialising influences which result from the interaction of political and socio-economic forces generates contradictions and conflicts.

Furthermore, these processes are complicated by the fact that, as a result of the strategic associations and sharing out of the political and institutional spoils, political forces do not simply direct but inhabit and fill up the state institutions with affiliated personnel, giving them an endemic party orientation. The intrinsic relationship between interests and politics that we have looked at, is mirrored in the link between interests and state institutions in which the pervasive political and party forces of mediation continue to operate. Probably the chronic weakness of the state institutions (manifested in that unconstructive 'self-interest' already mentioned) is the best comment on the action of the mass parties in usurping their functions in the area of social government and as guarantors of social order. To do this they have progressively occupied the state, which has further relinquished its autonomy. State institutions increasingly depend on the survival of the current régime and on the governing formulae which the parties can work out.

One must be careful not to underestimate the extent to which the state integrates the masses via an organisation of society which routes social relations through itself. Many social processes are subject to state administration and a large proportion of economic affairs is conducted in public or semi-public offices. The spectrum stretches from business which is completely drawn into the area of public, bureaucratic control to that which is determined by more or less spontaneous collaboration between social forces and the state. Through these connections all the contradictions and conflicts of one sphere are passed on to another, especially where state appropriation and the increasing public intervention of the state in economic and social matters occur in response to the problems of particularly critical areas. The state's intervention in the crisis becomes the channel through which the crisis spreads in the most intimate and pervasive manner to the state institutions themselves. This general tendency is summed up very effectively in the form taken by the crisis of the fiscal state which embodies the meeting of the two tendencies. In the Italian case matters are aggravated by the political permeability of the state institutions and by the social permeability (in the form of particular interests) of the political organisations, just as, conversely, by the profound politicisation and the ambivalent state connotations of general social relationships.

The Italian crisis began as a political crisis. But as social mobilisation spreads and more aspects of life are politicised, the crisis takes on an ever more social quality, putting it outside the scope of crisis management and beyond solution by purely political formulae. More solutions of this kind are attempted, but with less chance of success in response to the energy crisis, the fiscal crisis and inflation. Purely political measures (such as the governmental formulae or the alliances attempted since 1976), while they offer a certain defence of the state against collective demands, allow the social crisis to degenerate into one of real breakdown with the exclusion of certain collective movements born of the struggles of recent years. Thus the dimensions of the social crisis become even more broad. The growing difficulty in creating a new social climate in which the compromise between classes could be modified to favour greater integration of the working-class and which would also be satisfactory to numerous other social strata, makes the situation highly unstable. Demands have not been met, the institutions have not altered. However, certain reactions have occurred; on the one hand the institutions have become more authoritarian (rather than more rational), on the other there has been further exploration of the possibilities of compromise or reciprocal blackmail between the political forces all of which paralyses alliances or makes them very precarious. The possibility of changing from a system which revolves around the Christian Democratic Party to one based on different parties alternating in power becomes more distant. Although, politically speaking, we have seen the end of a cycle of social conflict which has left the dominant power structures virtually unaltered, there are still forces at work in society which erode the state (or create disaffection from it). This is clearly a risk not only for the dominant class but also for the workers' movement, caught as it is between opposition and government.

A new differentiation in the social system is taking shape which can be expressed as the separate development of three areas. First, that of large scale capital which expands by forcing through its own interests and by multinationalism. Secondly, that of medium and small scale 'local' enterprises tied by their symbiotic relationships with the political system. Thirdly, that of those social and territorial fringe areas which are unattached and 'parasitic' in as much as they depend upon resources dispensed from outside. These are the three 'sub-networks' which at present characterise the national society. Within the state and the political system some kind of synthesis is attempted via mediation between the first two on the basis of global political compromises and the exchange of specific resources. The dilemma of the workers' movement is whether to co-operate in this direction as the 'realists' among them propose or to continue to cultivate an alternative broad-based power structure. The 'third world' within the state – differentiated and divided as it now is – is considered a fixed quantity, not to be modified at this point of time but controlled by financial aid programmes and/or repressive measures. How these new differentiations in the social make-up are reflected in the state institutions is a topic for further study. The state certainly confirms the existing differences and enshrines them in the logic of its institutions and the manner of its political control. The problem lies in the state's meagre ability to realise any effective synthesis; the present situation is unstable and in need of a new equilibrium. Links with other capitalist countries and particularly with the EEC are of fundamental importance within this context. The most intense moments of crisis recently experienced can be interpreted as the expansion of a pluralist system where conflict surrounds the tendency towards working-class hegemony. In the new climate of moderation the process is carried forward by the joint actions of state institutions and socio-economic forces in a system of institutionalised and corporatist pluralism. Nowadays even protests and demands made from outside the system, and hostile to the state institutions, assume corporatist connotations. This is perhaps the social model most suited to the political system as we have traced it.

Summary

1. The transformations of the contemporary Italian state have to be analysed within the context of a case history specific to Italy and to the history of its institutions (with particular reference to the progress from fascism to the Republic). Generally it is difficult to speak of the state in a narrow sense; it would be more accurate to speak of the evolution of state institutions in terms of the logical development of the political system.

2. Certain specific features are explained by the manner in which national unification and the industrial revolution came about: a serious uneven development has resulted in the heterogeneous quality of the dominant bloc which has had two consequences: (a) the primacy of the executive function and of the art of mediation; (b) the necessity to delegate to moderate non-capitalist parties the responsibility of producing consensus (the relative autonomy of politics in Italy owes more to the rôle played by mass-support parties than to the State acting as 'ideal capitalist').

3. After the war the Christian Democrats became the mass-support party of the dominant bloc while opposition parties of the left remained powerless. There was no chance of an alternative to the Christian Democratic Party in power and the working masses were kept 'outside' the state. The fact that the Christian Democratic Party could not be removed from government gave it a central importance in the political system and eventually identified the party with the state. Thus, the Christian Democrats became the state party.

4. Briefly this transformation of the Christian Democratic Party and of the state came about in the following manner: during the period of De Gasperi's centrist government, management of the relatively autonomous public offices, of the less developed areas and the social consequences in general of capitalist development was entrusted to the Christian Democrats. It was expected that this would guarantee a climate of *laissez-faire* favourable to the development of large-scale capital within the oligopoly sector. These groups looked after their own interests as they worked together with the technical structures of state organisation – especially the Bank of Italy – and as they made transactions with various units of the state apparatus. With the passage of time a model took shape within which the major forces of

capital and the technical structures of the state directed economic policy while the Christian Democratic Party and its allies in government busied themselves with mediation and the like.

In the second half of the 1950s, however, the Christian Democrats begin to 'occupy' the state and to cultivate and expand the interests which it administered directly; that is, the interests of the middle classes. The party followed two lines of attack: the hypertrophic development of the semi-official state apparatuses (the *parastato*, which is to say the institutions and services of the welfare state), and the increase of state intervention in the economy (via the system of state participation in public enterprises). As a by-product of these transformations traditional clientelism became political and bureaucratic clientelism. This development reached its peak during the 1960s when the co-option of the Socialist Party into the Christian Democratic system occurred (the period of Centre-left government and the crisis of reformism). The crisis, which began in 1968, was a crisis of the Christian Democratic régime as the PCI and the trade unions came forward and assumed a central function in the political system. As the crisis developed compromise strategies became the order of the day which allowed complete legitimisation of the PCI and at the same time preserved the central importance of the Christian Democratic Party. Recent years have produced a situation in which the weakness of state institutions is fully compensated for in political terms by the power of the political parties (and of the unions which have assumed a political rôle). The parties tend to project themselves as a presence which influences the whole of society in the sense that they precondition the whole of social life in political and party terms. The competitive involvement of all parties in all walks of life transforms them as parties of mass organisation into inter-class parties each with a specific formula; moderate, corporative and populist in the case of the Christian Democrats, while the socialist line is pluralist and radical and the PCI national-popular. The reciprocal powers of veto among the parties tend to change the way in which public institutions, elements of the state apparatus, and systems of credit are controlled, by creating executive partnerships in which proportional representation is agreed. With public funding and the assumption of the rôle of defender of the institutions against the crisis, the parties are progressively more identified with the state and consider themselves organs of the state. Taking the tendency to its extreme one could say that the system of parties and the system of economic institutions actually are the state. In another sense one can say that the 'Christian Democratic system', that is, the sort of symbiosis realised by the Christian Democrats between collective identities, sectorial interests, public institutions and systems of power has imposed itself as a model even on the forces of the opposition.

5. The institutional continuity between fascism and the Republic can be traced in the personnel of public bureaucracy but especially in the fact that the Christian Democrats inherited from fascism various technical structures: the system of public banks, the system of sectorial economic institutions and the system of public enterprises. From within these structures emerged a small body of technocrats which thereafter directed the expansion of state intervention in the economy, the extraordinary measures of intervention in the South and the development of much of the financial system. The expansion of public involvement in the economy helped the Christian Democratic Party to gain greater autonomy (including financial autonomy) *vis-à-vis* private capital and to guarantee the growth of those social groups most closely linked to its system of power. This took place within the margins furnished by capitalist development especially between 1958 and 1968. Subsequently, the difficulties stemming from Italy's position in the world market, the energy crisis and above all, the growth in strength of the working-class, have badly affected the old system of alliances between large-scale capital and the Christian Democratic system. The Federation of Private Industries (*Confindustria*), under the guidance of Guido Carli, has for some time been pursuing a 'neo-*laissez-faire*' strategy and the idea of an alliance between the productive classes (capitalists and workers) against the 'parasitic' classes of the bureaucratic agents of the welfare state, protected as they are by the Christian Democratic Party. Despite the climate of economic austerity such proposals are unrealistic. The executive partnerships mentioned above are costly to capital but this is rewarded by the protectionism and liberal interventionism which the state continues to guarantee to capital.

6. The elements of which the state is composed can be listed as follows: the party system (and the appended system of representative democracy) the executive (divided into government, managerial élite, bureaucracy) and the semi-independent institutions. The latter, together with the managerial élite have shown signs of developing an autonomous rôle only very recently. The system of autonomous local bodies and of local political organisations represents a source of conflict with central power. The semi-official bodies and public enterprises must be mentioned as well for their political functions are as important as their economic ones. Relations between these elements of the state and their relations with organised interests have been modified with

the passage of time. In the years of centre government the interests of large-scale capital were satisfied by special relations with the Bank of Italy, the government and individual administrations. Interests that were peripheral to state functions were satisfied at local level and sometimes in Parliament. The political system is not, however, prepared to accommodate the interests of the working-class. In the years of the Centre-left, collaboration between interest groups and the public administration produced a kind of 'sub-culture' of government (*sottogoverno*), while the major forces of capital dealt directly with the government or its technical structures. Attempts at planning failed due to lack of collaboration with the unions and on account of the precarious political and administrative nature of the planning departments. The norms and the procedures for state intervention in the economy were made subservient to the interests of large-scale capital. After 1968 the situation became more complicated; a defence of workers' interests became possible with the combined efforts of the trade unions and the PCI, while a struggle took shape between private capital, public capital and state administration. A critical phase of the dominant bloc reached its climax and came to an end in 1976 with the political elections. The new situation had the following features: the organisations which protected sectorial interests were 'politicised' and expanded from mere pressure groups to something similar to union structures with proportional party representation in their leadership. This development then spread to all organised forms of Italian social life. The sectorial organisations established stable and business-like relations with the state apparatuses and with Parliament (which was only able to satisfy sectorial and private interests). Large-scale capital partly eluded the problems of this troubled phase by its multinational dimension and partly met them in negotiating with all political forces and all branches of the administration. (In this respect there was little difference between the behaviour of public and private capital.) The government operated as mediator between the factions within the major party, the different parties which supported it, sectorial interests and the imperatives of accumulation. In its work of mediation the government ignored the need for nationalisation of the structures involved because it knew that it would come up against the powers of veto. It sought rather to exploit, at the decision-making level, the relative degree of autonomy it could squeeze out of such a complex system of countervailing vetoes. In this way it managed occasionally and rather uncertainly to fill the rôle of ideal capitalist.

7. In Italy in 1968 the system of government entered a crisis which

is as yet unresolved. The legitimacy of the Christian Democratic power system came into question and, within that system, the traditional authoritarianism of the various state apparatuses. Growing collective demands produced a crisis of legitimation in the state apparatuses (it must be remembered that no reforms had taken place but new functions had simply been added to the state machinery). These processes had been set in motion by the workers' movement and by various social movements active throughout the period 1968–77. The failure of the hopes which inspired these movements caused certain changes to occur: the crisis over legitimacy was 'resolved' in practical terms by the fact that a great part of the population came to depend on the services of this populist, welfare state while apathy spread and a more cynical attitude to the parties developed. Terrorist violence born out of the breakdown of organised political movements was either repressed (but the real significance of this was that repressive machinery was strengthened for future use) or began to be taken for granted. The calling into question of the rational organisation of state apparatuses provoked a dual reaction. There was a growing tendency towards private appropriation of public offices coupled with an increase of private enterprise in essential public services which the public offices could not satisfactorily perform (health, transport and postal services). The public offices remained inefficient and permissive (in a selective sense, by exclusion of 'the general interest') towards any well-organised private interest. The concept of corporatist pluralism gained ground. A fiscal crisis occurred due to the uncontrollable rise of current expenditure (salaries and social spending programme) while the revenue remained rigidly fixed.

The most recent developments can be summed up as follows: the Christian Democratic spoil system was transformed into a quota allocation of spoils with resources divided and distributed by the various parties involved in the system. The network of public offices has increased both to provide ground for the new and competitive involvement of the parties and as a way of differentiating between areas of little importance for accumulation (such as schools), which are placed in the hands of the dominant party and of the government and areas which are more closely organised to serve the interests of large-scale capital. This second tendency could also lead to the takeover by private interests of certain parts of the state machinery. The party system and the collateral organisations which it controls (not simply organisations in support of particular interests but also entrepreneurial systems like the co-operative movement) have expanded in terms of personnel employed, and resources handled, consumed and produced. The state as an extended political system expands very much in connection with an aspect of the new socio-economic dualism; it does not represent the 'backward area' of the country as ideological supporters of large-scale capital would maintain, but the necessary outcome of managing the social consequences of capital accumulation. The 'reform of the State' means the reform of the model of accumulation; the present crisis is largely a struggle over how and to what extent the logic of the political system and the logic of accumulation can be made compatible. Upon the reality of this fundamental contradiction are grafted vestiges of the old anti-capitalist strategies and new embryonic ones for which in Italy there is still mass support.

References

Allum, P., *Italy: Republic Without Government* (Weidenfeld and Nicolson, London, 1973).
Allum, P., *Potere e società a Napoli* (Einaudi, Torino, 1973).
Amato, G., *Il governo dell'economia in Italia* (Il Mulino, Bologna, 1972).
Barucci, P., *Ricostruzione, pianificazione, Mezzogiorno: La politica economica italiana dal 1943 al 1955* (Il Mulino, Bologna, 1978).
Caciagli, M., *Democrazia cristiana e potere nel Mezzogiorno* (Guaraldi, Firenze, 1977).
Cassano, F., *Il Teorema Democristiano* (De Donato, Bari, 1979).
Cassese, S., *L'amministrazione pubblica in Italia* (Il Mulino, Bologna, 1974).
Cassese, S., *Burocrazia ed economia pubblica* (Il Mulino, Bologna, 1976).
Cassese, S., *La formazione dello stato amministrativo* (Giuffré, Milano, 1974).
Cassese, S., *Questione meridionale e questione amministrativa* (Giuffré, Milano, 1977).
Collidà, A. (ed.), *L'economia italiana tra sviluppo e sussistenza* (Angeli, Milano, 1978).
Di Palma, G., *Sopravvivere sena governare* (Il Mulino, Bologna, 1978).
Donolo, C., *Mutamento o transizione? Politica e società nella crisi italiana* (Il Mulino, Bologna, 1977).
Farneti, P., *Il sistema politico italiano* (Il Mulino, Bologna, 1973).
Galasso, G., *Potere e istituzioni in Italia* (Einaudi, Torino, 1974).
Galli, G., *Il bipartismo imperfetto* (Il Mulino, Bologna, 1966).
Graziani, A., *L'economia italiana: 1945–70* (Il Mulino, Bologna, 1972).
Pizzorno, A., *Partiti e sindacati* (Il Mulino, Bologna, 1978).
Pola, G. & Rey, M. (eds.), *Finanza locale e finanza centrale* (Il Mulino, Bologna, 1978).
Rusciano, M., *L'impiego pubblico in Italia* (Il Mulino, Bologna, 1978).
Tarrow, S., *Partito comunista e contadini nel Meridione* (Einaudi, Torino, 1972).
Tarrow, S. and Graziano, L., *La crisi italiana* (Einaudi, Torino, 1979).
Zanni Rosiello, I., *Gli apparati statali dall'Unità al fascismo* (Il Mulino, Bologna, 1976).

6 From Despotism to Parliamentarianism: Class Domination and Political Order in the Spanish State

SALVADOR GINER and EDUARDO SEVILLA

The Metamorphoses of Power and the Stability of Class Domination

This chapter explores certain political aspects of capitalist development, industrialisation and 'modernisation' in Spain from 1939 to the present day. The chief focus of our attention will be the state and the changes it has undergone during the period of Spain's transition from a backward economy to a fully modern one.[1] Spain poses interesting problems because, despite being a Western European society, it was, until the 1960s, what is usually called an underdeveloped country. In fact, it was one of the most backward in Western Europe. Yet, Spain, like Italy (and to a lesser extent Greece and Portugal), could only be called a semi-peripheral society,[2] as it was not a peripheral one either in terms of the international division of labour or in terms of its own internal characteristics. The spectrum of developed–underdeveloped societies (it is certainly not a continuum, and it should not be treated as a dichotomy) is a misleading one. Were we to accept it, however, it would be very difficult to place Spain within it during this period. Today, by contrast, if judged by the usual positivistic indicators (*per capita* income, industrial production output, private ownership of technological goods, and such like) Spain ranks among the small league of advanced and developed societies. The fact that its economy is still to a noticeably large extent 'dependent' ought not to make us blind to this new situation. What is crucial for the purposes of the present analysis is that Spain's transition to 'development' occurred and was conducted 'from above': as in Germany or Japan in other periods of their history, its traditional ruling classes were never unseated from their positions of power and privilege. Meanwhile, of course, partial and inevitable processes of upward mobility, élite substitution, wider recruitment patterns and occupational innovation very slowly changed some important features of Spain's society.

Our chief aims in this context are: (a) to explain the causes of the relatively peaceful transition to parliamentary democracy from dictatorship *via* the orderly dismantling of the Francoist autocratic régime; (b) to establish the nature of the Francoist state so that such transition can be satisfactorily explained; (c) to analyse the characteristics of the monarchical and parliamentary state which came to be fully established in 1978 in terms of class, power and the economy, and their connection with the various political forces that now support it, and finally, (d) to put forward some tentative hypotheses about the likely future of the Spanish polity by referring to certain relevant social-structural trends as well as to certain problems of legitimation. This we will do in outline, since the limits of this chapter do not allow for more.

In order to achieve some conceptual clarity we begin with what seems a pertinent discussion of a much neglected area: the study of modern despotic régimes. This will prove useful in putting the Spanish case in perspective by setting it in a much wider, comparative framework.

Backwardness, Capitalism and 'Modernisation' Through Dictatorship

The contemporary world has witnessed the emergence of a great number of non-democratic régimes in countries which find themselves in the geo-political and/or economic periphery of the metropolitan or 'core' countries in terms of technological and economic development. They have included a number of modern dictatorships in Egypt, Peru, Greece, Argentina, Cuba, Indonesia, Brazil, Chile, Spain, Portugal and many more countries over diverse periods. Though the political origins and specific social characteristics of each one of them differ considerably, some common traits can be discerned at the time of the establishment of such dictatorships. In all these and similar cases a large proportion of the population lived in poverty, was illiterate and dwelled on the land or in a non-industrial urban setting. (They were all largely peasant societies and often possessed large 'urban peasantries' in their shanty towns and slums.) This poor majority stood in stark contrast to the wealthiest strata in the country, which were in possession of considerable power and influence and were linked either to traditional ruling houses and castes or to the establishment left behind by the metropolitan power as its withdrawal created successor post-colonial states. In any case, the span of inequality between the powerful and the powerless was enormous in all these countries at the critical moment in question.

The exploitation of raw materials, local industry and the representation of foreign interests – when these were not directly held by foreigners – tended to be monopolised by a relatively small stratum of businessmen, entrepreneurs, financiers and politicians. Whilst a 'progressive' liberal and expanding bourgeoisie could be found in some of these countries, it was – and still is in many cases – too small to wield enough influence to consolidate a parliamentary democracy under the circumstances. The bourgeoisie, incessantly harassed and frustrated in its always problematic liberalism, has tended to reconcile itself with (or, indeed, wholeheartedly embrace) any autocratic form of government that could guarantee its continued existence as a prosperous and privileged class. In fact, the bourgeois stratum has given its allegiance to either 'law-and-order' right-wing military dictatorships (Chile, Argentina), conservative parliamentary régimes (Venezuela, Spain) or even socialist one-party régimes (Algeria) not according to any capricious switches of loyalty, but as coherent conjunctural responses to its position within the economy and in the structure of privilege, through calculations about its chances of survival and betterment in each case.[3]

The processes of trade, continued capitalist expansion and thirst for raw materials, international communications and others have prompted in the peripheral and semi-peripheral world a generalised desire to find the economic and political formula which could open the door to industrialisation, national aggrandisement, social wealth and military power. These have all become universal aims or government imperatives in the present age.[4] Of course, besides the unqualified acceptance of industrialisation and greater wealth for everyone as official goals, governments and political movements have understandably been much more reluctant to openly acknowledge the other, less noble intentions. The problem for governing élites (or élites aspiring to govern) under these conditions of legitimation generated by the political culture of the age (no matter how 'old-fashioned', 'backward-looking' or even 'feudal' they may be) has become that of effectively including that set of imperatives in one way or another in their overall policies. For a long time, it must be added, such élites have not had at their disposal any other experience in the path towards modernisation than that provided by the established 'great powers' in their own recent history. Consequently, struggles for power are strongly influenced by claims put forward by rising or ruling élites about their ability to set the country successfully along the path of modernisation and national aggrandisement.

Depending on a very complex set of factors (among which are international alliances, offers of help, and diverse forms of imperialist penetration or neutralisation) the countries in question have tended to veer towards either one-party, socialist régimes or towards military dictatorships (often rhetorically defined as 'socialist') intimately or openly linked to the international capitalist order. (This distinction is valid if we hasten to add that many socialist régimes, including China today are *de facto* actively linked to the capitalist order and support it by massive purchase of goods and services.) In what follows, and for obvious reasons, the 'socialist' response to the dislocations of modernity will not be examined.

The Nature and Varieties of Modern Despotism

We shall refer to contemporary dictatorships in underdeveloped (and sometimes also developing) economies as modern despotic régimes, or modern despotisms.[5] These, by and large, can be described as non-pluralist political systems which emerge from the historical crises created by capitalist expansion and industrialisation in more or less backward societies: they are 'solutions' to those crises imposed by force, which do not allow for the establishment of a negotiated and ongoing equilibrium of political forces within the state. Once established, these régimes claim to be the only viable and legitimate form of government and proceed to eliminate any movement or ideology which locates itself outside the ideological sphere within which they exist or which may challenge the class and corporate privileges which they serve.

Given the specific imperatives of the political culture of our age all modern despotic régimes must – in contrast with those of the past – try to represent certain wishes and aspirations present in the wider society. They cannot for long limit themselves to only defending the interests of the classes and groups which they serve. Thus, they must all have an explicit programme of social reforms, industrialisation, education, and improvements in the service and economic infrastructure. In other words, purely reactionary and obscurantist régimes are only partially possible now, for all modern despotic solutions must attempt to carry out some sort of partial (or even relatively far-reaching) 'revolution from above' even if it remains extremely circumscribed and is haltingly carried out, that is, even if it never becomes a proper substantial reform, let alone a genuine revolution.

These common characteristics notwithstanding, modern despotic régimes appear in different guises. There seem to be at least three varieties which are particularly relevant here. They may be defined thus:

(i) Autocratic Despotisms. They stem from the access to power of a notable or a military chief in countries with very low levels of modern organisation, which had resulted in serious confusion in the state administration. The weakness of the latter may be substituted by the barely disguised 'tribal' or ethnic arbitrary rule of one section of the society over the rest. This usually occurs through troops or police personally loyal to the autocrat. General Amin's Uganda illustrates this case.

(ii) Social-nationalist Despotisms. For want of a better name, we may call social-nationalist despotisms those régimes which arise from an alliance between military and certain 'progressive' sectors with a view to creating an autonomous 'anti-imperialist' state based on nationalism, and therefore on some components of the traditional culture, such as religious faith. The ruling groups assume the representation of the population at large *vis-à-vis* the privileged classes, which may be allowed to continue thriving in a number of cases. Naguib's, but more appropriately, Nasser's Egypt, provides an example.

(iii) Reactionary Despotisms. These are régimes which consolidate themselves after a forceful interruption of democratic political processes which were seen as leading towards a profound modification of society, entailing the elimination of traditionally dominant strata and groups. Spain after 1939 and Chile after 1974 are illustrations of this mode of domination.

Reactionary Despotism

Reactionary despotic régimes have been or are quite common in semi-peripheral societies and semi-developed ones. Chile, Argentina and Brazil are outstanding cases in Latin America. Countries on the fringe of industrial Europe – Poland, Hungary, Greece, Portugal and Spain – have also had reactionary dictatorships before the Second World War. Again, Greece, Spain and Portugal have had such régimes for diverse periods after the war. The case of Italy is not entirely exceptional if we recall that its fascism had certain 'weak' aspects which brought it closer to the other European examples.

If the exact nature of the reactionary despotic state (and its mode of domination) is to be thrown into sharp relief, it seems interesting to distinguish carefully between its features and those of totalitarian régimes, especially those with a reactionary, i.e., fascist, bent. Totalitarian régimes exercise their power from one single hegemonic centre which claims the complete monopoly of authority within their area of domination. Power, in totalitarian régimes, is conceived in zero sum terms: any non-recognised political group which stands outside its sphere of authority is seen as proportionally and illegally diminishing the status or power of the state. (In fact, any civic or voluntary association may be defined as a hostile political group.) Such groups are therefore seen as threats and systematically suppressed, annihilated or effectively neutralised. Under totalitarianism the fear of the autonomy of non-controlled groups and associations, coupled with a conspiratorial view of social relations leads to their incompatibility with the institution of privacy as a civil right. As we shall see, these characteristics are also present, though in a much more diminished and *ad hoc* way, in non-totalitarian forms of despotic rule, but they are used quite differently by them.

In totalitarian states the sovereign corporation is not the state, but the party. The relative (but considerable) autonomy of the party *vis-à-vis* other corporations (the army) and the state itself, but also the social classes, is one of the chief traits of totalitarianism. Dictatorships of the kind analysed here, by contrast, are far more class-bound: very often the modern despotic state is simply a dictatorship of the bourgeoisie through the military. Likewise, totalitarian states engage in the institutionalised mobilisation of the population via parties, propaganda, local activist cells, schools, youth organisations, and every conceivable form of guided indoctrination and enforced active participation. This is something modern despotic régimes usually avoid, though they may try to put it into practice at times, in a very limited manner, till the leaders realise that it is a dangerous course of action which can jeopardise the continuation of their rule. We shall look into this in greater detail in a moment, for it is a crucial feature of modern reactionary despotism.

The basic features of reactionary despotic régimes and, to a great extent, of the states whose power they embody seem to be the following:

(i) Class Domination. Reactionary despotism is a mode of class domination brought about by a reactionary coalition.[6] Régimes which follow its pattern inevitably claim to represent everyone's

interests – hence their recourse to populistic nationalism as a means for the control of the collective means of emotional production[7] – but are from the start entrusted with the preservation of the interests of the reactionary coalition. Usually they pave the way for a furthering of the process of capital accumulation and the development of capitalism according to the wishes of the ruling classes, though this last aspect of the régime soon comes into difficulties when confronted by other, equally important government imperatives. At any rate, these régimes neutralise the working-classes and other groups (such as dissident intellectuals and students) so that internal peace within a reactionary order is assured. Usually the reactionary coalition – landowners, industrialists, financiers – controls the state through the army, whose highest echelons are amply rewarded. The key office of chief of state and a large part of the government are often given over to the military.

Given the great complexity of the tasks to be confronted by government in a modern society, and the basic need for ample alliances with other subordinate classes – such as the middle strata – the government of the reactionary coalition assures the centralised control of the entire political and administrative apparatus in its intermediate and lower rungs with a *service class*[8] drawn from a relatively wide section of the population. The easy recruitment and solid loyalty of this 'class' is assured by the backward or semi-developed nature of the economy: job security, a steady income, health and medical advantages are even more highly valued in those societies than in more prosperous ones, where 'welfare state' policies are more successfully institutionalised.

Modern despotic régimes, therefore, combine traditional class domination with a tight control of the public administration, an efficient distribution of state rewards and a fairly adequate neutralisation – not involving mobilisation – of the subordinate classes. All this means that they can neither be seen as mere reflections of a mode of production (or even of an articulation of modes into a complex whole) nor as mere tools of the ruling classes. Each despotic state is, of course, partly a 'tool' of that nature, but the vested interests of the institutions and corporations on which it has to rely become structural constraints at the level of domination, i.e., limitations on power and orientations for policy stemming from the makeup of the régime itself. For these reasons modern despotic régimes and their states are among the most important structuring agents of the societies over which they rule. Once established they generate and maintain definite patterns of opportunity, occupation, inequality and recruitment which cannot be explained solely by the mere presence of inherited class structures nor by the dynamics of market trends, capital accumulation and other aspects of the economy. Once again, the intensity of their capacity to influence the social structure is less than that of totalitarian states. In fact, in the latter, the party is a central institution of power, privilege and class, whereas in the former (when it exists) it is secondary to the ruling class coalition: hence the reason why modern despotisms can more easily dismantle their party, police and 'trade union' façades and give way to other historically or economically more adequate political arrangements.

(ii) Restricted Ideological Sphere and Limited Political Pluralism. In so far as a coalition of different ruling classes differentially but firmly represents each one of them at the centres of political power it is to be expected that the officially sanctioned ideological spectrum will also include ideological components from each class. Likewise, the official ideological amalgam will explicitly exclude the ideologies and values of all the subordinate classes and outlawed parties and movements. (Some rhetorical concessions, however, will have to be made to 'democracy', the 'common good' and other notions.) This exclusion will entail a sustained and virulent propagandist attack on one main culprit (and its 'allies') whose progress is said to have been arrested by the establishment of the dictatorship. The culprit is usually 'communism', invariably not only the permanent scapegoat of reactionary despotism but also the convenient label attached to any liberal, socialist, separatist, or simply democratic opponents of the régime.

These régimes possess a syncretic ideological substratum, ranging from fundamentalist fascism to ultramontane monarchical legitimism from which the dictator and the government can freely choose at every political juncture. In fact, one of the main tasks of the Chief of State is to establish the successively adequate balances within the amalgam and to emphasise each one of its aspects according to time and place. One of the most arduous is to produce a convincing doctrine in terms of a reconciliation between the essentially reactionary nature of the régime and the rhetorically (and in some ways not so rhetorically) officially acknowledged aspirations of the subordinate classes.

A very limited but qualitatively highly important degree of political pluralism corresponds to all this: it is a political pluralism restricted to the ruling classes, factions and movements of the reactionary coalition, which is made extensive to the political employees of the régime – political police, propaganda personnel, single-party members, high civil servants, and the like – though these must also show the highest degree of discipline and subservience to the Chief of State at all times.

(iii) State Control Through the Service Classes. The victorious reactionary coalition inherits the state administration but is forced to set up a number of institutions of repression, economic development, welfare and education in order to govern, as the traditional Bonapartist straight military-bourgeois dictatorship can no longer be successfully implemented under contemporary conditions.

All associations and movements not sanctioned by the government are outlawed, excluded, or suffer a tight surveillance on the part of the forces of repression and manipulation. Non-organised individuals and people not stigmatised with a political past, in fact, the majority, are left alone in their enjoyment of property, the carrying out of private business, and their search for employment. Cautious non-interference with vast areas of social life thus becomes the hallmark of modern despotic régimes, coupled with a keen protection and encouragement of recognised 'apolitical' institutions such as the 'orthodox' national church and other associations devoted to the control of the means of emotional production, especially of those geared towards popular distraction and the sponsorship of patriotic notoriety in sport.

State power is thus implemented through the service classes. They legitimate the régime and its members are given, in return, the intermediate rungs in the diverse chains of authority. Part of the personnel in these 'classes' may not directly belong to the state apparatus, as tends to happen with the religious legitimisers of the traditional order upheld by the reactionary government: mullahs, priests, popes. (Perhaps lack of perfect integration and a greater access to popular aspirations makes the latter more prone to deserting the régime, as witness the behaviour of the Spanish priesthood in the late stages of Francoism or that of the shi'ite mullahs in Iran under the last Shah.) At any rate, the loyal service classes do not penetrate all the levels of the civil society: given the ultimately non-totalitarian nature of these states, certain degrees of tolerance or indifference to their life is to be expected. Thus their vigilance and use of institutionalised violence and terror is selective. It applies to suspects and 'trouble-makers', real or potential. But neither violence nor terror (especially torture) tend to be applied indiscriminately to the whole society. The political formula of any successful modern despotic régime includes the 'live and let live' tenet of traditional despotism as a very essential unwritten rule of existence.

(iv) Political Co-optation and Passive Obedience. All this means that recruitment into the sphere of state employment tends to be more on pragmatic than on ideological grounds, especially after the first phases of consolidation are over. Members of the service classes – mayors of towns, high and middling civil servants, university professors – may be asked to express allegiance to the official doctrine, yet, what is decisive is their personal loyalty to the chief or arbiter of the reactionary coalition and their explicit promise not to question the legitimacy of the political arrangement.

This sort of allegiance finds its counterpart in the selective form of repression just pointed out. The latter blocks the way to political participation for the perennial *classes dangereuses* – workers, students – and aggravates discrimination against ethnic, religious and national minorities, while avoiding unnecessary harassment of 'well-behaved' and 'law-abiding' citizens. The tight control of the mass media and the strict censorship of public opinion makes these tasks easier. Yet, it is important to stress that the entire repressive apparatus of the modern despotic state is geared towards obtaining the passive obedience of the subordinate majority rather than, as already indicated, its active mobilisation. Large scale militancy, even in favour of the régime, is avoided. Public occasions of multitudinous support are often arranged on special occasions, but tend to be as orderly and ritualised as possible.

No doubt, other features could be added to the ones pointed out here. Yet, perhaps the above, interrelated, characteristics suffice to give us a picture of what these régimes and their states entail. The picture is, however, incomplete, as nothing has been said about the historical patterns of change which can be detected in them. We have also ignored certain national varieties. Thus, in some countries a savage and apparently capricious repression by the political police takes place over a long period of time against suspects of all sorts (Brazil, Chile, Argentina) while in others (Spain) the physical elimination of the democratic enemy occurred during the Civil War and the following, less publicised bloodbath. This allowed for a long period of peace, where the traumas of war and political extermination made passive obedience much easier to implement. Ultimately, as a paradox, such traumas also make the transition to a pluralist polity easier, by virtue of a generalised desire to avoid the horrors of civil warfare, still in living memory. Such memory, however, may not be a sufficient deterrent for those classes, ethnic minorities and active democrats for whom hardly any truce or letup in the harshness of despotic domination is granted over the dictatorial period.

The Despotic State

Francoism and Class Domination

During the Francoist dictatorship (1939–77) Spain presented very clearly the elements of the model just described. Political authority was monopolised by one person, General Franco, who gave his name to the period. He was head of state, Prime Minister, chief of the armed forces, and chief of the reactionary-fascist political coalition called the National Movement. (In fact, he personally forced the fascist Falange to fuse with the right-wing legitimist and ultramontane Carlists into this single party.) He owed allegiance only to God and History, as he himself tellingly put it, and not to the people.

This extreme personal dictatorship was, however, set up by a military insurrection backed from the start by highly conservative and reactionary elements in the ruling classes. This is not the place to go into the question of the origins of the Spanish Civil War, though the well-known rally of the right-wing forces behind the army in order to stop the progressive advance of democracy, agrarian reform, further secularisation, and other such progressive trends may be the starting point of our analysis. A military victory with the help of mercenary Moroccans, 'active' non-interventionist Western powers and unflagging German and Italian fascist support, among other favourable factors, was forthcoming after three years of fighting against the popular forces. Thus victory through war became a perfect pretext for the liquidation of anything that smacked of republicanism and democracy. Policies – for instance, agrarian reform – which appeared to be closely linked to the vanquished Republic were shelved forever. Since such policies and reform programmes were invariably directed towards the redistribution of wealth and the creation of a socially less oppressive and more egalitarian Spain it is obvious that the war was won by the traditional ruling classes. They now had a dictator at their service though they found themselves landed with many overenthusiastic fascists who demanded autarchic state control of the economy, a 'national-syndicalist revolution' and a 'corporate' state along the path so successfully opened by the Germans and the Italians.

The fascist component, however, was never the backbone of the régime and never, not even during the first years of the Second World War, managed to 'fascistise' the state, let alone society. The Nazis might have been able to drive out the Prussian military establishment and slowly substitute it with their own men but for obvious reasons Falangist penetration of the Spanish army was a dismal failure: the Falange were given the Ministry of Labour (including the fascist 'vertical trade unions'), large slices of the propaganda, press and administrative apparatuses, and a chance to enrich themselves with impunity through the practice of widespread cleptocracy, municipal corruption, and the spoils of war. These rewards soon dampened their 'revolutionary' fascist fervour and domesticated them very effectively: every time the government took an 'anti-fascist' measure Falangists kept quiet. Some of their innovations, nevertheless, have remained to this day, as in Italy, quite untouched. Thus, autarchic policies created the INI (*Instituto Nacional de Industria*) and introduced state capitalist enterprise. It was easy to do away with import substitution policies when 'liberalisation' came in the late fifties, but not with the gigantic industrial plants set up by INI with Spanish state capital. (This was, of course, obtained through familiar modes of violent accumulation: salaries were frozen, strikes were banned, and the working-classes – especially the peasantry, the producers of the necessary agrarian surplus – were very efficiently repressed for a good two decades, if not three.)

From the beginning the government faithfully reflected the ruling-class components of the reactionary coalition. Though fluctuations in its social composition have been noticed[9] these are far from random. The Francoist régime at governmental level was a finely tuned compromise of factions. Apart from the military, law-and-order generals, and Falangist middle-class *arrivistes* and demagogues, it almost invariably contained right-wing monarchists, traditionalist Carlists, members of the extremely conservative Catholic Association, the ACNP (*Asociación Católica Nacional de Propagandistas*) and later, of another, more 'technocratic', 'modern' and semi-secret Catholic association, the Opus Dei. None dominated the government completely. Yet, together they made up a complex political class which faithfully represented the industrial, financial and land-owning oligarchies of the country and which was very often drawn from their narrow ranks. The long duration of the régime allowed for an important development directly connected with the domination of the state by the right-wing coalition: the slow coalescence of the several ruling classes and corporate groups (the Andalusian *latifundio* landlords, the military, the Catalan industrial bourgeoisie, the Basque financial and industrial bourgeoisie, and others) into one single 'national' upper class. Spain was, and still is, a country with a variety of social structures, but Francoism finally created one single ruling class, and finally put an end to the traditional clashes between the different local interests of each sectorial or regional ruling class. This occurred both through continued imperative co-ordination by the Chief of State himself and also through forty years of undisturbed rule, during which improvements in communication, the consolidation of a more modern 'single' economy for the whole country, and industrial expansion to areas hitherto only rural took place. All this must, of course, be seen against the background of important transformations in the social structure of Spain, which cannot be entered into here.[10]

Francoist Ideology and Restricted Political Pluralism

The ideological syncretism and pragmatism characteristic of modern despotic régimes found in Francoism one of its most paradigmatic expressions. The essentially *ad hoc* and highly realistic dimension of the ideological amalgam allowed it to adapt with ease to constantly changing conditions, both external and internal. This had led some to claim wrongly that it lacked an ideology in the strict sense of the term. In fact, the core tenets of Francoism hardly changed through time. They ranged from the notion that the Catholic religion was the ultimate identity of the Spanish nation (Spain being the country which best expressed the Christian virtues of sacrifice and militant proselytism) to the affirmation that its people were the 'spiritual reserve and defence' of an embattled West, its last bastion against Communist barbarism. The Manichean view that Spain – i.e., Francoist Spain – stood, indeed, led, the forces of Good against the forces of Evil (Free Masons, Communists, Atheists, Liberals) was a key feature of ideological Francoism. Other key features had to be clumsily touched-up or qualified in the course of time. Thus, when the 'corrupt democracies' of the forties – England, France and the United States – became uneasy friends but good allies during the Cold War years, Spain had to be redefined as the misunderstood bulwark of Western civilisation. (The similarities with South Africa are more than formal in this respect, while the Salazarist line in neighbouring Portugal was identical during the same decade.) After 1945, accordingly, traditional rhetorical fascist attacks on bankers and capitalists were suppressed, while the régime was re-baptised as an 'organic democracy' based on 'the overcoming of the class struggle through nationalist solidarity, hierarchy and order'.

Not only changes in ideological emphasis and content were noticeable but also, and perhaps more importantly, a slackening of the efforts made by the rulers to penetrate society through indoctrination. At first they believed that successful popular indoctrination through the official political ideology was necessary for the maintenance of the labour repressive economic system[11] of workers and peasants on which domination rested. Later, however, this was given up in exchange for sheer popular subservience and apolitical behaviour. The same shift in attitude could be observed in the universities, for a long time favourite targets of Francoist indoctrination. After a long and complicated series of confrontations the government abandoned further attempts at mobilisation and asked only for good 'hard-working' students. Later, as the situation deteriorated, it even acknowledged the *de facto* existence of a democratic ('Marxist') counter-culture in the ever-expanding student world. The government found no other solution to this than throwing a *cordon sanitaire* around it.[12] In fact, as the years went by and the legitimacy of the régime began to crumble even among those over whom it had established itself, the Francoist ideology shrank to defensive positions and vague justifications about the value of peace, tradition and, above all, the economic prosperity supposedly brought about only by virtue of the prolonged dictatorship of General Franco.

The muddled defensiveness and apologetics of the Franco government in its late stages recalls those of other despotisms, such as Greece under the colonels after 1967 or Portugal under the Caetano phase of Salazarism. In Spain the hesitations of the government helped the democratic movement to become bolder and more articulate. Government 'concessions' – such as its appeal to the obscure notion of a 'well-ordered competition of different criteria', i.e., different varieties of Francoism being allowed simultaneously – only emphasised the stark limitations of the political situation. That is, in our own terms, the régime's confused ideological withdrawal into official euphemisms only came to prove the severely restricted nature of the class pluralism the autocratic government was ready to permit. It was clear that once the hegemonic classes were to find this authoritarianism unacceptable for their own situation under the new economic and political conditions, they would begin to try to extricate themselves from the régime and turn in search of a new political formula for their continued domination. This they did in due course.

The State Apparatus and the Implementation of Domination

The ruling classes of Francoism were always in full ultimate control of the state apparatus. By contrast, and precisely because Francoism was not a totalitarian régime, the service classes and their bureaucracies had only delegated power. Hence, when the final crisis of the régime began to loom on the horizon the latter were not in a position to put up any serious resistance against the change of will of the hegemonic classes. Accordingly, after 1976 the political service personnel had to choose between conversion to parliamentary democracy and militancy into extreme right-wing or neo-fascist minority parties. A third possibility, especially for the lower ranks and the less adventurous, opened up: mere superannuation and the enjoyment of sinecures with full pay after certain ministries, notably that of the 'corporatist' fascist trade unions, were quietly dismantled. This possibility was, in fact, taken up by thousands of civil servants. However, a great number of higher civil servants of a new Francoist generation, who had risen within the Falange or in the inner circles of the Francoist state apparatus, went to form the UCD (*Unión de Centro Democrático*), the large conservative party in power since 1977, itself led by Sr Adolfo Suárez, an ex-Falangist and high dignitary of Franco's National Movement. Ideological change and continued enjoyment of political privilege was thus a smooth, uneventful and swift operation.

If ultimate and direct control rested on a Chief of State who consistently and unwaveringly ruled in favour of the reactionary coalition and its social classes, everyday political control was fully exercised through the institutions manned by the service classes of Francoism. Very briefly, these were the following:

(i) Institutions of Political Repression. The so-called 'Social-political Brigade' or political police in charge of the persecution of democratic movements and of the selective (and often not so selective) use of terror and torture was effective enough. In this it was helped by the massive repression and physical annihilation of republicans and democrats carried out by the government in the early post-war years, whose figures are staggering by any standard.[13] Given the relatively strong presence of the fascist organisation and that of other collateral

supports, however, the political police was on the whole less pervasive than other similar bodies elsewhere. Thus in Spain, when the régime ended, the political police did not become *the* target of liberation nor the chief symbol of popular oppression as did PIDE in Portugal in 1974 and SAVAK in Iran in 1979, though people were fully aware of its importance for the maintenance of Francoism as an ongoing political system.

The Civil Guard in the rural areas and the Armed Police in the urban ones were – and still are – paramilitary forces in charge of the maintenance of law and order. That, under Francoism, meant their constant use for political purposes. The Civil Guard was commanded, like its counterpart, by military officers, and was entrusted with the specific task of suppressing guerilla activity. In the 1947–62 period this was either Communist or anarchist inspired. Later it was carried on by the Basque separatist movement ETA. After 1973 urban terrorist groups, such as FRAP and GRAPO were also active. However, these two last ill-defined groups, whose motivations and ideologies, let alone their support, still remain unclear, should not be understood only as straight consequences of Francoism. They find important contemporary parallels in Germany, Italy, and Northern Ireland and perhaps require other, much wider, sociological explanations. At any rate, the paramilitary forces, and especially the Armed Police, were used throughout the duration of the régime, and very especially during its last years, as a force for the violent suppression of the mildest peaceful demonstrations and political gatherings. Their proverbial and often random violence went unabated in the Basque country well after the end of Francoism. This, together with the failure of the new régime to find sufficient legitimation in that sensitive area now poses one of the most serious threats to its consolidation as a parliamentary democracy.

(ii) Institutions of Economic Control. A number of state and para-state institutions were formally set up after 1939 with the official purpose of protecting or developing either weak or non-existent areas of the economy. Their chief function, however, was to serve the interests of the several components of the reactionary coalition. Their development corresponds as much to the successive economic con-junctures as to the political composition of the government. Thus, the early, more 'fascist' stages of Francoism saw the growth of autarchic policies and a relatively serious attempt at establishing a 'fascist' economy. Its most important result was the giant INI (*Instituto*

Nacional de Industria). Not unlike IRI, its Italian counterpart, INI has survived the régime that created it and represents the emergence, in Spain, of large-scale state-owned enterprise as well as of massive state investment and capitalism. At first, the political links of INI with the National Movement cadres gave the latter an easy ground for employment and personal advancement. Later, when greater efficiency was required, INI also became a venue for the growth of a new state bourgeoisie[14] whose 'apolitical' pretences were often belied by their Opus Dei or similar ideological allegiances. Likewise, the intense dominant-class nature of a great many allegedly 'egalitarian' state economic organisations, especially those linked to the agrarian sector is well documented:[15] invariably they benefited first and foremost the great landlords, local political bosses, high civil servants, as well as industrialists, investors and bankers.

The moment of victory in 1939, followed by the Second World War allowed the government to pursue a dual policy of state capitalism *and* protection of private industry and banking, forcing the more *laissez-faire* protectionist bourgeoisie to accept state intervention and monopolistic practices. By the time the private sector felt strong enough to curb the 'excessive' powers of the 'fascist' state (in 1959) the economic institutions created by the latter were too powerful to be dismantled. The same could be said of the welfare services developed by the state as one of its more solid claims for legitimacy. Thus, by the early sixties no one dared to propose a return to a non-welfare, non-investing, merely protectionist and law-and-order state.

(iii) Institutions of Ideological Legitimation. Despite its innate weariness of intense mobilisation, the Spanish form of modern despotism needed a minimum of ideological 'vitality' and even fervour at some points to generate enough legitimation. This was naturally provided by the anti-Marxist crusading spirit of the 'militant Church', the great-nation right-wing populism – made up of nostalgic imperial notions of Castilian hegemony – and, of course, the fascism of the Falange. However, as the fortunes of the Second World War began to turn against Franco's allies, the more moderate and, by far, much stronger forces of the reactionary coalition began to have the upper hand. The clerical-nationalist, anti-democratic ideological amalgam which characterised Francoist Spain for most of the time was supported by the Church and its organisations, which were given official sanction and thus became the central pillars of systematic legitimation through indoctrination, education and propaganda. A

vast exercise in desecularisation took place, not entirely successful in its early stages, though utterly impotent against other trends after the late sixties. Some of these trends – further secularisation, changes in mores, the penetration of alternative ideologies, such as Marxism, the growth of industrialism, hedonism, 'consumerism', and the like – were often, interestingly enough, fostered by the régime itself in its efforts at achieving economic success.

The belated, though in some ways remarkable, support given by certain sectors of the Church to the democratic anti-Francoist movement can be quite easily linked to structural crises in the Church itself (empty seminaries, pre- and post-Vatican Council renewal movements, and so on) rather than to any inherent ecclesiastical potential against the régime. With the noticeable exception of the Basque country, and, to a very limited extent, Catalonia, the Spanish church was thoroughly Francoist, and it was rewarded accordingly by the régime.

(iv) Institutions of Ideological Neutralisation. Much more diffuse than the above, these institutions were nevertheless vital for the maintenance of despotic class rule. In Spain they ranged from youth organisations (openly fascist in character) to rural 'television clubs' (in the early stages of this medium, in the sixties). They were all aimed at keeping the populace busy with 'healthy and wholesome' pursuits as apolitical as possible. These, however, came second to football and bullfights, both highly government-sponsored mass shows. The apparently erratic and whimsical censorship was a more overtly political support of the system. Though aimed at society in general it was clearly and specifically directed against the intellectuals, by keeping a tough and relentless grip throughout the period on works of a literary, cinematographic or artistic kind, and also against the workers and the students by a permanent ban on any non-government controlled or explicitly unacceptable publications.

(v) The Legal and Political Façade. This large, baroque and complicated network of wholly subservient institutions needs no detailed description here. They ranged from the utterly parasitical – such as the Cortes, or Francoist Parliament, an entirely unrepresentative body – to the politically-run courts of justice, especially the notorious 'public order' courts. The social composition of these bodies faithfully reflected the class nature of the régime.[16] They possessed no autonomy from these classes, and predictably evaporated when the régime came to an end, leaving no trace.

(vi) The Educational System. Modern reactionary dictatorships must all solve the delicate problem of underpinning the system of class domination and its reproduction and yet make them compatible with the capitalist world system of which they are part and parcel, i.e., make them compatible with its general dynamics, and innovative processes in the fields of technology and production of goods and services. No matter how subordinate and 'dependent' they may be within the hierarchy of capitalist states and international alliances they cannot avoid involvement with the 'development' ethos. They must be seen to 'modernise' and 'develop'. A point is soon reached when sheer state capitalism and public investment cannot occur without parallel expansion in education at all levels. By and large the Francoist régime attempted to cope with this problem by a traditionalistic reinforcement of the already existing highly prestigious élite engineering schools together with a closed university system, building alongside them a number of lesser technical schools for the middle management and technicians. These were open to the children of the lower middle classes and to a limited extent to those of the skilled workers as well.

The situation was under severe strain by the mid-sixties, however, when structural changes and economic growth were felt in earnest throughout the society. It was then that the government pinned its hopes on the 'development without democratisation' ideology of the Opus Dei 'technocrats', a Catholic faction which offered 'apoliticism' and economic growth without social upheavals in exchange for power. The strains and contradictions of this component of the implementation of domination apparatus soon became very acute. Hence, its partial breakdown predates the actual collapse of the régime by a long time.[17]

(vii) The Army. Within our conceptual scheme, the army is not just another service class though it is certainly the backbone of the despotic mode of domination. Having thrown in its lot with the system of inequality embodied in the hegemonic classes and pledged to its defence, it rises up when threatened by a real or apparently revolutionary régime. In the case of Spain, this was the 1931 Republic and, more particularly, the 1936 'popular front' government. The very diversity of interests of the several ruling classes making up the reactionary coalition gave the commanders of the army the power of imperative co-ordination and the express task of 'putting the house in order'. The Chief of State's dictatorial powers stemmed from this, as much as from the need to impose a 'martial outlook' on a society which was now seen as divided, chaotic and decadent.

Just as the army is not just another service class – for it has a substantial and direct share in the supreme power of the state – it does not participate either in the system of restricted class pluralism. In Spain associations for the corporate defence of army interests, army pressure groups and lobbies, vanished as soon as the uprising against the Republic took place, and were never permitted thereafter. The only exception that can be made to this generalisation that the army was not a service class of the régime nor one of its ruling classes, but some sort of institutional, corporate linchpin, is the fact that in the distribution of spoils, a great many officers were co-opted to serve as higher civil servants, ministers, provincial governors, and so on. Yet, they were never put there to infiltrate the civilian world, but rather as a normal consequence of the distribution of rewards in a highly militarised society. Another significant illustration of the peculiar position of the army is that, when the final break came, it was carried out with its permission, and largely under its supervision. Its men did not have to redeploy themselves or vanish like the members of the National Movement and its collateral organisations. They simply stayed in their army, and watched. In exchange for this they were given special guarantees, as we shall see, about their status and rôle in any future political system.

With these remarks about the army we may finish our cursory look at the Francoist state, although well aware that a number of important problems have not been dealt with. For one thing, though constant references have been made to the different moments in the history of the régime, we have not spelled out its different stages, much less attempted to draw up an adequate periodisation. For clarity's sake we have treated it practically as one historical unit. In some ways, of course, it was that: practically the same people held supreme power throughout the period, while rising factions (the Opus Dei) or slowly declining ones (the Falange) were so clearly linked to the mode of class domination as a whole that our interpretation does not suffer much from the necessary oversimplifications entered into thus far.

The Parliamentary State

The Spanish Path to Advanced Capitalist Development

Not only the victory of the reactionary forces in 1939, but also Western allied non-intervention after 1945 meant that Francoism as a political system was there to stay.[18] Its lifespan coincided with one of the longest and most profound cycles of capitalist prosperity which took place precisely in the countries with which Spain was most intimately connected economically, culturally and in other important ways, such as its sheer accessibility for the employment of migrant labourers, foreign capital, mass tourism and short-distance easy transport for imported and exported goods. It is obvious that by themselves these extremely favourable conditions – all of them external to Francoism itself – cannot enable a country to enter the metropolitan area of the world capitalist economy. If anything, they may increase dependence, hinder a well-balanced and varied industrialisation process, and create urban poverty and other evils.

In the case of Spain, however, they occurred in a country whose industrial base and economic infrastructure, let alone its educational and technological level though backward by, say, Scandinavian or British standards were even in 1939, not those of a typical 'underdeveloped society'. The chances for a passage from 'periphery', and especially 'semi-periphery', into 'core' are high and real when countries possess the characteristics Spain managed to acquire during the decades leading up to the Civil War. This fact alone, however, even perhaps in combination with the favourable international conditions just mentioned, would never have brought Spain into the central area of industrial capitalism. For semi-peripheral societies to do that it is necessary that their states play a very specific rôle.

This rôle varies according to the nature of the government in power and may lead to state capitalism and a totalitarian socialist order, as in the case of the Soviet Union, or it may lead to full incorporation into an oligopolistic, multi-national corporate economy within a political framework of supranational alliances (NATO, EEC, European Parliament, etc.) and a parliamentarian polity, as has occurred in Italy and Spain. In all cases it is clear that the function of the state in forcing the capitalist transformation or at least in speeding up sluggish, pre-existing tendencies, is decisive. The state alone, by a combination of protectionism and the introduction of a labour-repressive economic system, together with accelerated technical education, can create the internal markets and the adequate conditions for the 'shift to core'. A detailed account of the processes involved cannot be given here[19] but it is obvious that, in the case of Spain, once the 'state socialist solution' was ruled out by the outcome of the war – and also incidentally the 'libertarian path' which in that country was, at least, initiated – the only remaining alternative was reactionary stagnation or reactionary development. The Franco régime, by the devices pointed out in the above discussion – state capitalism, import substitution, protectionism, labour repression in countryside and city, and so on – created the basis for the latter.

Once this basis was consolidated, international investment, the opening up of the country to the inflow and outflow of capital, and a general drive to 'liberalisation' and even to a limited extent privatisation of capital took place. The phenomenal growth of the 1959–71 period could not mean that Spain was to join the league of highly developed nations as a fully independent power, since the nature of modern international capitalism excludes this pre-First World War pattern altogether. It meant, more modestly, a high rate of participation in a higher standard of living, high wages, full integration in the networks of multinational corporation industries, a notable – though often unmentioned – degree of Spanish private investment abroad both in the 'Third World' and in the industrialised world, and other similar phenomena. The precise place of the Spanish economy within the world's advanced economy cannot be described in a few lines, especially as it is now in an intense phase of restructuration, painfully shedding the remnants of the familistic property patterns which still characterised it in the late sixties. Suffice it to say that its problems – unemployment, inflation, further automation followed by lay-offs, decline in production in many fields – seem largely to be those of the developed, industrialised world.[20] In a restricted, but significant sense, it is wrong to speak of a 'Spanish' economy in the same way as it is now wrong to speak of any 'national' economy in the highly integrated Western capitalist metropolitan area.

The Political Readaptation of the Ruling Classes

There is no natural, ideal 'fit' between a given social structure and a political constitution. If anything, we have shown that the bourgeoisie may opt for forms of autocratic and anti-parliamentarian rule as the most adequate solution to its continued hegemony. Yet, it seems clear that at certain stages of economic development it may choose the vast negotiating process entailed by the liberal political framework as the best way for furthering its interests. In this context, it is interesting to note that in Spain, still without having switched their allegiance to a representative, multi-party system, the members of the industrial bourgeoisie were already moving towards unofficial collective bargaining and negotiation with the clandestine unions at a very early stage, bypassing the official channels. This started to happen as soon as wage settlements through peaceful means began to look more attractive than outright repression, from the late fifties onwards. The rise of collective bargaining between management and labour was also the beginning of the conversion of the industrialists to what they themselves called the 'Western political model'.

This change in attitude, together with vast socio-structural changes, cultural transformations – the rise of new subcultures, secularisation, the spread of new political creeds – precipitated the final loss of identity of the political formula of Francoism. The event had been heralded by the muddled defensiveness we have already pointed out, so characteristic of its late stages. Even certain sectors of the service classes – formerly highly loyal to the Chief of State and all he stood for – began to ask for the introduction of restricted democratic measures. Meanwhile, the most important legitimating body, the Church, had begun its orderly and skilful withdrawal of support. These trends were fully apparent after 1969.

The degree of autonomy gained by the dictator himself was so considerable, however, that he was able to prepare, unchallenged, the continuation of despotic rule through the nomination of Prince Juan Carlos, as successor (bypassing his father, as heir to the Spanish crown) having obtained his repeated and public commitment to the so-called Fundamental Laws of the State, i.e., to Francoism without Franco. All the dictator was prepared to accept was a very minor degree of constitutional cosmetics – the setting up of 'political associations' utterly loyal to the régime and explicitly hostile to any political multi-party system. Needless to say, such associations faithfully represented the restricted class pluralism which we have emphasised from the start. The political ineptitude of the last Francoist Prime Ministers, Carrero Blanco and Arias, however, was such, that the minimal reforms allowed by their leader were never successfully implemented. This made a Francoist reform wellnigh impossible.

When Franco died in November 1975 it was clear to a great many people of his political establishment – especially in the higher echelons of the service classes – that the powerful old guard of the régime were utterly incapable of establishing the 'Francoism without Franco' they themselves advocated, for even this needed some mild, but essential, technical reforms in the state structure. The eventual quiet defection of these far-sighted Francoists meant that the government and the old guard were left alone to confront the ever-growing democratic movement, increased labour unrest, guerrilla rebellion in the Basque country, and terrorism elsewhere. The emboldened opposition, which of course continued to be outlawed, gave political content to every demonstration, protest and rally. Demands for political amnesty, denunciations of police brutality and a wave of international popular support prompted by a series of summary executions and repeated states of emergency brought the crisis to a head in June 1976, when the last Francoist minister, Sr Arias, resigned.

His government was followed by that of Sr Adolfo Suárez, appointed by the king as someone whose Francoist credentials were immaculate but who was also committed to carefully dismantling the régime from inside, leaving the monarchical institution intact, the army as an unquestioned final arbiter of the situation, and the several groups and factions of the régime fully protected by whatever new system of legality was to be set up in the end. At this juncture the political skill of Don Juan Carlos and his mentor and adviser, Don Torcuato Fernández Miranda, played a crucial rôle. It would be foolish for any sociologist to ignore this personal and 'individualistic' dimension of the transition at that point. Sr Fernández Miranda implemented the Law of Political Reform (November 1976) and managed to present the monarch to a citizenry eager for change under a new image, as the very originator of political renewal and democracy (*motor del cambio*) and also as proof to the Francoist old guard and the most conservative sectors of the establishment that he guaranteed continuity, law and order. From then on two successive referenda and three general or local elections[21] produced, at a quick tempo, the necessary legal framework, which ruled out both the sheer continuation of the régime (*continuismo*) advocated by the extreme right and the democratic rupture (*ruptura democrática*) championed by the democrats. The latter notion had 'dangerously' begun to be embraced by an ever-growing circle of moderate democratic groups, which had become convinced that no real change could be expected from a recalcitrant and unimaginative government.

Through this delicate process the opposition obtained recognition (culminating with the legalisation of the Communist Party) as well as the basic liberal rights of assembly, freedom of opinion and organisation. In exchange, political parties had to accept a high degree of moderation in their demands. Thus no demands for justice that could even remotely appear as settlements of accounts between the two sides who fought the Civil War were to be made. The democratic parties had also to pledge not to question the privileges enjoyed by the universally and euphemistically called '*de facto* powers' (*poderes fácticos*) which included the army and a number of veto groups, such as high finance, nor to speak of the king himself and the monarchical institution. There was, thus, behind the 1978 Constitution (which is as liberal as any in the world) an unwritten pact whereby the army and the ex-Francoist Establishment promised non-intervention against the opposition in exchange for moderation on the part of the latter.[22]

Cleavage, Conflict and Legitimation Crisis in Spain's Future

Our analysis shows that the political metamorphosis which took place within the Spanish state from 1975 to 1978 entailed first and foremost the maintenance of the Francoist (or ex-Francoist) Establishment in power with all that implied in terms of class hegemony. Thus, the ruling party since the 1977 elections, Sr Suárez's UCD, is still over-whelmingly manned by the cadres of Francoism: Francoist provincial civil governors, under secretaries of state, dignitaries in ministries, 'technocrats' and highly-placed members of the now defunct National Movement bureaucracy. They all continue in power though their ideology is now conservative-parliamentarian. The specific mode of class domination has ceased to be despotic, so that the political forces which represent the upper classes, the state bourgeoisie, and other hegemonic sectors of society behave in a different way. They now have to obtain parliamentary approval for government programmes in the Cortes and have to make important concessions to public opinion. That they do this with obvious reluctance and imperfection can be put down to their long political socialisation under their former autocratic leader. This is understandably viewed with alarm by the left-wing opposition, whose tradition is republican. Yet, at some future date the UCD government may even by unseated through an election, though their unashamed control of the media and their manipulation of propaganda to their favour, together with their biased drawing of electoral constituencies has proved very effective so far. In the light of all this it is not surprising that some critics hold the erroneous view that post-1977 Spain is not very different politically from what it was earlier and that the new régime is fundamentally the same. Their judgement is marred by their simplistic reduction of the political to the class dimension of the social structure.

By contrast, the recognition that Spain now has an effective pluralist liberal constitution and that its citizens enjoy (with important qualifications as regards the rights of ethnic nationalities) the basic democratic rights of any other Western society, such as France or Great Britain, should not blind us to the specific characteristics of its situation, and the modes of conflict and domination which are now taking shape there. As they are directly related to the state and the strategies of the several political forces which work within its framework, we would like to conclude our exploration with a brief tentative comment on them.

The process of decomposition of any tyranny is frequently favourable for the growth of direct, if often ephemeral, forms of popular democracy. The last phase of the Franco régime saw the spontaneous formation of many grass-roots political movements, such as 'workers committees' (*comisiones obreras*), democratic committees, professional democratic associations and many other civic organisations. Some, like the Assembly of Catalonia, acquired very considerable proportions and posed a very serious threat to the legality of the government in a key and sensitive area of the country. Political parties, of course, were actively present in all these popular movements, and though accusations of 'manipulation' were soon raised against them, it is clear that they were for a long time controlled only by themselves. They helped create an enthusiasm for democracy and self-management (*autogestión*) which was reflected in the programmes of the parties and especially in the very high (nearly 80 per cent) popular turnout at the June 1977 elections. By contrast, the turnout at the December 1978 referendum was alarmingly low: by then the professionalisation of politics had, on the one hand, fully taken place and, on the other, the opposition parties of the left had embraced the social democratic path and settled for a 'social contract' on wages and unemployment with the government.

The professionalisation of politics, the deradicalisation of the Socialist and the Communist Parties – the former through its official abandonment of Marxism, the second of Leninism – and the acceptance of the democratic-parliamentary rules by the Francoist Establishment guaranteed the success of the new political formula. It is a formula which is in many ways identical to that which prevails in the rest of Western Europe. This is not a coincidence: given the stage reached by industry and the economy in general and the new social structure of Spain it is difficult to see how else its major political parties on the left could behave. The Communist Party, much smaller than the Socialist, but the third in size in the Cortes and powerful through its control of one of the chief trade unions, is a good illustration. Its leader, Don Santiago Carrillo, is one of the principal architects of Eurocommunism. He has taken his followers away from the programmatic 'dictatorship of the proletariat' (i.e., dictatorship of the party) into the public acceptance of political pluralism and parliamentarism. This decision may have been made because otherwise the party would have never acquired legal recognition but also because such is the accepted formula within the advanced Western European capitalist area of which Spain is now part. The alternative for Sr Carrillo's party would have been the loss of the crucial middle-class vote, a large part of the relatively well-off skilled worker's vote and that of other sectors supporting the reformist and moderate policies of his party. As in Italy and other 'comparable' countries, radicalism today means smallness and relegation. Yet, as in those countries, the deradicalisation of once revolutionary parties also means the frustration of many fundamentalist groups and even their resort to violence and extremism.

Paradoxically, perhaps the main political contradiction now taking shape in Spain is that which arises between the relatively autonomous organised political forces thriving within the framework of the state and the popular forces at work which, under the country's specific situation, fail to be adequately represented in it. Obviously this *décalage* exists even in the most democratic countries, but what is specific of Spain today is the excessive width of the gap, in many areas, between the two levels. On the one hand, the nature of the political reform, its limits, have accelerated the shift of all forces towards their integration into a 'corporate society' model of polity.[23] By this we do not mean any form of societal organisation reminiscent of fascist corporatism but rather something else; the hegemonic presence, in a society, of large political, economic and cultural corporations engaged in a constant and vast process of negotiations with each other, through which they share goods, allocate resources and manage their respective social constituencies. Again, the rise of corporatism is not a specifically Spanish phenomenon but rather a characteristic of the modern world in its present historical period, and is directly connected to other currents, such as further bureaucratisation and industrialisation, as well as the need for large-scale social control in the face of an excessive population, an energy crisis, and technologically advanced armed forces. However, this very rise (in a society such as Spain's a large part of whose social structures and certainly of its culture is still closely linked to its recent semiperipheral and 'backward' past) makes the tensions between what we may call the popular level and the corporate level highly acute.

We do not rule out the possibility that in the near future the large parties, the unions, the government, the multinational companies, and all the corporate groups now engaged in an intense, though clearly peaceful struggle for the establishment of boundaries and areas of influence within the newly acquired Spanish territory will manage to control or sufficiently neutralise the forces that now seem to escape them to a noticeable degree. That will depend on their strategies as much as on the final strength of these forces. Yet, it is clear that continued strife and perhaps even certain forms of open conflict will hardly be avoided. Yet in order to substantiate this very general point we must look at the evidence. Though it can be found in many areas of social life, it is particularly striking in those of nationalism, the labour movement, and political terrorism.

First, ethnic nationalism. Next to the 'dangers' of a socialist, libertarian, or communist revolution (the three appeared possible according to the right in 1936) the reactionary forces feared separatism, at the time confined to the two most distinct stateless nations of the society: Catalonia and the Basque country. In the past the irrational fear of 'national' dismemberment took hold of the deeply centralist right-wing (and also not so right-wing) political parties as a result of ancient prejudices, new misunderstandings and last, but not least, vested interests in the inherited machinery of the state structures. For these and other reasons the oppression of the national minorities, the destruction of whatever degree of home rule they managed to acquire before 1939, and a policy of systematic cultural genocide were part and parcel of the Francoist régime. Social conflict increases when cleavages and oppositions of a different nature superimpose one another: in the Basque country and Catalonia the humiliation of national pride compounded the enduring injuries of despotic rule and the suppression of age-old patterns of civility and local democracy which are so characteristic of those two small nations. For reasons which are not too difficult to explain, but that would require some space, the development of Catalan and Basque separatism under Franco and after has followed different paths: while the Catalans, honouring their long tradition for patient compromise and painstaking negotiation have secured the provisional restoration of their parliament, the Generalitat, and the return from exile of their president, Sr Josep Tarradellas to lead it, the Basque forces have been more divided, and therefore less successful at first in getting concessions from the central government. Some of the Basque political parties, and a large part of the Basque people, have opted for confrontation, maximalism, hardly disguised separatism and, for an important sector, guerrilla warfare against the central government. As if to prove that the Suárez administration is in some essential ways the true heir of Francoism, its treatment so far of the Basque problem has been politically disastrous, for wanton repression and indiscriminate police brutality have not ceased. This makes the usual comparisons with the Ulster problem utterly out of place.

The government 'solution' to de-localise the so-called nationalities problems by giving every historical region of Spain the same degree of autonomy and promising a certain degree of federalism within an essentially non-federal constitution is doomed to failure unless a sufficiently strong Statute of Autonomy is granted to the Catalans – who are showing a growing impatience with the mild concessions so far made – and a corresponding withdrawal of terror tactics occurs in the Basque country, followed by negotiation and the granting of real home rule based on the Guernica House of Assembly and a locally recruited police force.[24]

Secondly, precisely because Spain is at the bottom of the industrialised league and it lacks oil, coal or some other basic source of raw material the position of its working people is still highly vulnerable. Tourism and migrants' remittances are *not* Spain's North Sea Oil as some journalists are inclined to put it, because these are more subject to the fluctuations in the economic fortunes of other nations, as we have seen after 1973. When a recession or even a crisis occurs in the advanced metropolitan area the first countries to suffer nowadays are those which are weakest within it.

The Spanish working-classes possess a higher degree of independence from the large trade union federations (*centrales sindicales*) than their other European counterparts and the latter have had only a very short period to organise and spread in earnest under conditions of legality. At the moment of writing two unions (the anarchist CNT and the socialist USO) are not linked to a political party, though significantly, they are much smaller than the Communist CCOO and the Socialist Party's UGT, with whom both government and employers negotiate. A vast number of workers (blue and white collar) remain outside them, and tend to constantly disobey the guidelines of the wage agreements reached by the two large federations as well as their appeals to discipline. This situation of restlessness, and frequent confrontation through unofficial strikes cannot be solely attributed to lack of unionisation, as it also occurs in other parts of Europe. In the Spanish case it is also linked in significant areas with older traditions of workers' self-management, libertarianism (anarco-syndicalism), and diffidence towards bureaucratic management of the labour movement. On the whole, however, the further strengthening of the two large party-linked unions, with their reformist ideologies and highly professionalised hierarchies goes unabated, so that the chances for an 'uncontrolled' movement of the subordinate classes seems unlikely. If a crisis arose in the near future, however, it is clear that the Spanish party-linked federations would be at pains to master the constituency they claim to represent.

Thirdly, the Spanish state in the late seventies is far less weak, unstable and vulnerable than it was before, by virtue of the process of political consolidation and international economic integration so far described. However, the point has not been reached when all forces at play have concluded that this is so. De-stabilising techniques are being used by groups (perhaps with foreign support in some cases, but the evidence is lacking) through the use of political assassination. Though the left has been often the victim of terrorist attacks, it is those on the right (often carried out by the notorious and obscure GRAPO) which are clearly aimed at de-stabilisation, i.e., provoking the army to undertake a coup and overthrow the liberal constitution and its bill of rights. Mild and erratic prosecution of anti-left terrorists or mysteriously inefficient measures against 'pseudo-left' de-stabilising attackers of right-wing victims shows how defective the renovation of the state personnel has been under the new régime. The police, for one thing, are the same people, and have not been adequately re-organised or disbanded. For another, the ruling party, and especially the Ministry of the Interior, is still manned by people whose sympathies for democracy and republicanism are known to be either problematic or nil.

It is clear, in the light of these brief points, that the process towards the full consolidation of a Western-type pluralist, industrialised and welfare-state 'corporate society' though well under way, will not be easily completed. The chances of this happening, however, are fairly high. Spanish economic and political integration into Europe (first through the EEC, then through the European parliament, and finally through further military subordination) will only signal the culmination of the country's path towards that kind of society.[25] In that event the Spanish people will have to confront the same general problems already faced by others in the advanced capitalist and industrial West: problems of cultural and inequality legitimation, of resource allocation and distribution, of welfare state malfunction, of overbureaucratisation, unemployment and anomy. Some will consider these disadvantages as a necessary sacrifice to be fully offset by the obvious advantages gained by Spain's belated re-entry into its legitimate historical sphere, Western Europe. Yet, many more are bound to feel that the new world now taking shape beyond the Pyrenees is not the kind of free and egalitarian society for which, for a time spanning several generations, a great many Spaniards fought with grim and perhaps characteristically quixotic determination. But this is an entirely different matter.

Notes

1. The first two parts of this essay are a much abridged and modified version of an essay written by us in 1974 and published in *Cuadernos de Ruedo Ibérico*, Paris, nos. 43–45 (1975), pp. 83–104 (Italian translation *Quaderni di sociologia*, Turin, vol. XXV, no. 1 (1976), pp. 11–40). A revised and updated version, drawn up by our colleague Manuel Pérez Yruela, appeared in *Papers de sociologia*, Barcelona, no. 8 (1978), pp. 103–41. We wish to thank our friend for his important collaboration. The present version largely omits theoretical and doctrinal polemics with other interpreters of Francoism, and reduces bibliographical sources considerably. Readers interested in either may consult the preceding versions. We must stress the fact that the chief hypotheses presented here about why the Francoist régime metamorphosed into a parliamentary democracy were already present in the first version and are inherent in our early notion of an 'economically developing reactionary despotism'. Our reflections on the nature of present-day Spanish political pluralism are therefore not *ex post facto*, as they were put forward well before the end of the Franco era.

2. 'Semi-peripheral', and, of course, 'peripheral' and 'core' as in I. Wallerstein's *The Modern World System* (Academic Press, New York, 1974); see also E. Shils' much earlier distinction between 'center' and 'periphery' in his *Center and Periphery* (University Press, Chicago, 1975) which not only refers to single societies but extends to the international level.

3. Thus the view that the frequent changes in régimes through coups and countercoups, or even elections, in certain areas, such as Latin America, are capricious and unconnected to questions of development, investment, nationalisation of goods and services, etc., is untenable. This may seem a banal remark, but much work by political scientists on régime changes in certain areas of the world seems to ignore all links with the economy and international economic trends, not to speak of geopolitical and international interventions, of which they are somewhat more aware. In this chapter I cannot develop this question, though in the following pages the pertinent ties of the Spanish ruling classes to the changes in the structure of the economy and the class composition of the country are of course sharply emphasised.

4. E. Gellner, *Thought and Change* (Weidenfeld, London, 1964) points out that, in our time, a social order has 'rightful claims to the loyalty of the members of the society under two conditions', namely industrialism leading to an affluent society and 'co-cultural' authority, i.e., the satisfaction of nationalism (p. 33).

5. We are aware of the old-fashioned ring of the word 'despotism' which, as Melvin Richter points out, is the least known of that family of concepts which includes 'tyranny, autocracy, absolutism, dictatorship (in its modern sense) and totalitarianism' (in P. Wiener (ed.), *Dictionary of the History of Ideas* (Scribner's, New York, 1973), vol. II, p. 1). After its wide use by Montesquieu and Rousseau it has become increasingly less common. Its terminological advantages for the phenomena analysed here will become quite apparent as the argument unfolds.

6. 'Reactionary coalition' as in Barrington Moore in *Social Origins of Dictatorship and Democracy* (Penguin, Harmondsworth, 1973), pp. 436 ff.

7. The term 'means of emotional production' is borrowed from R. Collins' discussion of the manipulation of the materials and techniques used to stage rituals producing strong emotional bonds. (Bonds of obedience, we would like to add.) This typically entails the 'contagion' which results from the gathering together of a large number of people focusing on a common object and participating in a co-ordinated sequence of gestures. Political and religious ceremonies and certain sporting events provide good examples. R. Collins, *Conflict Sociology* (Academic Press, New York, 1975), pp. 58–9.

8. 'Service class' in a sense akin to K. Renner, *Wandlungen der Modernen Gesellschaft* (Wiener Volksbuchhandlung, Vienna, 1953), p. 119. See also M. S. Archer and S. Giner, *Contemporary Europe: Class, Status and Power* (Weidenfeld and Nicolson, London, 1971), pp. 1–59.

9. A. de Miguel in his *Sociologia del Franquismo* (Euros, Barcelona, 1975) gives a descriptive account of all the 'Francoist' groups, which is very useful if correctly reinterpreted. His work is tinged by Juan Linz's view of Francoism as some sort of paternalistic right-wing dictatorship, not bereft of benevolent facets. Our own critique of their approach is contained in the sources referred to in note 1 and in S. Giner's review article of A. de Miguel's book (pp. 151–2) in *Papers de sociologia*, vol. 8 (1978), with rejoinder by the author. All this does not diminish the importance of Juan Linz's and his disciples' work on the political sociology of Spain. It is certainly the most elaborate we possess from a positivist–functionalist 'Lipsetian' perspective.

10. For our own analytical account of the contemporary social structure of Spain, see S. Giner, *La estructura social de España* (Tecnos, Madrid, 1980); this is an expanded and reworked version of 'La estructura social de España' in A. López Pina (ed.), *Poder y clases sociales* (Tecnos, Madrid, 1978), pp. 73–149. A first approach to this, in English, appears in M. S. Archer and S. Giner (eds.), *Contemporary Europe: Class, Status and Power*, pp. 125–62.

11. The notion of 'labour repressive economic system' is akin to B. Moore's expression 'labour-repressive agricultural system' as in his *Social Origins of Dictatorship and Democracy* (p. 434), extended, though, to the entire economy.

12. For an analysis of the relationship between Francoism and higher education and the students' democratic movement see S. Giner, 'Power, Freedom and Social Change in the Spanish University' in P. Preston (ed.), *Spain in Crisis* (Harvester Press, London, 1976), pp. 183–211. See also J. M. Maravall, *Dictatorship and Political Dissent* (Tavistock, London, 1978), pp. 98–117.

13. Even as mild a critic of Francoism as S. Payne is forced to accept the harrowing figures of the post-war extermination of republicans, democrats and any persons who had the slightest connection with the vanquished régime. See S. Payne, *Franco's Spain* (Routledge & Kegan Paul, London, 1968), pp. 110 and ff.

14. From the aptly called *borghesia di stato*, an expression used by some Italian sociologists.

15. As in other parts of this paper we omit a detailed enumeration of these institutions as well as a description of their evolution, volume of production and trade, etc. For a detailed substantiation of our claims about the ruling class-nature of Francoist agrarian policies, see E. Sevilla, *La evolución del campesinado en España*, with an Introduction by S. Giner (Península, Barcelona, 1979); for the economy in general, J. Ros Hombravella *et al., Capitalismo español: de la autarquia a la estabilización* (Edicusa, Madrid, 1973), vols. I and II.

16. For the social composition of the Cortes, see J. M. de Miguel and J. Linz, 'Las Cortes españolas, 1943–70', *Sistema*, nos. 8 (1975), pp. 85–110 and 10 (1975), pp. 102–23.

17. For a specific study of the ultimate failures of the régime as regards its educational policies see, again, the two sources quoted in note 12; also V. Pérez Díaz, *Cambio tecnológico y procesos educativos en España* (Seminarios y Ediciones, Madrid, 1972).

18. For obvious reasons in this chapter we 'ignore' the international factors which helped maintain the Franco régime from Yalta – if not earlier – till its demise in 1975–7. We are well aware, of course, that it cannot be explained only internally. and that a simple-minded explanation of its duration through the standard 'Fascist help cum Franco–British non-intervention policies' during the Civil War is notoriously insufficient. There seems to be abundant evidence, for instance, that the USA were against any help to the democratic anti-Franco forces from an extremely early stage, certainly well before the end of the Second World War.

19. For a discussion of the chances and prerequisites of any semi-peripheral society in its efforts to put into effect its own shift to the core, see I. Wallerstein, *The Capitalist World Economy* (Cambridge University Press, Cambridge, 1979), pp. 66–118.

20. For a substantiation of these points about the degree of development reached by the Spanish economy see, apart from references given in note 15, above, A. de Miguel and J. Salcedo, *Dinámica del desarrollo industrial de las regiones españolas* (Tecnos, Madrid, 1972), and very especially 'Después de Franco ¿qué?: La reestructuración del capitalismo español', *Revista Mensual–Monthly Review*, vol. 2, no. 5/6 (1979), and R. Esteve Secall, 'Tourism and the Economy', (pp. 98–115) in the same issue. Also J. Harrison, *An Economic History of Modern Spain* (Manchester University Press, Manchester, 1978), among other standard sources.

21. Referendum of December 1976; General Elections to the Constituent Cortes, June 1977; Approval of the Constitution Referendum, December, 1978; General Elections to the Cortes, March, 1979; General Local Elections (finally dismantling the last vestiges of Franco-appointed offices, save that of the King himself), April 1979.

22. Our own interpretation of the transition may be compared with Raymond Carr's and J. P. Fusi's as it appears in their book *España de la dictadura a la democracia* (Planeta, Barcelona, 1979), which contains an interesting, historiographic account of Francoism. For the first time Professor R. Carr somewhat abandons the line taken in his former and influential *Spain 1908–39* (Allen and Unwin, London, 1979) and treats the Civil War as a case of 'class war' (p. 14). It is to be regretted, however, that the authors have not attempted to *explain* the course of events in the very descriptive final parts of their book. They also show a systematic ignorance of the many serious contributions which have appeared in the journal *Cuadernos de Ruedo Ibérico* (Paris) since 1965. See, too, the Francoist historian Ricardo de la Cierva's *Historia del Franquismo* (Planeta, Barcelona, 1978) vol. II. This is the last of the many works of this privileged insider and cannot be ignored, as the author has had access to documents which could not be obtained by scholars of other persuasions.

23. For a detailed account of our views on this matter, see S. Giner and M. M. Pérez Yruela, *La sociedad corporativa* (CIS, Madrid, 1979).

24. Since this was written statutes of limited autonomy have finally been granted to both Catalonia and the Basque country.

25. About Spain's – and other Southern European societies' – path towards a new type of structure contrast our views with those of Juan Linz in 'Europe's Southern Frontier: Evolving Trends Towards What?', *Daedalus*, vol. 108, no. 1 (Winter 1979), pp. 175–209.

7   Some Preliminary Notes on the State in Contemporary Portugal

NUNO PORTAS and SERRAS GAGO

To speak of the state in Portugal today implies making an analysis of the profound social and political changes brought about in the years 1974–5. The fall of the fifty-year-old dictatorship and 'the end of the Empire' marked a turning-point of the greatest importance in a centuries-old history and, above all, constituted the final stage of a modern epoch heralded by the loss of Brazil in the 1820s, and the alternative strategy of exploitation of Africa (Angola, Mozambique), by means of which the dominant class attempted to recreate 'a new Brazil'. In 1974 changes in the colonial situation were once again associated with a change of political régime. The social and political transformations of the 25 April imparted very special characteristics to the Portuguese political process, to which we shall return later.[1]

The so-called corporatist state in Portugal came into being at the end of the 1920s, and was consolidated in the early 1930s as an open reaction against the Republican parliamentary system. On 28 May 1926 there was a successful coup d'état which was military, nationalist and antiplutocratic and had the declared intention of 'regenerating political morality' and putting an end to the 'disarray of politicians and parties'. This was the régime of the *Ditadura Nacional*, in which a certain predominance of the military was at first evident. The period between the date of the coup d'état and 1933 was marked by a succession of 'coups within the coup' which in essence relegated from leadership of the movement those political forces that wished, quite simply, to 'clean up' the former political parties by means of a *temporary* military and authoritarian action of pacification and revitalisation of structures (the state and the parties). Within the *Ditadura Nacional*, power fell more and more into the hands of the representatives of the major proprietors of wealth in the banking sector and of the oligarchy, who were pressing for a complete break with the system of political democracy.

In 1933 the new constitution was promulgated whereby the régime was defined as an 'organic democracy'. The text of this document guaranteed freedom of expression and of association – an article immediately suspended once circumstances safely allowed this provision to be applied. The National Labour Law was also published based on the Italian *Carta del Lavoro*. The monied upper middle class and the large agrarian landowners came to constitute the leading faction in the new ruling class. The régime adopted a 'policy of austerity', of wage constraint, making the workers 'pay for the crisis'. As for external affairs, it adopted a policy of rejecting the progressive indebtedness of the country to foreign creditors, who at times imposed very hard conditions Salazar gained the support of the most nationalistic and conservative sectors of the middle class that had their roots in the land or who were part of the state bureaucracy. The Church, which had been the mainspring of Salazar's rise to power, gave its aid to the régime that had put an end to the 'terror' of the anticlerical and masonic republicanism of the PRP (Democratic Party), the leading party of the urban left-wing lower middle class.

The fact that the leading faction in the Salazarist bloc was conservative in character does not imply that it upheld the thesis of the absolute 'retrograde' character of the régime that grew out of the 1933 Constitution. There was no attempt to return to any lost archetype; there was a continuing search for ways of averting the outbreak of the social conflicts characteristic of other large industrialised European societies. For example, to avoid the great concentrations of exclusively working-class housing by adopting a system of town planning 'to accord with the individualistic nature of Portuguese people'. The state, furthermore, had to 'control the economy'. The policy of anti-foreign indebtedness implied a slowing-down of economic activity since a situation of deflation and recession, of 'planned stagnation', was considered to be preferable to a policy of development financed from abroad. Consequently, the working-class suffered heavily from the effects of this 'national reconstruction'. As yet there existed none of the great financial groups which were to be expropriated by the 1974 April Revolution. Thus, the forty-year history of the *Estado Novo* is also the history of the formation and development of these groups, of their concentration and centralisation and of the close relations they enjoyed with the corporatist state.

The 1933 Constitution made provision for the existence of two chambers: the *Assembleia Nacional* and the *Càmara Corporativa*.

The latter was a body of a consultative nature whose members were nominated by the state and which played a leading part in co-ordinating various economic interests. Before the formation of the great financial groups it was to be one of the essential decision-making centres in the determination of economic policy and a privileged place for the expression of the interests of small and medium-sized firms. It was, moreover, to have a considerable importance in the preparation of various development plans (*Planos de Fomento*).

Salazar's party, the *União Nacional* (UN), the sole party for over forty years and renamed by Caetano (1968–74) as the *Acção Nacional Popular* (ANP), was one in which personal loyalty to the uncontested leader was of great importance. During the 1930s and immediately after the War, there were great gatherings of mass support, 'in the German manner', that vilified 'the chaos of democracy' and thanked the dictator for having 'spared us the horrors of war'. These meetings brought together tens of thousands of people. Thus, the UN party together with the *Assembleia Nacional* constituted the 'political' branch of the régime, while the *Càmara Corporativa* was predominantly its 'economic' branch.

The period of 'liberalisation' of the Marcello Caetano government (1968–74) accentuated the fundamental economic characteristics of the last years of Salazarism but introduced original features concerning patterns of political consumption. With respect to this, two distinct periods need to be distinguished. During the first – 1968–70 – an illusion of democratisation obtained a certain degree of credibility, while in the period up to 1974, it became obvious that there was no question of evolution where the dictatorship was concerned. The 'colonial question' was a major point of polarisation for the forces of the régime. An increase in the extent of social and political struggles in European Portugal (1972–4) created conditions suitable for the unification of internal and external struggles against the régime. For example, the forms by which international capital penetrated Portuguese society, a development that had begun in the early 1960s, disrupted and weakened the logic of the corporatist system whereby the state 'controlled' the economy. Numerous and often divergent positions were taken up within the party and in certain sectors of the state administration. These centred around the question, 'Which way should Portugal go?' and were a clear indication of a deep division within the ruling class. Was it to be 'the way to Europe' or 'the way to Africa'? One or other of these options was absolutely necessary.

The 1974 April Revolution confirmed the incapacity for simultaneous development of both of these two options within the context of the world capitalist crisis in the early 1970s, and thus the impossibility of: (a) an industrial base which was both dependent upon the economic exploitation of the colonies through the continual development of extractive industries, and yet compatible with a European economy into which Portugal was encouraged to integrate; (b) ensuring the expansion of exploitation and the destruction of pre-capitalist relations of production in the colonies. In this Portuguese capital was associated with foreign investment in a position of legal preference, protected by the state and by the physical occupation of territories by white colonists; (c) ensuring in Portugal forms of exploitation in which political and social conflicts would continue to have little legitimacy but where there would be the gradual acceptance of a system of negotiation with working-class organisations; and (d) preserving, with respect to major international capital interests, a margin of autonomy on the one hand, and a level of association on the other, indispensable to the functioning of world capitalism. From the 1960s, therefore, the position of the Portuguese bourgeoisie could be described as consisting of three essential contradictions; those which put it in direct opposition to colonial peoples, to major *international* capital interests, and to workers as a whole, whose attitudes had been polarised by the multiple effects of the colonial war. The build up of the process that led to the explosion of 25 April 1974 was the history of the transformation of each of these contradictions. The decisive factor was that they were very closely connected in a systematic manner; that is, transformations in any one implied cumulative effects in the others. The Caetano period was accompanied by increasing complications in this web of contradictions. Thus, the development of a new type of relationship between the 'centre' and the 'periphery', the changeover to direct investment in the industrial productive sector, 'dependent industrialisation', emigration, the armed struggle of the colonial peoples, the increase in financial needs created by the war, and the spread of social political struggles in Portugal itself, strengthened the deep-rooted tendency towards the disruption and collapse of the ruling political régime.

The 1974 April Revolution nationalised important areas of monopoly capital which had been developing under the overall protection of 'conditioned industrialisation' in the corporatist system. There was also the introduction of Land Reform which expropriated the great landed estates in the South that had been the strongest pillars of the Salazar régime. Even before 1974 important splits had become manifest within the dominant rural class; the process of capitalist accumulation had created a 'dynamic' class of large capitalist farmers who were beginning to occupy positions of authority in the *Alentejo* and in those sectors of the state machinery concerned with agrarian questions, thereby reducing the power of absentee landowners. With nationalisation and the expropriation of the large estates, the destruction of Salazar's sole party, the *União Nacional* (modernised by Caetano as the *Acção Nacional Popular* (ANP)), and the introduction of the 1975 Constitution which specified the objective of a 'classless society', a new question arose; how are economic and social inequalities reproduced under the new democratic régime? The revolution had broken the link between the great financial groups and the political élite of the state. The largest capitalists disappeared as did the most notorious political personages of the former régime. They either went into exile in Brazil and Spain or simply retired from politics. But the state machinery and the technocratic structure of the great financial groups remained essentially unaltered. However, the large financial concerns were reorganised as public enterprises and through the framework of the Institute of State Holdings (IPE), they became an important instrument of the party system in the renewal and enlargement of the state bureaucracy.

During the period from April 1974 to June 1976 (between the parliamentary and presidential elections), the rôle of ensuring that the rules were respected was shared by the political parties and the Armed Forces Movement (MFA). This was the period of successive MFA-party pacts which demonstrated the political weight of the military *avant-garde* as against the nascent hierarchy of the party machines. These were not yet legitimated by the popular vote, and not yet credible as legitimate entities as compared with those that had swept away the dictatorship. The MFA-party pacts conditioned the whole revolutionary period as well as the constitution and the type of state that was to emerge from it. They reflected not only the relationship of forces that existed between the military and civil spheres, but also the situation within the military, divided as it was between those who wished to 'push on' and those who wanted to 'return to the barracks', appealing for obedience to the civil power; that is to say, to the representatives of the people, chosen through the ballot box. Of the four major political parties that dominate the political scene today, three were consistent signatories to these pacts; the PS (Socialist Party), the PSD (Social Democratic Party) and the PCP (Communist

Party). The fourth, the CDS (Centre Social Democrats) situated further to the right, adopted a position of hostility that reached its height in their refusal to vote for the constitution on the grounds of its socialist nature. The holding of four elections (two parliamentary, one local government, another presidential) gave a legal basis to the party system, accentuating within the military the need for a 'return to the barracks'.

The PS (Socialist Party) won the two parliamentary elections and the local elections, adopting the position of a 'party of equilibrium' with a very broad class base. It was the party that was the least regionalised and the most evenly represented throughout the electorate on a national basis. Its appeal extended in all political directions, given the fact that it not only had a clear anti-fascist image but also had led the mass movement against the Communist Party in the summer of 1975. This dual appeal enabled it to create a dynamic that had brought together a large, somewhat nebulous following drawn from all classes, consisting of 38 per cent of the electorate. The PSD (Social Democratic Party), the second largest party in terms of electoral support, was led by those who in 1969, believing in a gradual and smooth change in the régime, had been part of the so-called 'liberal' wing during the Caetano period. The Secretary-General of the PSD, Sá Carneiro, an independent deputy under Caetano, later renounced his mandate as a deputy and made a social democratic profession of faith. This group had hoped for a slow but certain change in the corporatist system, a 'creeping europeanisation' as opposed to the 'way to Africa' of the extremist supporters of Salazar. The CDS (Centre Social Democrats) more clearly has its origin within the old régime. Even more than with the PSD, its leadership consisted of those who, because of their age or the restrictive mobility of the corporatist system, had not yet been promoted to high positions of political trust. It was more clearly anti-socialist and favourable to the market economy than the PSD. Their alliance with the PS that formed the basis of the Fourth Constitutional Government represented, in a context in which the socialists explicitly abandoned the aim of building Socialism, an attempt to occupy the centre, thereby placing the PSD to its right.

The presidential election of June 1976 introduced on the political scene the notion of a presidential majority consisting of the PS, PSD and CDS; the parties that had supported the candidature of General Eanes. From this date onwards, there was to be a conflict between the notion of a presidential majority and a parliamentary majority, the latter often being impossible to obtain. This conflict continues to threaten to block the political system. What will be the outcome? With respect to the Assembly, shall we see a strengthening or a weakening of the President's power? Under the present system, the 'presidential threat' has operated more to bring pressure to bear upon inter-party bargaining than as an overall and coherent alternative to the present party system.

The social basis of the state has remained relatively stable despite political developments since 1974. From a strictly political point of view, the Salazar and Caetano régimes resisted to the end any attempt at democratisation. They never allowed the forces of the 'resistance' to organise themselves legally, whether they represented the die-hard democratic republican middle class or the workers' organisations. They were always inaccessible even to those political forces that in certain cases and in other circumstances would have been integrated into a democratic-parliamentary process constituting one of the bridges leading to gradual change in the régime. Indeed, the impossibility of reforming the régime from within was, even at the moment of its fall in 1974, a conviction held even by the political forces that today occupy positions on the centre-right.

The 1933 Constitution should have resolved at the outset the paradox of a state that develops the productive forces with minimal costs for the reproduction of labour power and at the same time presents itself as 'the state that builds for the people'. With this objective, apart from the corporatist structure that should have led to the economic integration of the workers, and the repressive machinery that should have liquidated the clandestine workers' resistance organisations, a very highly centralised administrative system was set up. This suited the small size of the country and the low level of economic development. It was a matter of dismantling and doing away with republican patronage at the local and regional levels and taking decisions in the central administration on all matters concerning the improvement of the living conditions of the people, which although carried out at low cost were magnified by a propaganda machine conceived on a new model, 'in the German style'. The cornerstone of this activity consisted of two government departments; one for Public Works, led from 1933 to 1943 by a superb technocrat, who created peripheral regional bodies and supervised throughout the country the construction of schools and rural roadbuilding, etc., and the other of Finance, through which Salazar imposed a budgetary dictatorship on the whole Administration. Thus, an important feature of the 1933 Constitution was the destruction of the municipalities with the exception of the capital, Lisbon. They were abolished both as democratic entities capable of transmitting complaints and, thus, of putting pressure on the central bureaucracy and as administrative and executive bodies; functions which the central government never delegated to the local authorities until after 25 April 1974. The 1940s and the 1950s were characterised by a stagnation in the level of investment required for the reproduction of labour power in favour of investment in basic infrastructures such as, for example, hydro-electric schemes, the road network, and the ports. This had the aim of making Portugal self-sufficient in electricity and strengthening the industrial matrix. Improvements in the conditions of the reproduction of labour power were only brought about when the régime became incapable of repressing discontent in urban areas or among the rural proletariat of the Alentejo. Thus, the régime built a number of low-cost housing estates and roads in the South in order to reduce seasonal unemployment. But on the whole, with respect to the reproduction of labour, the only effort of the régime was concentrated upon the enlargement of the primary and secondary school system during the early 1970s, led by the liberal Veiga Simão, under the influence of OECD guidelines.

It is impossible to dwell in detail upon the class nature of the state produced by the 1974 Revolution. Certain characteristics may be briefly mentioned; the military coup, organised by the lowest echelons of the military hierarchy (the MFA) was followed by mass demonstrations. These signified on the one hand the unpopularity of the régime (war, inflation, unemployment, repression, the lack of political activity) and, on the other, the already existing signs of the divisions to come. From 25 April 1974 until 11 March 1975 the important divisions were to be produced within the MFA with regard to decolonisation and, at the same time, the type of society to be constructed. The decisive turning-point occurred on 11 March 1975; the MFA decided on the nationalisation of the banks, insurance companies and the great financial groups, and there was the beginning of the occupation of the estates of the great landowners in the South. It was from this date that the idea began to develop according to which one could 'bypass certain stages' in the construction of socialism, in view of 'the uniqueness of the Portuguese case', by cutting out a long and, in principle, necessary democratic stage. The development of this thesis led to political leadership being formed that was to increasingly alienate itself from the middle strata of society, the small capitalists and a great part of the working-class, especially in the North of the country. The events of 25 November 1975 (more coups d'état within the coup) – marking a further turning-point (this time to the right) – were the outcome of a process that led to the formation, through a popular mass movement, of a large bloc that disagreed with and was antagonistic towards revolutionary power.

The great mobilisation and participation of the masses in exerting strong pressure on the state machinery is one of the essential characteristics of the revolutionary period of 1974–5. It was a phenomenon observed above all in urban and coastal areas, and in the South. In this, the new lower middle class, especially the technical and younger professional workers, played a leading part. The capitalist development of the 1960s, the great economic, demographic and urban concentration in the Lisbon region and along the littoral, had accentuated the strong dualist characteristics of the social formation. It was not by chance that the strongest reaction against the new political process should come from the rural regions and from the interior of the country. This, however, does not mean that it was an essentially peasant reaction; the rôle of the provincial middle class, the merchants and the shopkeepers, was a determining factor in the formation of a conservative bloc.

Among the institutional experiments of this 'revolutionary' period may be noted a low-cost house-building programme for slum or shanty-town districts, from whence the most aggressive urban struggles originated. This was a policy carried out in the summer of 1974 by the Second Provisional Government by which the state undertook to delegate certain prerogatives and functions of the administration to local popular movements. These were made responsible for the choice of sites, the content and priorities of the programme, the implementation and control of the projects, and the allocation of dwellings to families. The enormous dynamism of this programme contrasted with the defensive passivity of the classical programmes of the pre-revolutionary administration. But it also explains why the central state bureaucracy, especially after the 25 November, immediately raised objections, slowing down the initiatives put into practice by these popular movements. The state bureaucracy claimed they were politically partisan, while the movements themselves, accused the state of 'bourgeois legality' and held it responsible for preventing the devolution of power to the people.

Fluctuating between making a radical change in structures and, on the other hand, postponing the transformation of the state machinery was an ever-present dilemma during the early revolutionary period; it presented itself in every sector of the state. An insufficient transformation of the state machinery, limited to a number of changes among higher officials on political grounds, implied its condemnation as inadequate because of a lack of legitimacy; it was in the position of having no control over ever-increasing contradictions. It had never been accepted by the increasingly powerful social forces; these were mistrustful of what had been an instrument of constant oppression in the hands of the former ruling class. To accord priority, on the other hand, to rapid and far-reaching transformations of the state machinery implied that it had ceased to be an instrument capable of transmitting and executing orders in accordance with a coherent and overall strategy of social change, above all, in the period during which old relationships were still making their presence felt. The absence of this second strategy prevented an adequate and dynamic intervention in connection with social movements, the demands of which increasingly contributed to causing splits within the social bloc giving its support to the revolution. The highly dismembered nature of the state machinery prevented, in a large measure, its utilisation as a mediator between the various interests which could, and should of necessity have been, integrated into a sufficiently enlarged revolutionary bloc.

When the revolution took place, the administrative machinery of the state – centralised and bureaucratic, relying on an antiquated system of badly-paid and ageing civil servants, most of whom had recourse to a second private income – found itself in an unenviable position. On the one hand, the new political aim of 'provisional governments' was that the population should understand, through concrete social projects, that the change was being made in the workers' interests (for example, the programme of the MFA). On the other hand, the instantaneous eruption of multiple forms of organisation and the struggle of those same masses brought about an attitude of rejection within the state administration. None of the democratic parties, not even the MFA, had a coherent strategy for controlling and inclining the state machinery towards the new class interests, except for the very simple idea of replacing the heads of the former régime by trusted men from the new parties in key positions within the hierarchy. Formal legalism and revolutionary legality divided, in one case after another, the forces of the left. However, this did not prevent the left in the Constituent Assembly in 1975–6, from implementing far-reaching political reforms. These included the setting-up of a strong municipal system; administrative regions with considerably increased responsibilities; recognition of autonomous organisations of the people as voluntary organs, representative of local interests; and the acceptance of workers' control. Nevertheless, the urban social movements – those whose effects were the most far-reaching – did not have the broad class base for the formation of an enlarged social bloc able to give its support to revolutionary changes but, rather, were in the nature of an opposition to what was called the 'bourgeois state', conceived as a monolithic bloc without any autonomy. These movements were also very divided and some with radical leaders interested in confrontation with the forces of the parliamentary left and with those responsible for various municipal bodies. Furthermore, these urban social movements were elements of conflict within the different MFA factions and thus an obstacle to the consolidation of the political rôle of that movement. After 25 November 1975 these popular organisations were gradually demobilised and the population returned to their defensive and resigned attitude towards the state administration.

The question of the restructuring of the state administrative machinery still remains; for example, the impossibility of implementing a binding economic and social plan, as laid down in the Constitution, is a symptom of this. With a Constitution that establishes the existence of three different spheres – the state, the private and the co-operative – the state machinery has always resisted attempts at decentralisation. The nationalisation of the large Portuguese financial institutions has augmented and weighed down a state machinery which has a strong bureaucratic tradition. Although there are pressures from the political right for denationalisation, the existing extent of state enterprises is protected by the Constitution. The pressures that these enterprises are able to exert on the private sector of the economy run counter to certain notions of private capitalist development and constitute one of the major reasons why there is currently an intense political struggle over the form that the revision of the Constitution should take in 1980.

Note

1. In contrast to what happens in other countries where the absence of censorship and readily available facilities for research have long since brought forth fruitful results, in the case of Portugal the small number of serious and detailed texts, whether on the whole theoretical concept of the state or on its more concrete and empirical aspects, advises great prudence in dealing with these problems. Research teams have scarcely begun to be formed. Interesting and serious studies are only now beginning to appear.

8 Capitalism and the Development of the Greek State

NICOS MOUZELIS

Introduction

This chapter will try to give an overall account of the modern Greek state up to the present date, laying particular stress on developments from the interwar period onwards, when the capitalist mode of production became dominant in the Greek social formation. Within this context the main focus of analysis is the manner in which the development of Greek capitalism,[1] closely associated with the successive phases of Western imperialism, interconnects through transformations of the class structure with the changing forms and functions of state institutions.

The State in Pre-capitalist Greece

Since I believe a proper understanding of state developments in contemporary Greece to be impossible without some reference to the nineteenth century, this section will provide a general picture of the Greek state during the pre-capitalist phase of Greek social formation.

Despite its early integration into the world capitalist system, nineteenth-century Greece, as far as its internal structures of production were concerned, was clearly a pre-capitalist social formation. After the spectacular development of English industrial capitalism had destroyed early attempts at an industrial take-off in pre-independence Greece,[2] indigenous Greek capital kept out of the spheres of both industrial and agricultural production and oriented itself towards the more lucrative and safe commercial and financial investments. During the first fifty years of Greek independence (1821–70) therefore, Greece was predominantly an agrarian society with a relatively inflated service sector – a large part of which consisted of a huge state apparatus which absorbed into its ranks all those who had left the countryside and for whom a non-existent industry could provide no occupation.

241

It has been calculated that during the 1870s, the number of civil servants per 10,000 of the population was approximately seven times higher in Greece than in the United Kingdom.[3] This huge administrative growth is even more remarkable if it is remembered that the top state bureaucrats received salaries which compared very favourably with those of the economically dominant classes. So whereas the average annual income of the ten largest landowners (before the annexation of Thessaly which augmented big landed property) did not exceed drachmae 20,000, and the largest Greek textile establishment had an annual profit of dr 5,000, a state minister – in addition to obvious fringe benefits – received an annual salary of dr 10,000, and an army general one of dr 8,300.[4] At this pre-capitalist stage, therefore, the importance of the state apparatus lay not simply in its size, but also in the fact that in the absence of any well-organised and powerful indigenous interest groups, the state personnel syphoned off a significant part of the economic surplus.

As regards the internal structure of the state, control of the state apparatus was shared with the throne (at this early period the major institutional channel through which the foreign powers exercised their tutelage over the country), and with a handful of oligarchic families, the so-called *tzakia*. The latter, even after the introduction of universal male suffrage in 1864, managed by means of traditional patronage to maintain total control over local voters in favour of their own political advantage.[5] In consequence, parliamentary conflict during this early period of oligarchic politics tended, in the absence of the middle and working-classes from active politics, to centre not around issues emerging out of the exploitative division of labour, but around personal struggles over the distribution of spoils. Thus, the overall picture which emerges in this strictly pre-capitalist era is of a huge state apparatus, controlled by the crown and a more or less fragmented political oligarchy at the head of extensive clientelistic networks. The lack of class-based pressure groups and the relatively vast size of the state did not mean, however, that the latter enjoyed the degree of control over civil society found in totalitarian political systems. It was not only clientelism that paralysed the state's capacity for effective collective action, but also the strict limits imposed on internal politics by Greece's dependence on the great powers and, to a lesser extent, on the big Greek diaspora capital.[6]

Given Greece's peripheral position in the world capitalist market, it is not surprising that the first major structural transformation of the Greek state was a direct reflection of the changes taking place in

Western imperialism during the final quarter of the nineteenth century. After the industrialisation of the western continent had posed the first real challenge to the industrial supremacy of England, there ensued a wholesale campaign by Western nations to plunder dependent societies in fierce competition for new markets. For the Balkan states this meant that the previously politico-military control the West had exercised became rather more directly economic.[7] It was particularly in relation to the 1873 crisis, when Western capital had to compensate for falling domestic profits, that it looked to the Balkan (and Latin American) economies for quick, high gains. This was the first time foreign capital investments were really substantial[8] and, furthermore, had the full backing of their respective governments.[9]

In Greece, this influx (which mainly took the form of government loans and railway investments) was accelerated by the huge Greek diaspora capital. This capital had previously thrived by playing an intermediary rôle between metropolitan and colonial or quasi-colonial societies, but was now feeling the effects not only of the crisis, but also of the rise of nationalism in Central and Eastern Europe. A large part of Greek diaspora capital, therefore, either relocated itself in countries where English imperialism was still strong (Egypt, the Sudan), or looked for refuge in Greece proper.[10]

The massive influx of foreign and diaspora capital had a major impact on the Greek economy and society. True, most of this capital was not invested in industry. It either took the form of government loans and railway investments or, even worse, it was used for the purchase of land and for speculative financial operations which multiplied the fortunes of the already rich new diaspora arrivals, simultaneously accentuating the dependent, peripheral character of the Greek economy. Yet despite this, it was in the fifty years or so spanning the turn of the century that most of the fundamental preconditions were laid for the eventual dominance of the capitalist mode of production. This period saw the development of social overhead capital (railways, roads, ports) which, in combination with the concomitant expansion of Greek territory and population[11] contributed to the creation of a national market, the improvement of educational institutions, the adoption of protectionist measures for the development of industry, the initiation of legislative measures for agrarian reform, etc.

Moreover, the state made valiant attempts at creating a more rational system of public administration, capable of playing an active rôle in the economy. Prior to this, not only had state action been paralysed by the persistence of large-scale brigandage, but the state administration itself was so susceptible to pressure from political bosses and local interest groups that it was quite incapable of acting as a corporate, collective body. Given the lack of secure tenure for civil servants[12] and the non-existence of any criteria of merit in their recruitment, the position of every state employee depended wholly on his political patron remaining in power, or on his connections with powerful bandits or influential notables. The radical reforms of Trikoupis (1880–95) and later of Venizelos (1910–20) gradually eliminated these aspects of the state apparatus; brigandage was overcome and legislative attempts were made to establish educational standards for civil servants, introduce life tenure for most state employees, tighten state control over the banking system, and to set up new and more specialised ministerial branches of government.

This administrative rationalisation was accompanied by an unprecedented expansion of the state budget, as state income as well as expenditure rose in a spectacular fashion.[13] In contrast to the preceding period, the additional financial resources the state managed to extract through exorbitant (mainly indirect) taxation, through increased customs duties and large-scale internal and external borrowing,[14] were used not merely for the maintenance and expansion of the civil administration: they also went into the creation of a modern army and, as mentioned, into developing the country's communications system. It was during this transitional period (1875–1920), that the Greek state ceased to be a mere 'caretaker' and took the first steps towards regulating the economy in a more direct manner; both by adopting more protectionist policies and by providing the basic legal and economic infrastructure for the 1920s' development of industrial capitalism.

These crucial changes in the state–economy relationship had, of course, repercussions on the distribution of power within the state itself. The economic changes of the late nineteenth century generated a new middle class which was no longer willing to leave the political game to the monopoly prerogative of a handful of oligarchic families (the *tzakia*). The changing socio-economic conditions weakened the hold of oligarchic politics, and created a fertile ground for the 1909 military coup which designates the transition from oligarchic to middle class politics in Greece. This transformation is reflected in the composition of the parliamentary forces from the 1910 elections onwards,[15] as *ancien régime* politicians (the so-called *paleokommatiki*) had to make room for and share power with lawyers, doctors and diaspora capitalists. At the same time, the gradual decline of the *paleokommatiki* meant an erosion in the power position of the throne, since the newcomers were less loyal to the king, or rather less ready to accept military and foreign affairs as the exclusive preserve of the monarchy.[16]

The inevitable clash did not take long to come. It took the form of a disagreement between the liberal prime minister Venizelos and King Constantine I over the policy Greece should adopt during the First World War. The disagreement led in 1916 to the *dichasmos*, the schism between Venizelists and anti-Venizelists which was to profoundly affect the course of Greek politics during the entire interwar period.

It was the advent of middle class politics, therefore, that disrupted the balance between the throne and the oligarchy which had for a very long time (1864–1909) provided a stable régime framework for a restricted/oligarchic parliamentarianism in Greece. Broadening the base of political participation not only lost the throne some of its control over the state but, by identifying its political fortunes with one fraction of the bourgeoisie, made it incapable of continuing its balancing rôle between the bourgeois parties. From now on, chronic governmental instability, which had always been a characteristic feature of Greek politics, was complemented by régime instability as Venizelists and anti-Venizelists attempted to impose their respective constitutional solutions on the political crisis.[17]

Capitalism and the Transformation of the Greek State: 1922–38

In 1922, as a result of the disastrous defeat of the Greek forces in the Greco–Turkish war in Asia Minor, more than one million refugees from the previously flourishing Anatolian Greek communities moved into Greek territory. But while this sudden influx of uprooted people brought major disruptions, their arrival also created conditions for the subsequent take-off of the Greek economy. In agriculture it accelerated the reform programme (originally initiated in 1917), and gave the final blow to large-scale landed property in Greece. From the 1920s onwards, the small family plot has been the dominant form of land ownership in the Greek countryside. In industry the settlement of a large number of refugees in the main urban centres meant the availability of abundant cheap labour[18] and entrepreneurial skills[19] at a time when Greece was experiencing a massive injection of foreign funds in the form of government loans, international aid to the refugees, and private investments in public works, etc.[20] With the favourable preconditions established in the previous four decades, the combination of entrepreneurial skills, cheap labour and abundant capital gave a decisive boost to the development of Greek industry.

What was even more influential was the 1929 economic crisis which forced the Greek state radically to reorient its policies *vis-à-vis* the world market and the management of the economy. In fact, given the collapse of world trade and the incapacity of the Greek economy to export its traditional agricultural products, the state had to embark on a programme of import-substitution by adopting a highly protectionist customs policy, by favouring industrial capital in a variety of ways, and by becoming more involved with the general management of the economy. Consequently, in 1932 the Venizelos government initiated a series of legislative measures (the abolition of the free drachma convertibility into gold, quantitative restrictions on imports, bilateral forms of exchange not requiring the use of foreign currency, etc.[21]) which, in combination with earlier measures,[22] facilitated the development of industrial enterprises and provided a framework conducive to an effective breakthrough in the industrial sector. From 1923 to 1939, industrial production doubled in horse power and value, and tripled in volume.[23] Between 1928 and 1938, electricity production quadrupled and during the same period, according to United Nations statistics, Greece had the highest increase in industrial production (65 per cent) after the Soviet Union and Japan.[24]

Without doubt, this period marks the decisive entrance of capital into the sphere of production. Before this, not only was the industrial sector as a whole relatively small, but the number of capitalist enterprises proper (i.e., those using a large number of wage labourers)[25] was insignificant. With the twenties and thirties came a considerable concentration of capital, as well as closer collaboration between banking and industrial capital – i.e., the emergence of finance capital. This was the time of the multiplication of holding companies, trusts and cartels which, although they did not acquire the dimensions of their West European counterparts, were quite impressive by Balkan standards. At the same time there was a marked differentiation of banking capital, as some of the functions previously performed by the all-pervasive and all-powerful National Bank of Greece were shared among several specialised institutions: the Bank of Greece (founded in 1927) which became responsible for the issue of currency, the Real Estate Bank (1927) and the Agricultural Bank (1931). The creation of the Bank of Greece which, after great resistance from vested interests,[26] took over the prerogative of currency control from the National Bank, was a significant move in the state's attempt to establish firmer control over the economy.

The growth of finance and industrial capital came at a time when large-scale landed property had virtually disappeared and when merchant capital, in the wake of increasing state control over the import–export trade, was at a standstill.[27] From the thirties onwards there is no doubt that the capitalist mode of production had become firmly established in the industrial sector, to function as the dynamic pivot of the Greek economy – where dynamism is meant to imply not only high rates of growth, but also the systematic transfer of resources from the simple-commodity sector (prevalent in agriculture and small industry) to the industrial capitalist sector. Of course, it was still the state which played the crucial rôle in creating and maintaining these transfer mechanisms; these took the form of state subsidies to large-scale industry, scandalous credit facilities, indiscriminate tariff protection enabling highly inefficient firms to achieve quasi-monopolistic positions, and the prevalence of indirect taxation which hit low income earners very hard,[28] etc. It was not surprising, therefore, that the profits of large-scale industrial and finance capital attained spectacular dimensions,[29] whereas in the simple-commodity agricultural and artisanal sectors, the plethora of small family units found it difficult to make ends meet.[30] Inevitably, growing inequalities and the relative marginalisation of all those involved in simple-commodity production became two major features of the Greek model of capital accumulation.

These points illustrate not only the increasingly close partnership between state and capital, but also the fact that in this collaboration it was the state which was the major partner. This was because interwar industrial capital was, to a large extent, its creation: it had only come into existence because of the conditions which the state, forced by the world economic crisis, had created in its favour. The circumstances of the *dependent* way in which capital had entered industrial production, refutes the naïve argument which portrays the interwar Greek state as a passive instrument of capital. This argument not only ignores the fragmentation and precarious position of interwar capital, but also underestimates the overriding power position which the Greek state occupied even before the dominance of the capitalist mode of production. In this I agree with the Greek Marxist economist Vergopoulous when he says that 'the functioning axis of the Greek social formation was not bourgeois civil society, as a certain liberal theory would imply, but the state. Ever since the middle of the nineteenth century, nothing could be done in Greece without it necessarily passing through the machinery of the state. The state apparatus, as Gramsci would say, was the social machine *par excellence.*'[31] Of course, the dependence of capital on the state does not contradict the fact that the latter, being in charge of the capitalist system's enlarged reproduction, could not perform its function without favouring industrial capital. In other words, the state choosing to adopt pro-capitalist policies was not so much the result of manipulations or pressures from a well-organised, powerful bourgeoisie, but rather because of the systemic structural constraints partly generated by the Asia Minor fiasco and by the later 1929 economic crisis. One could argue further that, because of these factors, the capitalist mode of production became dominant in the economy *without* the economically dominant industrial bourgeoisie exercising control over the state apparatus. Finally, when talking of the dependent position of capital *vis-à-vis* the state, we should always keep in mind the chronic external dependence of the latter – a situation which was dramatically aggravated in the 1930s. For instance, it has been calculated that in 1932 the annual repayment of Greece's foreign debt – both private and public – absorbed 81.08 per cent of the foreign currency Greece was earning from its agricultural exports. In comparative terms, the *per capita* external public debt in the same period was $43 in Greece, $27 in Yugoslavia, $18.8 in Bulgaria, and $12.1 in Czechoslovakia.[32]

Turning to the structure of politics during the twenties and thirties, the most striking feature is that, despite the influx of refugees and the large-scale disruptions created by the development of capitalism in both the countryside and the towns, the rural and urban working-classes[33] failed, with few exceptions, to organise themselves in a politically autonomous manner. In contrast to all other Balkan societies, which over the same period developed strong agrarian movements with populist orientations, the Greek peasants were kept firmly within the clientelistic confines of the two major bourgeois parties (these, as mentioned earlier, were deeply divided over the issue of the monarchy, the *dichasmos*). The same holds true for the refugees who, by ascribing all responsibility for the Asia Minor débâcle to the royalist government, massively gave their vote to Venizelos who was actually the main architect of the Asia Minor folly.

The *dichasmos*, this deep intra-bourgeois split, operated as a powerful conservative mechanism in interwar Greece, preventing the appearance of both the urban and the rural working-classes into the spheres of active politics. At a time when Bulgarian peasants under the leadership of Stambuliiski were putting forward and implementing a radical, anti-capitalist, populist programme of reforms which seriously threatened the bourgeois *status quo*,[34] when similar processes of industrialisation in many Latin American countries led to the rise of powerful populist movements in both rural and urban areas,[35] the Greek peasantry and poor urban dwellers were drawn into an intra-bourgeois type of conflict which had very little relevance to their own vital interests and kept them politically organised in a clientelistic/vertical manner.[36] The fact that clientelism persisted during the whole of the interwar period does not mean that there were no fundamental differences between nineteenth-century pre-capitalist and interwar capitalist politics. The spectacular expansion of the state bureaucracy and its acquisition of new functions dealt the final blow to the traditional/oligarchic type of patronage, where local notables were monopolising all links between villages and the national centre. The local oligarchies had increasingly to share 'brokerage' functions with the 'new men' the doctors, lawyers, teachers and bureaucrats.

These developments were related to changes in the structure of the major clientelistic parties. In the previous century, local political potentates had had such control over their voters, and enjoyed such a high autonomy *vis-à-vis* national political leaders, that parties on the national level could only be extremely loose coalitions of political barons. In the interwar period, the rise of the middle classes and the relative decline of the old oligarchic leadership meant, despite the continued absence of mass politics, the strengthening of the parties' central organisation as orientations, allegiances and resources shifted from the local to the national level. These developments demanded that traditional clientelism had to give way to more 'modern' forms of party and state-oriented patronage; the autonomy of the local notables being eroded not only by the expansion of the state administration, but also by the increasing power of those who controlled the party machinery at national level. These changes signified that clientelism had not only changed its form; it had also become increasingly fragile and precarious since broad economic developments and class-based issues were able to cut more easily through clientelistic networks and traditional particularistic ties. This 'loosening-up' process, which was to accelerate in the civil-war and post-war period, was evident in the crucial rôle which the Greek Communist Party – organised along non-clientelistic, 'horizontal' lines – started playing as early as the 1930s.[37]

Let us finally take a look at the internal structure of the state. If the masses were kept away from active politics, a new force was about to join the throne and the bourgeoisie in their competition over state control. As mentioned earlier, the disruption of the throne-oligarchy balance, because of the rise of the middle classes and the issue of the *dichasmos*, had set the scene for the emergence of the army as a distinct pressure group keen on promoting its own interests, and unavoidably drawn into the political game as both participant and arbiter among the quarrelling bourgeois factions. The size of the army had increased very considerably after the Balkan Wars and the First World War.[38] As it became more accessible to the middle classes and when, because of the long war years, career opportunities improved, the officers' corps lost some of its quasi-aristocratic, *tzakia*-style character and it developed a more middle-class orientation.[39] Since this coincided with the new régime's growing instability, the army's intervention was an almost foregone conclusion. Despite its politicisation in the interwar years, however, the army did not become an autonomous political force, as, for example, in Turkey.[40] It was either the politicians themselves (e.g., Venizelos' unsuccessful coup of 1935) which brought the Greek military into politics, or when the military took the initiative, they first assured themselves of the active support and collaboration of the politicians.[41] Thus, in the absence of mass politics (i.e., the absence of any real 'threat from below'), the army had never prior to the 1936 Metaxas dictatorship tried to establish a long-term military rule. Its frequent interventions in politics were not aimed at permanent control of the state machinery, but rather at creating a new balance among the forces competing for control.

The Post-war Period

The German occupation disorganised the Greek state apparatus and the clientelistic networks of the major bourgeois parties to such an extent that it gave the left, and particularly the Communist Party, the opportunity to mobilise the urban and rural population in such a way that by the time the occupation forces withdrew, most of the Greek territory was under its direct control. The subsequent protracted Civil War ended, for reasons which cannot be discussed here, with the total victory of the right. With the help of the Americans, a quasi-parliamentary régime was established in the country: a régime of 'guided democracy' which outlawed the Communist Party and, through a variety of legal and illegal mechanisms, systematically persecuted the defeated left-wing. The army and other parts of the state apparatus were purged not only of communists, but even of anti-royalists and similar 'subversive' elements.[42] Chief responsibility for the control and smooth functioning of this system of repressive parliamentarianism was assigned to the major victor of the Civil War: the Greek Army, and especially to the group of anti-communist officers belonging to the notorious secret IDEA organisation.[43]

In view of the decisive rôle which the Greek Army, first with British and then with American help, had played during the Civil War, it is not surprising that after the war it was the army that occupied the dominant power position in the throne–parliamentary forces–army triarchy. The fact that the officers who controlled the repressive state apparatus were royalists did not mean that the army was, as it had been in the nineteenth century, a mere tool of the throne. Given the long-term decline of the monarchy's power position within the state, and the emergence of the army as a distinct pressure group as early as the interwar period, it is understandable that King Paul should have been suspicious and apprehensive of the rôle the army in general and the IDEA officers in particular were assuming in post-civil war Greek politics.[44]

During the long period of uninterrupted right-wing rule (1952–63), when the system of 'guided democracy' and the revived clientelistic networks of the right were operating smoothly, the differences among the three forces within the ruling bloc were at a minimum, and the IDEA group, once it had put its anti-communist stamp on all branches of the state, underwent a period of inactivity. However, these differences were to emerge again as soon as the system of repressive parliamentarianism could no longer cope with the effects of social change and the popular dissatisfaction created by the post-war development of capitalism. It is precisely this development which provides the key to an understanding of the structure and dynamics of the post-war Greek state.

The large-scale destruction caused by the German occupation and the Civil War notwithstanding, the Greek economy, with the help of Marshall Aid and in the context of the general post-war European economic expansion, quickly managed to start functioning again more or less along the pattern established in the 1930s.[45] With an average annual growth rate of around 6 per cent in the mid-fifties, pre-war levels of output were soon reached and then exceeded. By 1959 the volume of industrial production was double that of 1938, and by 1964 it had tripled. Production of electrical power which had been

270,000 kwh in 1938, was ten times as much by 1961. The growth of tourism and the merchant marine were the most remarkable; in 1938, only 100,000 tourists had visited the country each year but by 1961 the number was multiplied by five, and by the end of the sixties by twenty. When the merchant marine resumed operating in 1945, it had a mere one hundred 10,000-ton American Liberty ships; two decades later it had become one of the largest merchant fleets in the world.[46]

With regard also to the relations of production, progress was rapid. The concentration of capital continued to increase and a series of complicated mergers put banking capital into a monopolistic position such that two giants – the National Bank of Greece and the Commercial Bank – controlled the bulk of all financial transactions. In 1962 their combined assets amounted to 96.3 per cent of the total held by all Greek commercial banks;[47] the fact that Greek banking capital was growing much faster than industrial or merchant capital[48] emphasises the enormous power of these two Goliaths. Not only did they handle 90 per cent of the country's considerable savings, but they were also directly involved in the ownership and management of a large part of industry and insurance.[49]

As far as the state is concerned, the interventionist pattern adopted after 1932 not only continued, but was reinforced to such an extent that one may speak of a *qualitative* change. First, the remarkable concentration of banking capital and its tight hold over the economy is a clear indication of increased state control. The larger of the two banks, the National Bank, has always been owned by various public corporations through which the state has exercised majority control, while the Commercial Bank has also quite recently come under direct state control. Furthermore, the all-powerful *State Monetary Commission* not only regulates in a detailed manner the credit policies of all banking establishments, but also sets an overall credit and monetary objective, with a view to influencing both short- and long-term economic fluctuations. For example, through a policy of differential interest rates and by the imposition of quantitative credit controls over the amounts banks may lend to certain sectors, the Commission has the power to regulate specific branches of the economy, in line with its overall policies.[50] Finally, the state, in a way and on a scale unthinkable in the interwar period, also influences the economy through its massive investment programme. In 1959, as much as 34 per cent of the total fixed capital of industrial enterprises was owned by the state (at the same time the percentage was 32 in England, approximately 27 in Italy and Austria, and 25 in France[51]). Whereas in 1957 the state's direct investments in the economy amounted to approximately $113 million, i.e., 4.7 per cent of the Gross National Product, this rose to $538 million or 9.2 per cent of the GNP in 1970. Furthermore, if one remembers that the state budget, which before the war constituted 16.17 per cent of the GNP, now amounts to more than a third, it becomes understandable why many Greek Marxist economists speak of state-monopoly capitalism in post-war Greece.[52]

However, despite impressive rates of growth and increasing state intervention, the Greek economy by the late fifties had not managed to overcome a major feature of its underdevelopment: its weak manufacturing sector. Regardless of various state incentives, Greek capital was unwilling or unable to direct itself into those key manufacturing sectors (metallurgy, chemicals) where growth has great transformative power and important multiplying effects on the rest of the economy.[53] Consequently, by the end of the first post-civil war decade, Greece still exhibited the familiar features of an underdeveloped economy: an over-inflated, rapidly expanding tertiary sector, a badly organised and inefficient agricultural system employing more than one-half of the labour force, and a feeble, stagnating manufacturing sector. The contribution of the industrial sector to the GNP was only around 25 per cent, and manufacturing was the slowest growing industrial sector. (Its contribution to the total industrial output was in fact decreasing, whereas that of construction, transport and public utilities was increasing.[54])

The serious extent of Greece's backwardness in manufacturing is shown by a comparison with the country's now communist neighbours, who had been behind during the interwar period. In 1938 the index of manufacturing production (taking 1958 as 100) was 52 in Greece, 28 in Yugoslavia, and only 10 in Bulgaria. But by 1959, the score was 101 for Greece, 114 for Yugoslavia and 121 for Bulgaria.[55] Given this type of *impasse*, which clearly illustrates the limitations and weaknesses of the capital-accumulation model adopted, and given the state's commitment to the principle of free enterprise, the only solution for the further development of Greek capitalism was to resort to the help of foreign capital which, through the spectacular post-war development of the multinationals, started invading and exploiting peripheral societies in novel and ingenious ways.

Although Greece had initiated legislation to attract foreign capital as early as 1953, it was only in the early sixties that large amounts started to come to Greece in the form of direct investments. In 1960 the annual inflow of foreign capital was about $11.5 million, but by

1963 it had gone up to $50 million, and by 1966 to $157.5 million.[56] This was the third injection of foreign funds into the Greek economy. On the two previous occasions, in 1880 and 1922, the bulk of capital influx, mainly from England, had been in the form of public loans and social overhead investments. In the sixties it arrived as direct investments in industry, and came mainly from multinationals of American origin.[57] The relatively modest amount was more than offset by its going into those key sectors where Greek capital was reluctant to invest,[58] and thus greatly boosted Greek manufacturing and the industrial sector generally. As a result, industry not only expanded at a faster rate (its share in the GNP overtook that of agriculture from 1962 onwards), but there was a strong shift in investments from light consumer to durable and capital goods. (The share of light industry was 77.5 per cent of total manufacturing output in 1948–50, but down to 60.9 per cent in 1963–70.[59]) There was a parallel change in the composition of Greek exports, where agricultural products and raw minerals decreased in ratio to considerable exports of industrial goods.

There is no doubt that the post-1960 influx of foreign capital gave a considerable push to capitalist industrialisation in Greece, though this type of dependent, foreign-induced industrialisation did not eliminate the peripheral, underdeveloped character of the Greek economy; it simply changed its form. In Greece, just as in many other countries (especially in Latin America), the foreign-dominated dynamic and technologically advanced sector of industry was much better integrated with the requirements of the developed capitalist economies involved, than with the technologically backward but persistent simple-commodity sectors of agriculture and artisanal industry at home.

Contrary to what happened in Western Europe, Greek industrial capitalism has taken on an 'enclave' form. It has neither destroyed non-capitalist modes of production (i.e., the simple-commodity family unit which still prevails heavily in agriculture and small industry), nor has it become articulated with them in an organic, positive manner.[60] In fact, the linkages between the capitalist and simple-commodity sectors are predominantly negative: the effects of high productivity and technological progress originating in the advanced capitalist sector have not spread to the rest of the economy. Instead, through a variety of partly state-induced mechanisms, resources are systematically shifted from the simple-commodity to the capitalist sector, and then abroad.

The lack of complementarity, i.e., the disarticulation of simple-commodity and capitalist modes of production, is nowhere better illustrated than in the incapacity of the technologically advanced industrial sector to absorb the labour force leaving the countryside (hence the massive migration into Western Europe), and in the low value attributed to Greek industrial production. This in turn means that further industrialisation generates an increase in the level of imports of capital-goods which far outstrips the import-substitution currency gains from the additional indigenous production.[61]

The persistence/marginalisation of simple-commodity production explains to a great extent why inequalities in Greece are not only greater than in Western Europe, but also growing at a faster rate. In addition to the usual inequalities between labour and capital, there are huge inequalities between the technologically advanced and backward sectors of the economy. It has been estimated that, after deduction of taxes and social security benefits, 9.5 per cent of the national income goes to 40 per cent of the lowest income groups, whereas 58 per cent is channelled to the 17 per cent in the top income brackets.[62] Between 1954 and 1966, the national income almost doubled, profits tripled, and from 1960–71 banking profits quadrupled.[63]

Under the legislation of 1953, foreign capital is the most privileged in terms of cheap energy supplies, credits, taxation, and the re-exportation of profits, etc.[64] Indeed, it can be argued that industrial expenses and risks are socialised, while the profits from successful industrial ventures accrue to private/foreign interests. In other words, the state revenue from taxation on low incomes is used chiefly for the consolidation and development of big capital. This is obvious from the fact that indirect taxation provides not only more than one-half of state revenues but also tends to increase in comparison to direct taxes. Furthermore, even direct taxation is a heavier burden on small and medium than on higher incomes.[65] In the underdeveloped condition of Greek capitalism, such state policies are perfectly logical and indeed necessary. Where the economy depends on the continued willingness of foreign and mixed capital to keep investing, then any serious attempt to redress inequalities would only result in making the investment climate less favourable, so that foreign capital might prefer safer investments in the developed capitalist world, rather than run the risks inherent in a politically unstable environment. Thus, the state can do very little to redress inequalities; indeed, its own taxation and industrial incentives policies are at the root of such inequalities. The influx of foreign capital and the industrialisation of the sixties have brought the state and big capital ever closer together, even if the partnership has changed somewhat: despite its continuing expansion and interventionism, the state no longer occupies the dominant position. In the interwar period, indigenous capital was the junior partner, but this has ceased to be the case now that foreign capital plays such a key rôle.

It is not that foreign interests have set up some sort of formidable pressure group which dictates what economic policies the Greek government must follow. Although this is true to some limited extent, it is mainly the Greek state's structural/systemic constraints which force it to adopt an anti-popular, pro-big capital orientation. The real strength of foreign capital lies less in its ability to exert pressure, than in its threat of potential defection. Given the process of the increasing internationalisation of capital which is taking place in the Greek economy, the state can control big capital less and less. For instance, many interwar Greek firms owed their monopoly position to the good will of the state, but in the post-war era the monopoly exercised by foreign firms is more a function of modern technology than of state protectionism.[66] It is this which has led to the weakening of the bargaining position of the state, and to the greater autonomy and privileges of foreign capital. From these privileges and this autonomy, big indigenous capital tends to profit as well – as when, for example, large amounts of indigenous capital slip illegally abroad, in order to re-enter the Greek economy as foreign capital, with all the privileges of the 1953 law.[67]

Furthermore, the important rôle played in the post-war economy by big shipping capital is another indication of the shifting balance of power between capital and state. Since shipping capital whenever it feels itself 'bothered' by the state, can easily move elsewhere, shipowners enjoy all the state privileges accorded to big capital, without having to assume any obligations in return. Moreover, since shipping capital lies beyond the effective control of the state, it is becoming an increasingly easy avenue by means of which merchant capital can escape abroad. So if the migration of labour robs Greece of its more valuable human resources, shipping plays a similar rôle with respect to its financial wealth.

The large-scale social disruptions and shifts (rural exodus, migration, urbanisation) created by the Greek post-war model of capital accumulation have weakened traditional ties and orientations, and thus not only made inequalities larger, but also more visible. This is why the rising standard of living[68] which eliminated extreme forms of poverty, instead of appeasing, only intensified popular discontent. It is a truism that relative pauperisation in conditions of rapid change creates more frustration and dissatisfaction than the stable, traditional type of absolute poverty. This mounting popular dissatisfaction, in combination with dramatic events in Cyprus, was at the root of the political mobilisation of the late fifties and early sixties which was to call into question the post-civil war system of 'guided democracy'. The point had been reached where neither state repression, nor the right's clientelistic networks could retain for much longer their control over an urban and rural population already radicalised during the civil war, and increasingly aware of the pattern of growing inequalities. As the forces of the left were gathering political strength,[69] the repressive apparatus of the state, under the active guidance of IDEA, underwent reactivation.[70] But, given the level of popular dissatisfaction, the more the state and the para-state were trying to manipulate the parliamentary forces (e.g., by rigging the 1961 elections), the more the opposition forces gained popular support and consolidated their organisational cohesion.[71]

It lies outside the scope of this chapter to examine the complicated set of events which led to the 1967 military dictatorship.[72] Suffice it to say that as the growing political turmoil was translating itself into political forces, it threatened the post-civil war balance of power between the throne, the army and parliament, within which the army rather than parliament held the dominant position. To put it more generally, the Greek model of capital accumulation had by the middle sixties created conditions which were incompatible with the repressive political superstructure. By favouring big capital at the expense of almost all other sections of the population, the Greek state had nurtured a socio-politcial discontent which its system of repressive parliamentarianism could no longer cope with. This system had either to be liberalised and opened up to the masses, or rigorously reinforced by the total abolition of parliamentary rule. To understand why the second alternative came to prevail requires a closer analysis of the throne–parliament–army configuration within the state. It has already been mentioned that the power position of the throne had been steadily declining since the early twentieth century. Moreover, after the Civil War and during the rapid post-war capitalist development, the intra-bourgeois 'throne' issue gradually ceased to play its earlier important rôle as this was displaced by the 'threat from below' issue as Greece moved rapidly to the stage of mass politics. With the crown largely out of the running, therefore, the two major contestants for power were the army and the parliamentary forces. Since the popular mobilisation did not have a revolutionary orientation, the political right did not feel sufficiently threatened to support a military solution. Instead, it opted for an electoral confrontation with the rising centre and centre–left forces.[73] The army, on the other hand – or rather those who occupied key repressive positions within the various branches of the state and para-state – had a great deal to lose from an 'opening up' of the parliamentary system. The liberalisation of the régime, that is, the entrance of the masses into the political arena, even if initially organised under the banner of a liberal bourgeois party, would result in the broadened parliamentary forces gaining firmer control over state apparatuses, including the army itself. This situation would threaten directly not only all those holding crucial repressive jobs within the state, but also the overall structural dominance of the army.[74] So it was the military component of the ruling bloc that decided in favour of a dictatorial solution.

If repressive parliamentarianism had failed to direct the 'orderly' entrance of the Greek masses into politics, the dictatorial solution which attempted to block their entrance could not claim success either. As the colonels followed even more ruthlessly the model of capital accumulation set by their predecessors, all the trends already present merely became accentuated. Given the growing popular discontent, and the fact that the military did not even manage to get the active support of important bourgeois factions (which felt that dictatorship was unnecessary for maintaining bourgeois rule), they failed to build up any mass organisations which might have con- solidated their power. In other words, the seven-year dictatorial régime was not only quite different from the inter-war military interventions (where the different rôle of the military made interven- tion less repressive and more ephemeral), it was also very different from fascist or quasi-fascist régimes like Franco's in Spain or Salazar's in Portugal, which managed to mobilise considerable mass support in both the towns and the countryside. It only needed the 1974 economic depression and the Greco–Turkish crisis over Cyprus for the military régime to fall, and to give way to a presidential parlia- mentary régime which, although not as repressive as the post-civil war 'guided democracy', has not basically reversed the dominant rôle of the army over the state apparatus. The persistence of army dominance is explained by the fact that the change of régime was not brought about by popular action, but from above; mainly by army factions which tried to safeguard the prestige and dominance of the army by dissociating it from the disastrous foreign policy of the short-lived Ioannides dictatorship. The armed forces turned to Karamanlis for the same reason that seven years earlier they had decided to abolish parliamentary rule: in order to preserve the dominant position of the army within the Greek post-war state.[75]

The significant political development within the present parliamentary system is the emergence in the 1977 elections of a well-organised socialist/populist party (under the leadership of Andreas Papandreou) as the main opposition party in Parliament. At last, Greek populism has, if somewhat belatedly, made its large-scale appearance in Greek politics.[76] This means that for the first time in Greek parliamentary history, the liberal–conservative intra-bourgeois split which had by clientelistic means managed the 'vertical' organisation of the working-classes in politics, has been replaced by a political split more directly linked with the underlying structures of economic exploitation. It also means that, sooner or later, this new mode of polical integration of the Greek urban and rural working-classes will have its impact on the existing army–parliament balance of power within the state. But it remains to be seen – if and when Papandreou challenges the present structures of state controls – how the military will react to such a threat to its dominance within the state. What seems certain is that, within the Greek framework of underdevelopment, the entrance of the masses into politics remains an insoluble problem in the sense that, as I shall argue later, neither parliamentary modes of integration nor dictatorial modes of exclusion seem able to cope in the long run with the disruptions created by dependent, unbalanced capitalist growth.

On the Peripheral Character of the Greek State

The Major Trends

Up to now we have examined the modern Greek state in relation to the development of the economy from the pre-capitalist phase in the nineteenth century to the present day. From this examination have emerged the following main features.

(a) Given the dependent/peripheral character of the Greek social formation, the basic structural transformations in the state–economy relationship have always had their origin in the changing nature of Western imperialism. Thus, the first decisive attempt at administrative rationalisation and state intervention in the economy was linked with the European economic crisis of the 1870s, and the relatively massive inflow of foreign and diaspora capital into Greece (railway investments, etc.). The second attempt, which involved a serious drive at import-substitution industrialisation, was the direct result of the 1929 world crisis accelerating and putting into a new, highly protectionist context processes of capital accumulation which had started a few years earlier; again as a result of an international crisis (i.e., the 'eastern' question which involved Greece in a disastrous war with Turkey in 1922). The reconstruction and capitalist expansion of the 1950s which, for the first time, involved the state in direct large-scale investments in the economy, was linked with post-war European expansion and American aid for reconstructing the ruined European economies. Finally, the industrialisation breakthrough of the 1960s, which brought the state into very close collaboration with foreign capital is, of course, related to the present multi-national direct investment phase of Western imperialism.

(b) Since state intervention aims at buttressing rather than combating capitalism, increasing state participation in the economy does not necessarily mean increasing state control over capital. If in the interwar period industrial capital, as the passive creature of the state, was under its tutelage, the state–capital power relationship was reversed in the sixties: despite direct public investments in industry and the huge state budget, the imperative need for attracting foreign capital meant that the latter, by reason of its very structural position, increasingly became a major force in the state–capital relationship.

(c) In terms of the power structure of the state (the throne–parliament–army triumvirate), the broad trends were the gradual decline of the throne's power position in the transition from oligarchic to mass politics brought about by first, the middle classes (first quarter of the twentieth century), and then the urban and rural working-classes (Civil War and after). This gradual broadening of political participation was, of course, reflected in the organisation of the political parties and the changing character of clientelistic politics: 'monopolistic' patronage of local notables was succeeded by a more 'open' state and party-oriented clientelism, and the emergence of 'horizontal' political organisations which weakened patronage networks. The strengthening of the parliamentary forces was accompanied by the development of the armed forces, their formation into a distinct and highly powerful interest group, and later by the changing character of army interventions in politics: from seeing itself as an arbiter and participant in the interwar intra-bourgeois squabblings, the army promoted itself in the post-civil war era to guardian of the bourgeois system against popular threats.

(d) In view of the underdeveloped character of Greek capitalism, neither the army nor the parliamentary forces has been able to establish a long-term and irreversible dominance over the other. Instead, there is a pendulum movement of 'openings' and 'closures' of the political system, a periodic alternation between quasi-parliamentary and dictatorial forms of state control while Greek capitalism continues to be unable to deal with the popular mobilisation that its very growth unavoidably fosters.

The 'Over-extended' Character of the Greek State

The literature on post-colonial or peripheral states[77] always stresses the *overdeveloped* and relatively *autonomous* character of the state in dependent capitalist formations. It will not be possible here to enter into a complicated debate on the nature of this so-called overdevelopment and state autonomy. I shall merely try to point out briefly *some* of the factors which must be taken into account in an explanation of the extensive nature of state interventionism in Greek civil society, and the extent to which it is possible to speak of the relative autonomy of the state in peripheral societies. Although most of my points refer primarily to the Greek situation, they are also relevant, I believe, for other peripheral states, especially those which try to operate more or less intermittently within parliamentary institutional forms (e.g., Latin American societies).

The fundamental consideration to be emphasised in this context is that underdeveloped capitalism is less *self-regulatory* than developed capitalism. With the large-scale persistence of non-capitalist modes of production and the disarticulation (negative linkages) between the capitalist and the non-capitalist modes, the peripheral state has in comparison with the metropolitan state a much more difficult and complicated reproduction task. It has to intervene in the economy in a two-fold and contradictory sense: on the one hand, the need to develop industrial capitalism means that there must be massive transfers of resources from the non-capitalist to the capitalist sectors; on the other, as these two sectors are neither self-contained nor complementary, the state must increasingly step in to fill the 'gaps' in order to maintain the economic system as a whole.[78] To give a few examples: the lack of development of a serious capital market in the Greek economy[79] means that the state is forced to assume financial/credit functions which in a developed capitalist economy are performed by the stock exchange (in which case the state intervenes *indirectly* to regulate stock exchange operations, rather than *directly* to provide substitute solutions for their weak development).

Secondly, in the simple-commodity sector, the lack of a strong co-operative movement in the Greek countryside and the more general absence of any regionally autonomous modes of organisation mean that the state has to perform functions (e.g., agricultural credit, price regulation, etc.) which could be performed more effectively and advantageously for agricultural producers if the rural sector were organised in an economically and politically more autonomous fashion.[80]

Thirdly, the lack of self-regulation becomes even more noticeable at the political and ideological levels. As has been frequently pointed out, peripheral capitalist formations, including the Greek case, are characterised by a weak, atrophied civil society. It is not only that the Greek working-classes of both the cities and the countryside are poorly organised (trade unions and co-operative organisations are mostly passive extensions of the state administration),[81] but even the economically dominant classes do not manage to constitute well-organised and cohesive pressure groups. Because of the persistence of patronage politics, even bourgeois parties and interest groups are articulated within the state machinery in a clientelistic/personalistic manner. This type of articulation means – as I shall argue below – that state policies promote the interests of particular types of capital, rather than the interests of capital as a whole.

Finally, the lack of organisation in even the dominant classes is reflected on the ideological level by the weak development of a 'hegemonic' ideology in the Greek social formation; that is to say, of legitimating mechanisms which more or less autonomously integrate ideologically the dominated classes without direct state indoctrination (through the existence of strong voluntary organisations, and of a conservative intelligentsia which is not totally isolated from popular aspirations and orientations, and so on). Since the poorly-structured Greek civil society has only very weak self-regulating ideological mechanisms, the state has to take on additional politico–ideological functions; for example, strict control over the mass media, great regimentation and control of educational curricula, and close surveillance of university and religious institutions. Since such additional controls, given the disruptions created by underdeveloped capitalism and the bureaucratic inefficiency of the peripheral state, can never be executed successfully, the state's repressive apparatus must inevitably keep on expanding.[82]

However, it is important to stress that my attempt to explain state characteristics in terms of the reproduction requirements of under-developed capitalism by no means implies that I consider such a 'functionalist' explanation sufficient in itself. To show, for example, that peripheral capitalism 'requires' an over-extended state apparatus does not explain *how* and under *what* specific conditions such a state came into being in any particular social formation – hence the need for the more historical analysis of the previous sections.

The Relative Autonomy of the Greek State

Given the very serious structural constraints within which the Greek state must operate, in what sense is it possible to speak of its relative autonomy? Examination of the relation between class structure and politics will show that this relation, not only in pre-capitalist Greece but even after the dominance of the capitalist mode of production, is more *indirect* than in Western capitalism: in contrast to the West, the persistence of large-scale vertical/clientelistic modes of integration even after the advent of mass politics cuts across and prevents the development of horizontal, class-type political organisations.

This is not, of course, to say that political clientelism has not changed with the entrance of the masses into politics. As I have stressed in the sections above, not only is 'modern' clientelism very different from its 'traditional'/oligarchic predecessor, but it is also much more precarious and fragile. It is constantly disrupted by emerging 'horizontal' organisations which, however, are *equally fragile and precarious*, and it is this which prevents the patronage networks – unlike their Western counterparts – from declining irreversibly. Indeed, the uneasy coexistence of vertical and horizontal political organisations, and the weak institutionalisation of both, is another distinctive characteristic of peripheral capitalist states, especially those with quasi-parliamentary forms of control.

In so far as the linkages between the state and civil society operate to a much greater extent through clientelistic/vertical networks than in the West, and in so far as a relatively autonomous political organisa-tion of the dominated classes is not possible, it is quite legitimate to argue that political conflict and developments within the state are not *directly* linked with 'objective' cleavages emanating from the social and economic division of labour. The state is, therefore, relatively independent (by comparison with the metropolitan state) from the pressures of well articulated class interests. In other words, objective class locations are *not directly* linked with political practices. It is obvious, for instance, that in political systems characterised by non-personalistic/clientelistic, mass-based bourgeois parties, the autonomy of the state *vis-à-vis* the dominant classes is not as high as in cases where such parties do not exist. In the latter case, as the 1967 Greek military coup has shown, it is easier for shifts of power to occur within the state, which then present the bourgeoisie with a *fait accompli*.

Relative state autonomy with respect to class organisations does not, however, imply that the peripheral 'autonomous' state is able to act against the interests of capital. In its rôle as the general co-ordinator of the total social formation, the state has to provide a favourable institutional framework for the enlarged reproduction of capital, that is, it has to use its resources to safeguard and promote bourgeois interests, even if these are poorly organised. Such an institutional framework requires, among other things, that the state ensures the working-classes remain fragmented and badly organised; it is precisely when this fragmentation decreases that individual capitals are forced to organise better.

The Relative Weakness of the Greek State

Relative autonomy *vis-à-vis* organised class interests does not necessarily mean that the state has the ability to achieve even class-based collective goals; indeed, *relative autonomy* can coincide with *structural dependence*. The peripheral state is restricted much more by structural constraints than by group pressures. In fact, structural constraints are so limiting that capitalist interests do not have to become organised in order to get the state to work for them. This combination of high autonomy *vis-à-vis* poorly organised class interests, and high structural dependence upon both the national and international capitalist system, is one of the specific characteristics of the peripheral state. In Greece, externally generated structural constraints are such that, despite the non-existence of strong class structures, they leave the state with very little room for manoeuvre. Apart from the inherent uncontrollability of foreign capital, Greek industrialisation is based on the import of capital goods which create an increasingly large trade deficit; in other words, a gradually deteriorating structural dependence, which is much more difficult to overcome than pressures on Greek governments emanating from NATO circles or the CIA.

If we consider internal structural constraints and if, *pace* Offe, the capitalist state has built-in mechanisms which enable it to achieve both instrumental (reproduction of the capitalist system) and legitimation goals,[83] these mechanisms are less effective in the peripheral state. We have already mentioned the difficulties the Greek state has to face in its attempts to legitimise capitalism (lack of a hegemonic ideology; growing inequalities, the maintenance of which demands high levels of repression; etc.). Concerning state performance with regard to 'instrumental goals', the persistence of clientelism and the large-scale political corruption which accompanies it, means that it lacks the organisational tools (an 'impartial' and efficient administration, well-organised bourgeois parties operating as effective transmission belts between rulers and ruled) for achieving the general interests of capital. In fact, capitalist growth is often blocked or retarded by the ability of individual capitalists or very narrow regional interests to influence state policies in their own favour. There are, for instance, numerous examples in Greek parliamentary history of laws tailored to suit particular, politically influential capitalists, and of cases where huge state resources are channelled into an area where the political clientele of the relevant minister is located. Although these particularistic practices can also be found in Western political systems, they never take the dimensions that exist in clientelistic politics. In the latter, such practices are so pervasive that they seriously hamper and obstruct the implementation of collective capitalist interests. At the same time these practices create an extreme formalism which constantly confronts 'non-influential' citizens in their dealings with state bureaucrats. This can partly be explained historically, by the wholesale importation and imposition in nineteenth-century Greece of Western European administrative and parliamentary institutions which are totally incongruent with Greek infrastructural realities.[84] But they can also be explained as deliberate strategies by which state bureaucrats try to enhance their power position and extract a variety of benefits. However, what matters here is that the combination of extreme particularistic and formalistic practices makes the state apparatus both too pliable and too rigid for not only the people's general interest, but also for the general interests of capital.

The Greek State's Régime Instability

The point just made brings us to another fundamental and distinctive characteristic of the peripheral Greek state: its inherent incapacity to deal effectively with the entrance of the masses into active politics. What is often omitted in the literature on the peripheral state is that it is not only foreign capital over which the peripheral state is gradually losing control: it is also losing control of the mass mobilisation process, intensified by the disruptions and inequalities which its very policies continue to engender. In fact, capitalist growth in the Western parliamentary régimes, being more indigenously generated, has created a framework within which the material fruits of technological progress and economic growth have been more evenly and widely spread among the population (for example, the development of the welfare state). This framework has been favourable for the gradual broadening of political participation, for the development of relatively autonomous[85] and cohesive political organisations of the working-classes, and for the irreversible decline of clientelistic politics. Such a mode of political integration is much more difficult, if not impossible, to achieve in underdeveloped capitalist formations. Their basic economic structure is incompatible with an 'open' solution to the problems of mass political participation. If the urban and rural working-classes were to be permitted to organise in a politically autonomous manner, they would do so in order to press, if not for the overthrow of capitalism, at least for a radical redressing of growing inequalities. But if this were done to any serious extent it would jeopardise the type of foreign-led, dependent, disarticulated industrialisation which is based on these very inequalities. What this means is that the autonomous political organisation of the working-classes tends to be, in the long view, incompatible with the model of underdeveloped capitalist accumulation. In other words, the chances of the relatively autonomous organisation of the disadvantaged classes are much less in peripheral than in developed capitalism.

What solutions are available to the peripheral state for dealing with the political participation problem? There are two major alternatives: (a) either the masses are brought into the political arena through *dependent modes* of integration, through vertical/clientelistic political organisations controlled by the dominant classes (as was the case in Greek interwar politics), and/or through horizontal dependent ones (like most Latin American populist parties); or (b) when such dependent modes of parliamentary integration fail to work (for example, when populalist parties like Bulgaria's Agrarian Union get out of control, or when strong class-based communist/socialist parties seriously disrupt the clientelistic networks of the bourgeoisie), the capitalist state steps in to impose *dictatorial modes* of control. What is important to note, however, is that *neither dependent modes of integration nor dictatorial modes of exclusion can constitute a permanent solution to the problem of mass participation in politics.*

The dependent mode of integration is not only inherently unstable at advanced stages of capitalist underdevelopment (rapid urbanisation inevitably disrupts clientelistic networks)[86] but, as the Greek case has shown, dictatorial solutions are equally brittle and precarious. The long-term consolidation of a dictatorial régime presupposes the building up of mass organisations and the mobilisation of large-scale popular support; conditions which are difficult to achieve in a socio-economic context which favours big capital at the expense of most other sections of the population. In view of the ineffectiveness and instability of both solutions, therefore, what happens in many peripheral capitalist formations is the regular alternation of dictatorial and dependent modes of control, as the bourgeois state tries to cope with the complicated reproduction problems of underdeveloped capitalism.

In fact, I would argue that the characteristic which most clearly distinguishes the peripheral capitalist state from both the metropolitan state and the state in collectivist régimes such as those of Eastern Europe, is its inherent régime instability, its incapacity to institutionalise in a more or less permanent manner either an open or closed mode of political integration. The institutionalisation of an 'open' solution would, as already argued, require the granting of some political autonomy to the dominated classes, an autonomy which is not compatible with the reproduction requirements of peripheral capitalism. The institutionalisation of a long-term dictatorial system of state controls, on the other hand, would require the total subjugation of both labour *and* capital; in other words, the abolition of the capitalist mode of production. It is only when dictatorial regimentation is not one-sided but all-embracing, and therefore capable of imposing a radical economic and social levelling, that it acquires enough legitimacy for its lasting consolidation. Another way of putting this is to say that the peripheral state can neither achieve the régime stability which is based on a relatively self-regulated, well-articulated civil society, nor the stability based on its complete subjugation to totalitarian state rule. The fact that the peripheral capitalist state is as unable to destroy civil society as it is unable to articulate with it in any effective manner, is the most important reason for the regular changes of its form.

Notes

1. Capitalism in this paper is defined in its narrow sense as referring to a mode of production characterised by the use of wage labour and hence by the direct producers being divorced from the means of production. With this definition, the integration of an economy into a world capitalist market, or the commercialisation of some of its sectors, do not automatically make it capitalist.

2. During the middle of the eighteenth century, the already important Greek merchant capital started quite successfully to enter shipbuilding and textile production. This early promising start was cut short at the beginning of the nineteenth century, just before the 1821 Greek war of independence against the Ottoman empire, when both these industrial sectors started to decline again rapidly. See V. Kremmidas, *Introduction to the History of Modern Greek Society* (in Greek) (Exantas, Athens, 1976).

3. See G. Dertilis, 'Social Change and Military Intervention in Politics', unpublished PhD thesis, University of Sheffield, 1976, Table XIV. Also, according to another calculation, at approximately the same time, a quarter of the non-agricultural labour force was employed by the state; see C. Tsoukalas, 'The Reforms of Trikoupis', in *History of the Greek Nation: Modern Hellenism 1881–1913* (Ekdotiki Athinon, Athens, 1977), p. 13.

4. C. Tsoukalas, *History of The Greek Nation*, p. 13.

5. In fact, as in *ancien régime* Western Europe, the nineteenth-century centralisation and expansion of the state did not imply the total political ruin of the previously autonomous local oligarchies. Most of them, once they realised the futility of resisting state expansionism, successfully compensated for the reduction of their political functions at local level by occupying powerful positions within the state apparatus.

6. See G. Dertilis, 'Social Change and Military Intervention in Politics', for an excellent analysis of the relationship between the diaspora bourgeoisie and Greek politics.

7. L. S. Stavrianos, *The Balkans Since 1453* (Holt, Reinhart and Winston, New York, 1952), pp. 413–544.

8. A recent calculation puts the influx of foreign capital into Greece between 1879 and 1893, which arrived in various forms including state loans, private investments, etc., at the considerable amount of 750 million gold francs.

9. L. S. Stavrianos, *The Balkans Since 1453*, pp. 416–17. With regard to the inflow of diaspora capital, whereas between 1830–80 it had been channelled into donations to the state and remittances to village relatives, after 1880 it not only increased in extent, but changed direction into finance, transport, shipping and land purchases. See also G. Dertilis, 'Social Change and Military Intervention in Politics'.

10. For example, C. Tsoukalas, *History of The Greek Nation*.

11. First by the annexation of Thessaly in 1881, and later, as a result of the Balkan Wars and the First World War, by the incorporation of Epirus, Macedonia, part of Thrace, the Aegean islands and Crete.

12. Except for judges and the military.

13. This significant trend started with Trikoupis and continued with Venizelos. Especially in the second decade of the twentieth century, when Greece was permanently at war (the Balkan Wars, First World War), state expenditure rose and remained at a very high level even after the wars had ended. In addition, the national protectionism created by the hostilities and the enormous war profits realised by Greek entrepreneurs did contribute to some limited industrialisation, a process which was to be speeded up dramatically after 1922.

14. For figures on levels of taxation and state borrowing, see C. Tsoukalas, *History of The Greek Nation*, pp. 199 ff.

15. For statistical evidence see K. Legg, *Politics in Modern Greece* (Stanford University Press, California, 1969), Chapter 5; and D. Kitsikis, 'L'Evolution de l'élite politique Grecque' in M. B. Kiray (ed.), *Social Stratification and Development in the Mediterranean Basin* (Paris, 1973).

16. The relative decline of the throne was a very gradual process. Though no modern mass parties emerged under Venizelos' premiership, there was considerable development and strengthening of *national* party organisations, giving political leaders more control over their members and more bargaining power *vis-à-vis* the King. As party discipline increased, the King's ability to manipulate politicians and elections lessened. It had not entirely disappeared even by 1965–7, but it was certainly less easy to effect: whereas King George in 1868 had easily been able to dismiss Prime Minister Koumoundouros, King Constantine in 1915 found it considerably more difficult to rid himself of Venizelos.

17. On this point see N. Mouzelis, *Modern Greece: Facets of Underdevelopment* (Macmillan, London, 1978), Chapter 6.

18. The abrupt restriction at approximately this time of migration to America increased the availability of labour even further.

19. The fact that even as late as 1961 a quarter of Greek industrialists originated from outside Greece, mostly from Turkey, demonstrates the crucial contribution of Asia Minor refugees with regard to entrepreneurial skills. See A. Alexander, *Greek Industrialists*, Research Monograph Series (Centre of Planning and Economic Research, Athens, 1964), p. 128.

20. From 1923 to 1930, imported foreign capital amounted to 1,162.8 million gold francs. Considering the short period during which this capital came into the country, it was quite an unprecedented influx in modern Greek history. See M. Nikolinakos, *Studies on Greek Capitalism* (in Greek) (Nea Sinora, Athens, 1976), p. 55.

21. For a detailed examination of these measures, see C. Vergopoulos, 'The Greek Economy from 1926 to 1935', in *History of the Greek Nation: The New Hellenism 1913–41* (Ekdotiki Athinon, Athens, 1977).

22. Measures taken between 1923 and 1926, referring to tariff protection, expropriation of land for the development of industrial enterprises, etc. See C. Vergopoulos, *History of the Greek Nation.*

23. S. Gregoriadis, *Economic History of Modern Greece* (in Greek) (Athens, 1974), p. 48.

24. Figures taken from C. Vergopoulos, *History of the Greek Nation*, p. 330.

25. For Marx, 'capitalist production only then really begins when each individual capitalist employs simultaneously a comparatively large number of laborers; when consequently the labor process is carried on on an extensive scale and yields relatively large quantities of products'. *Capital* (International Publishers, New York, 1967), vol. I, p. 322.

26. On this, see C. Vergopoulos, who views the National Bank's resistance as representing all those interests which were associated with a commercially 'liberal' agrarian society against the emerging protectionist, import-substituting industrial capitalism. *History of the Greek Nation*, p. 334.

27. Since the main Greek exports were luxury goods for which international demand was relatively inelastic, Greek exporters became more and more dependent on foreign buyers. See M. Serafetinidi, 'The Breakdown of Parliamentary Institutions in Greece', unfinished thesis, London School of Economics.

28. A close analysis of how these mechanisms link small-commodity agricultural production to industry is given by C. Vergopoulos, *The Agrarian Problems of Greece* (in Greek) (Exantas, Athens, 1975), pp. 176 ff. A more theoretical treatment is contained in S. Amin and C. Vergopoulos, *La Question paysanne et le capitalisme* (Anthropos, Paris, 1974).

29. No serious studies on income distribution in Greece exist. For some interwar figures concerning the growth of upper class incomes, see G. Dertilis, 'Social Change

and Military Intervention in Politics', Chapter 2, Table XII. For post-war figures see M. Malios, *The Present Phase of Capitalist Development in Greece* (in Greek) (Athens, 1975), pp. 139 and 141; also D. Karageorgas, 'The Distribution of Tax Burden by Income Groups in Greece', *Economic Journal* (June 1973).

30. C. Vergopoulos, *The Agrarian Problems of Greece*, pp. 238 ff.

31. C. Vergopoulos, *The Agrarian Problems of Greece*, p. 15 (my translation).

32. C. Vergopoulos, 'The Greek Economy 1926–35', in *History of the Greek Nation*, pp. 336–7.

33. The Greek Communist Party, which had started to play an active rôle in Greek politics in the 1930s, was numerically very weak during all the interwar period.

34. See J. D. Bell, 'The Agrarian Movement in Bulgaria', unpublished thesis, Princeton University, 1970.

35. J. M. Malloy (ed.), *Authoritarianism and Populism in Latin America* (University of Pittsburg Press, Pittsburg, 1977).

36. For an examination of the reasons which explain this fundamental difference in political organisation between Greek and Bulgarian interwar peasants, see N. Mouzelis, *Modern Greece*, Chapter 5.

37. For more details on these developments see N. Mouzelis, 'Class and Clientelistic Politics: The Case of Greece', *Sociological Review* (August 1978).

38. Although general conscription was introduced in 1880, it was only during the Balkan Wars that numbers increased markedly. For statistics on that point, see D. Dakin, *The Unification of Greece 1770–1923* (Benn, London, 1972), p. 316.

39. Tuition fees for the Evelpidon School, the top military academy in Greece, were abolished in 1917 and its exclusive student body – all of whom needed wealthy families or a good marriage to be able to maintain an officer's life style – began to be diluted with middle class elements. See T. Veremis, 'The Greek Army in Politics 1922–35', unpublished PhD thesis, Trinity College, Oxford, 1974.

40. The relatively dependent position of the interwar military is understandable in terms of its historical origins. Contrary to the case of many newly independent countries, there was no continuity in Greece between the forces who fought in the war of independence against the Turks, and those who constituted the modern Greek Army. The reason for this was that after the establishment of the monarchical state under Bavarian King Otho in the early nineteenth century, the local chieftains, who more than anyone else had contributed to the successful outcome of the war, were brushed aside in favour of a new military organisation with Bavarian officers and troops which were controlled by the throne. See I. Makriyannis, *Memoirs*, trans. H. A. Liderdale (Oxford University Press, London, 1966).

41. T. Veremis, 'The Greek Army in Politics, 1922–35', Chapters III and XII.

42. For a detailed account, see G. Katiphoris, *The Barbarians' Legislation* (in Greek) (Athens, 1975).

43. IDEA was founded in Athens in 1944. A most interesting insider's account of the group is given by G. Karayannis, *1940–52: The Greek Drama* (in Greek) (Athens, n.d.), pp. 105–69, who was himself an IDEA man.

44. A clear indication of the power and autonomy of the army *vis-à-vis* both the throne and the bourgeois parliamentary forces was the rise of Marshal Papagos, the leader of the Civil War army, whom the King mistrusted. Papagos' enormous prestige among officers and his successful entrance into politics in 1952 through the creation of a popular right-wing movement (the Greek Rally) were obvious signs of the dominance of the military within the state.

45. The average growth rate in the fifties was 6 per cent. See *National Accounts of Greece 1948–70* (in Greek), pp. 120–1.

46. S. Gregoriadis, *Economic History of Modern Greece*, pp. 70–8; G. Coutsoumaris, *The Morphology of Greek Industry* (Centre of Economic Research, Athens, 1963).

47. D. Psilos, *Capital Market in Greece* (Centre of Economic Research, Athens, 1964), pp. 185–6.

48. The assets of the commerical banks increased twenty-fold between 1955 and 1969. See M. Malios, *The Present Phase of Capitalist Development in Greece.*

49. For a detailed account of the development of banking capital in Greece, see M. Serafetinidi, 'The Breakdown of Parliamentary Institutions in Greece'.

50. For details on the structure and functioning of the Monetary Commission, see J. Samaras, *State and Capital in Greece* (in Greek) (Sinhroni Epohi, Athens, 1977), pp. 159 ff.

51. J. Samaras, *State and Capital in Greece*, p. 107.

52. Cf. the works of M. Malios, *The Present Phase of Capitalist Development in Greece*; J. Samaras, *State and Capital in Greece*; and G. Farakos, *Problems of the Greek State Monopoly Capitalism* (in Greek) (Sinhroni Epohi, Athens, 1976).

53. An indication of this unwillingness was the fact that the two big banking concerns were unable to dispose of the 15 per cent of their funds they were obliged to advance for the development of the manufacturing sector. See D. Psilos, *Capital Market in Greece*, p. 194.

54. In 1938 manufacturing output amounted to 85.6 per cent of all industrial output, but declined to 79.9 per cent in 1948–9, and to 73 per cent in the 1959–60 period. See G. Coutsoumaris, *The Morphology of Greek Industry*, p. 55.

55. *United Nations Statistical Yearbook 1966*, Table 50.

56. Taken from G. Giannaros, 'Foreign Capital in the Greek Economy', in E. Illiou, *et al.*, *Multinational Monopolies* (in Greek) (Exantas, Athens, 1973), p. 404.

57. For details, see D. Benas, *The Influx of Foreign Capital in Greece* (Papazizis, Athens, 1976).

58. In fact, 76.5 per cent of foreign capital was invested in the manufacturing sector. See D. Benas, *The Influx of Foreign Capital in Greece*, p. 18.

59. B. Nefeloudis, *Demythisation With Numbers* (in Greek) (Athens, 1973), p. 146.

60. For an early analysis of Greek underdevelopment in terms of modes of production cf. M. Serafetinidi, 'The Breakdown of Parliamentary Institutions in Greece'.

61. S. Babanasi and C. Soula, *Greece on the Periphery of Developed Countries* (in Greek) (Athens, 1978), pp. 115 ff.

62. D. Karageorgas, 'The Distribution of Tax Burden by Income Groups in Greece'.

63. M. Malios, *The Present Phase of Capitalist Development in Greece*, pp. 139 and 141.

64. For details see D. Benas, *The Influx of Foreign Capital in Greece*, Part I.

65. B. Nefeloudis, *Demythisation With Numbers*, p. 96.

66. The influx of foreign capital has dramatically accentuated the monopolisation tendencies of the Greek economy. For instance, the enormous size of such giants as ESSO–PAPPAS or PECHINEY, or the fact that out of the 200 largest firms in terms of fixed capital 17 were fully foreign-owned and in another 39 the foreign participation varied from 10 to 90 per cent, is a clear demonstration of this. See, for example, A. Photopoulos, 'The Dependence of the Greek Economy on Foreign Capital' (in Greek), *Economicos Tahidromos* (July 1975), p. 10.

67. D. Benas, *The Influx of Foreign Capital in Greece*, p. 29.

68. Gross *per capita* income, approximately $550 at the beginning of the sixties, had reached the $1000 level by the end of the decade, (*Statistical Annual of Greece 1971*), p. 378.

69. A clear sign of this were the spectacular 1958 election gains of the left-wing EDA party which, for a short period (i.e., before the unification of the political forces of the Centre), became the main opposition in parliament.

70. Thus IDEA participated fully in the elaboration of the notorious 'Pericles' contingency plan, devised for the purpose of neutralising the communists in case of war, but used instead by the right to achieve victory in the 1961 elections. See S. Gregoriadis, *The History of the Dictatorship* (in Greek) (Athens, 1975), vol. I, p. 14.

71. Thus George Papandreou's Centre Party managed to challenge the electoral supremacy of the right in the 1962 and again in the 1963 elections. In the latter case, he won an unprecendented majority of 53 per cent.

72. For a more detailed analysis see N. Mouzelis, *Modern Greece*, Chapter 7.

73. Kanellopoulos, the right-wing leader, finally accepted the risk of an electoral confrontation which was set for April 1967, and came to a secret agreement with George Papandreou.

74. It was not by chance that the catalyst of the political crisis was a conflict over the control of the armed forces.

75. I would argue that the major reasons for the rise and fall of the 1967 military dictatorship are to be found in the internal structural imbalances of the state, rather than in external intervention (by the CIA, etc.). For a justification of this position, see N. Mouzelis, *Modern Greece*, pp. 131 ff.

76. The main reasons why populism did not make its appearance during the interwar period of import-substitution industrialisation (as it did in most Latin American and Balkan countries) are connected with the *dichasmos* and the Civil War. For a development of this point see N. Mouzelis, 'On the Greek Elections', *New Left Review* (April 1978).

77. Some representative works of this literature are: H. Alavi, 'The State in Post-colonial Societies: Pakistan and Bangladesh', *New Left Review* (July–August 1972); Colin Leys, 'The "Over-developed" Post-colonial State: A Re-evaluation', in *Review of African Political Economy* (January–April 1976); John Saul, 'The State in Post-colonial Societies', in *Socialist Register* (1974); W. Ziemann and M. Lanzendörfer, 'The State in Peripheral Societies', *Socialist Register* (1977).

78. This point is made by W. Ziemann and M. Lanzendörfer, 'The State in Peripheral Societies'.

79. D. Psilos, *Capital Market in Greece*, Chapter 10.

80. This important point is fully developed in K. D. Karavidas' classical work *Agrotika* (new edition by Papazisis, Athens, 1978). The lack of organisational self-regulation and autonomy which Karavidas sees in interwar Greek agriculture was further accentuated in the post-war period. See also N. Mouzelis, '*Agrotika*: The Comparative Study of Inter-war Balkan Rural Structures', *Greek Review of Social Research* (Summer 1978).

81. J. Kordatos, *The Workers' Movement in Greece* (in Greek) (Karavacos, Athens, 1956); C. Jecchines, *Trade-unionism in Greece* (Chicago, 1967), and G. Katsanevas, 'The Functions and Present Organisation of Industrial Relations in Greece', unfinished PhD thesis, London School of Economics.

82. However, it should be noted that in one respect underdeveloped capitalist formations are more self regulated than developed ones: in so far as extended kinship structures and more traditional forms of provision for old age and sickness are still operating (especially in the non-capitalist sectors of the economy), the peripheral state's labour reproduction costs are much lower. But despite relatively low welfare expenditures, state expenses for capital accumulation are so exorbitant that O'Connor's concept of a 'fiscal crisis' (having its roots in the increasing socialisation of production costs and the continuing private appropriation of all gains) applies equally if not more in the case of the peripheral state. See J. O'Connor, *The Fiscal Crisis of the State* (St Martin's Press, New York, 1973).

83. For Claus Offe it is not so much structural constraints or group pressures in the state's distant or immediate environment which make it capitalist, but rather internal, inbuilt mechanisms which ensure (a) negatively, the elimination of all policies representing non-capitalist or very narrow capitalist interests; (b) positively, that the 'proper' decisions from the point of view of the general interests of capital are taken; (c) that the state policies favouring the general interests of capital are shown as favouring the general interests of all classes. See C. Offe, 'Political Authority and Class Structures', in P. Connerton (ed.), *Critical Sociology* (Penguin, London, 1976).

84. On the extensive degree of political formalism in Greece, see N. Mouzelis, *Modern Greece*, Chapter 8.

85. According to Poulantzas, the fundamental precondition for the reproduction of capitalism is the political fragmentation of the working class. See N. Poulantzas, *Political Power and Social Classes* (New Left Books, London, 1973). Even if generally speaking this has indeed been the case for both developed and underdeveloped capitalist formations, it must be strongly emphasised that this fragmentation is more noticeable in underdeveloped capitalism. The fact that political fragmentation and a reformist orientation are characteristics of the West European working-classes should not be allowed to obscure the very marked differences in terms of political autonomy and power that exists between them and their counterparts in underdeveloped countries.

86. Empirical evidence on this is contained in a still unfinished research project on the development of the patronage system in two Greek provinces during the 1960s. See C. Comninos, 'The Development of the Patronage System in Etolo-Akarnia and Kavala', unfinished thesis, London School of Economics.

Index

275